IDEALISM WITHOUT ILLUSIONS

OTHER BOOKS BY GEORGE WEIGEL

*Peace and Freedom: Christian Faith, Democracy,
and the Problem of War*

*Tranquillitas Ordinis: The Present Failure and Future Promise
of American Catholic Thought on War and Peace*

Catholicism and the Renewal of American Democracy

*American Interests, American Purpose:
Moral Reasoning and U.S. Foreign Policy*

Fieles y Libres: Catolicismo, Derechos Humanos, y Democracia

Freedom and Its Discontents: Catholicism Confronts Modernity

Just War and the Gulf War
(with James Turner Johnson)

*The Final Revolution: The Resistance Church
and the Collapse of Communism*

Edited Volumes

*Retos Contemporáneos: Reflexiones desde el realismo
bíblico de la tradición católico*

*A Century of Catholic Social Thought: Essays on
'Rerum Novarum' and Nine Other Key Documents*
(with Robert Royal)

*The American Search for Peace: Moral Reasoning,
Religious Hope, and National Security*
(with John P. Langan, S.J.)

*A New Worldly Order: John Paul II on Human Freedom—
A 'Centesimus Annus' Reader*

Being Christian Today: An American Conversation
(with Richard John Neuhaus)

*Building the Free Society: Democracy, Capitalism,
and Catholic Social Teaching*
(with Robert Royal)

Idealism without Illusions

GEORGE WEIGEL

ETHICS AND PUBLIC POLICY CENTER
WASHINGTON, D.C.

WILLIAM B. EERDMANS PUBLISHING COMPANY
GRAND RAPIDS, MICHIGAN

ISBN 0-8028-0746-1

For
Bob Andrews

"We few, we happy few, we band of brothers."
King Henry V, IV. 3. 40

Contents

Acknowledgments

It was Robert Pickus, founder and president of the World Without War Council, who first suggested that I write a regular commentary on the peace, freedom, and security debate when, in 1986, I was launching the James Madison Foundation, the Council's sister-organization, in Washington, D.C. That newsletter, *American Purpose*, subsequently moved with me to the Ethics and Public Policy Center in 1989. Several of the chapters that follow first saw the light of day in *American Purpose*, and although they have been extensively reworked for this volume, it seems appropriate to acknowledge, once again, Bob Pickus's enduring influence on my life and thought.

I am also grateful to Norman Podhoretz and Neal Kozodoy for their invitation to write for the distinguished monthly *Commentary*, in which others of these chapters first appeared, as I am to Richard John Neuhaus and James Nuechterlein for opening the pages of *First Things* to my work. Thanks, too, to John O'Sullivan of *National Review* for the invitation to "dance on communism's grave."

Other friends, colleagues, and occasional correspondents have shaped my thinking about the matters discussed here, and I thank them all: Elliott Abrams, Peter L. Berger, Pavel Bratinka, Rocco Buttiglione, Yigal Carmon, Douglas Feith, Timothy Garton Ash, Carl Gershman, Patrick Glynn, the late Senator Henry M. Jackson, James Turner Johnson, Max M. Kampelman, Charles Krauthammer, John Langan, S.J., Samuel W. Lewis, John Miller, Menahem Milson, Michael Novak, Piotr Nowina-Konopka, Brad Roberts, Eugene V. Rostow, Robert Royal, Richard Schifter, Nina Shea, Josef Skvorecky, and Harry Summers. Amy Sherman, Christopher Ditzenberger, and Derek Mogck have been serially indispensable in making *American Purpose*, and the functioning of my office in general, possible. Thanks, also, to the Board of Directors of the Ethics and Public Policy Center and to the Center's benefactors for their generous support of my work. On the home front, Joan, Gwyneth, Monica, and Stephen Weigel have been patient above and beyond the call of affection and duty.

Carol Griffith, senior editor of the Ethics and Public Policy Center, has done a fine job of weaving many essays into a coherent argument—and in tempering some of my rhetorical exuberance. In an age when serious editing is becoming as rare an art as the successfully executed sacrifice bunt, Carol Griffith stands out as a skilled and engaging practitioner of an ancient and honorable craft.

I am dedicating this book to a friend of many years' standing, Robert Andrews, whose conversation, counsel, and encouragement have been a steady source of pleasure and stimulation as I've tried to think my way through the thicket of issues involved in defining an American purpose in the world. In a town where patriotism can too often be the last refuge of scoundrels, Bob Andrews is the real thing: an American patriot with a large vision of freedom's cause in the world, who did not bend to the winds of fashion after the debacle of Vietnam. I owe him a lot. So does the United States. Multiply Bob Andrews by a thousand, and what they call the "decision-making process" in the nation's capital would be very different, indeed.

G.W.

All Saints, 1993
Washington, D.C.

INTRODUCTION

Breaking the Realist/Idealist Logjam

For a considerable part of the past seventy-five years, a seemingly endless argument between idealists (usually identified with Woodrow Wilson) and realists (Hans Morgenthau and his intellectual progeny) has dominated the U.S. foreign-policy debate. To be sure, the isolationist/internationalist struggle held center stage in certain periods, and that ancient feud has been rekindled in the aftermath of World War III, the Cold War. But when it was understood that the United States *had* to have a foreign policy, the battle lines were typically drawn between Wilsonians, who believed that negotiations, arbitration, and international law could domesticate world politics, and the Morgenthauian devotees of Realpolitik, who claimed that any such domestication was impossible—and that policy devoted to that end was inherently foolish, not to say dangerous.

This analytic and prescriptive division has cut across many of the other boundaries of American life. There have been immigrant realists and immigrant idealists. Catholic, Protestant, and Jewish ethicists can be found in both camps, as can Republicans and Democrats, industrialists and trade unionists, farmers and financiers, urbanites and suburbanites, scientists and military officers, traditional conservatives, neoconservatives, and liberals.

Viewed from one cultural-historical angle, the idealist/realist controversy has been about whether the United States is (and ought to behave like) simply another great power on the traditional models of European statecraft, or whether America is an "exception" by reason of its founding principles and the universal moral claims embedded therein. Viewed from a different, and I believe more illuminating, angle, the argument has been about the rela-

1

tion between morality and politics: which is to say, it has been an argument about human nature.

Realism and Its Discontents

This deeper dimension of the debate was evident in the argument touched off in the internationalist camp by President George Bush's call for American leadership in erecting a "new world order." (The isolationists, of course, had their own reasons for nervousness at this presidential formulation; but they will be dealt with later.) Realists fretted about "new world order" language and imagery on any number of counts. Some worried about the Bush administration's reading of the dynamics of world politics. Others were concerned about the country's, and the administration's, staying power in crises. Still others feared that our commitments in the world were vastly exceeding our resources.

But, at bottom, realist skepticism about any "new world order" reflected realist views of human nature, and specifically the conviction that human nature does not change. There could be no "new world order" because there weren't going to be any "new" human beings—just the same old kind who had been doing politics since Thucydides wrote *The Peloponnesian War*. The world was still divided into Athenians and Melians; and you had better have read Thucydides' "Melian Dialogue" if you wanted to know what international hardball was and is all about.

This realist conviction about the continuity of human nature is an important part of the intellectual armamentarium of any thoughtful student of international affairs. The capacity for evil and injustice does seem built into the species, and ignoring it causes great damage, usually to the weakest nations and peoples. Moreover, utopian schemes of human perfectibility do not simply fail: they often lead to tyranny, as the illuminated few seek to accelerate the progress of the dimwitted herd. Madison's realist dictum in *The Federalist*, that men are not angels and therefore need governments, is ignored at the statesman's—and the nation's—peril.

But realism can be led astray, too. Realism can degenerate into cynicism, particularly in an intellectual climate like that of the contemporary United States, where the academy is dominated by a skeptical relativism about virtually everything (except, of course, the unquestionable moral rectitude and social necessity of the tenure system!). And a deteriorated realism can lead to foolish policy, just as a naïve idealism can (and has).

Examples of a certain form of realist myopia were evident in the endgame of the Cold War. To be sure, realists were better equipped to cope with the challenge of Communism after World War II than were their idealist brethren; indeed, the realists were right in thinking that that quintessential Wilsonian, Franklin D. Roosevelt, did a lot to make the Cold War inevitable by failing to take the measure of "Uncle Joe" Stalin. But if the realists were right about the origins of World War III, and if they were more right than wrong about its conduct, still most of them were caught rather off guard by its last act, the Revolution of 1989 and the New Russian Revolution of 1991. Not only did realists fail to see these cataclysms coming: most of them didn't seem to think it possible that Communism could implode the way it did. Furthermore, the realists have, as a camp, been slow to comprehend the singular moral qualities of these most distinctive of revolutionary upheavals. Realism knows, correctly, that the bad guys often win. But realism tends to forget that the good guys sometimes win, too. Sometimes they even win big.

The Possibility of Progress

The realist account of human nature is not, in the final analysis, persuasive, nor does it illuminate as well as it ought to (and frequently claims to) the dynamics of politics. Man may not be an angel whose occasional lapses are due solely to unfortunate circumstances; but neither is he a demon with occasional twinges of conscience. The realist insistence that facts must be faced is wise moral (and political) counsel. But one of these facts is that human nature does change, and for the better, in the sense that human moral intuitions and understandings develop over time. And as they do, some things are put off the board, definitively.

Although the multicultural despisers of Columbus tended to ignore such unpleasantnesses during the 1992 quincentenary, human sacrifice was a staple feature of human societies for millennia; it is now definitively off the board. From the earliest days of recorded history until the mid-nineteenth century, slavery was considered a normal part of the ordering of society; slavery is now off the board, save in some backwaters of the African and Arab worlds.

Perhaps most provocatively, moral attitudes toward war have changed. For thousands of years, war was understood as part of the normal rhythm of human affairs. To take but one example: Over the past several years, I have had occasion to read a lot of Polish history and literature; and you can't read through that material without being powerfully struck by the "normality" of violent conflict over almost a thousand years of national life. Poland is, admittedly, a singular place, cursed by a singular geography. But still it may stand as an apt representative of a more general human phenomenon: the ubiquity of war throughout recorded history, and the subsequent, widespread conviction that war is "in the nature of things." (This has not been a traditional American sentiment, given our fortuitous residence on an island continent. But here is a point on which American "exceptionalism" surely does confuse our reading of history.)

That conviction about the inevitability, the "normality," of war has now changed: somewhat. It has changed in the West and in those parts of the world most directly influenced by the West, primarily because of the experience of the three world wars of this century. The great Western religious traditions now flatly condemn the notion of "holy war," and some religious (and secular) ethicists, not all of them frivolous or naïve, are deeply skeptical about the possibility of a justified war under modern conditions. Indeed, in much of the West, war is now considered an aberration, an outbreak of what a teenager would call "terminal weirdness." Some would maintain (correctly, in my view) that war is sometimes a necessary last resort, precisely in the service of peace with freedom and justice. But the idea that war is not "in the nature of things" is commonplace today.

That conviction is ready prey for utopianism, as the perennial moral and political confusions of the "peace movement" sadly attest. But I think it would be a mistake to dismiss as mere credulousness the widespread conviction throughout the Western world that war, like human sacrifice and slavery, need not be in the nature of things. We do not think of war today in terms qualitatively different from those of the people of the eighteenth century simply because of mindless sentimentality in a decadent and spineless West (although we surely suffer from decadence and spinelessness aplenty). Something else is at work here, something that looks suspiciously like growth: like a genuine development of our common moral intuition. It could degenerate into appeasement. But that would indeed be a degeneration. Or so it seems to me.

In any event, and no matter what we think about this business of humanity's moral evolution on the matter of organized mass violence, the realist account of human nature—and thus the realist "take" on world politics—surely needs some tempering. If the realist account were fully on the mark, we would be living in Metternich's world. That we are not seems, to borrow from Mr. Jefferson, self-evident.

It's the Morality, Stupid

The realist/idealist debate has also tended toward the repetitious, indeed toward the circular, because of a defective understanding of moral reasoning that is epidemic in American culture and society.

Both realists and idealists tend to conceive "morality" as something reducible to the injunctions of the Sermon on the Mount. The idealists then try to figure out how to apply, to America's business in the world, the counsels to poverty of spirit, meekness, mercy, purity of heart, and so forth. The realists, agreeing that these counsels sum up the meaning of "morality," insist that they cannot be ascribed to corporate units like states and conclude that foreign policy is the realm of amorality. In other words, realists and idealists alike tend to assume that, in the morality-and-politics equation, everyone agrees on what "morality" is, and thus the only real arguments are about the possible political applications of that "morality."

But that assumption is exactly wrong.

Neither realists nor idealists seem able to imagine a form of morality that is distinctive to *political* life: a morality whose principles are derived from rational reflection on the ends of politics as these can be discerned by human moral imagination, and whose practices are mediated through the virtue of prudence —the moral skill of applying principle to circumstance so as to maximize the chances of doing good and minimize the chances of making things worse than they already are. Which is to say, neither realists nor idealists seem able to conceive of a form of moral reasoning adequate to the distinctive tasks of the statesman. And that incapacity is the source of both the circularity of the realist/idealist argument and the confusions of the general public debate over America's obligations in world affairs.

I believe it is possible to make a persuasive theoretical case for such a distinctive morality: a realistic social ethic of idealism without illusions. But it would be far more useful to illustrate such a form of moral reasoning at work. That is what I have tried to do in this book.

Part One examines the collapse of European Communism: how it happened, why it happened, who did (and didn't) make it happen, and what it means for our times. This is not an exercise in nostalgia. The dynamics of the Communist crackup are widely misunderstood in the West, and this failure of understanding reinforces the sterility of the realist/idealist debate, hastens the onset of a new form of isolationism, and makes the formulation of post–Cold War policy all the more difficult, intellectually and politically. Both realists and idealists have much to celebrate, and much to learn from, in the Revolution of 1989 and the New Russian Revolution of 1991. What, is the business of Part One.

Part Two is an attempt to pin down some elements of America's role in the post–Cold War world: to think about some of the component parts of a general strategic framework that would do for the policy analyst and statesman of the 1990s what "containment" did for us from 1947 through 1991. Chapter 6, "Beyond Moralism and Realpolitik," may be considered the central argument of the entire book, and Thesis 7 in that chapter—on the dialectic of interest and purpose in America's action in the world —is the linchpin of that argument.

Then, in Part Three, I try to apply Part One's lessons of the recent past and Part Two's strategic principles to five issues that rapidly reminded post–Cold War America that the global neighborhood is getting smaller all the time—and that there is no escape from engagement and prudent statecraft in that kind of world.

All of which will be, I hope, of interest to strategists and ethicists, citizens and public officials, alike.

PART ONE

The Past Is Prologue

"Courage is the secret of power."
HOMER, *The Iliad*

1

The Revolution of 1989 and the Restoration of History

The euphoria, the explosive joy at the sheer improbability of it all, embodied in those still-stunning pictures of the breaching of the Berlin Wall: it lasted about a year, perhaps a little less. Then came the "terrible twos," as the children of the Revolution of 1989—the new democracies of central and eastern Europe—tried to get a grip on their emergent personalities. Things got a little rough, but the afterglow of the Revolution was warm enough to ward off any chills of grave concern about the future. It would all settle down, people both east and west of the old iron curtain told themselves. The turn toward democracy and the free economy had been secured.

But then the terrible twos seemed to stretch into the terrible threes. And the prospect of a healthy and happy, if inevitably messy, childhood seemed to recede. Might the terrible twos and the terrible threes give way to the ferocious fours and the fearsome fives? Were the children of the Revolution of 1989 becoming political cannibals? What was going on in the old Warsaw Pact, anyway?

What was (and is) going on in central and eastern Europe is the restoration of history, with all its trials and tribulations, after more than four decades of political-psychological hypothermia produced by Stalinism and neo-Stalinism. Moreover, history—which includes ancient ethnic, religious, national, and personal animosities, as well as more recent experiences of revolutionary brotherhood—has been jump-started in *Mitteleuropa* amidst levels of economic, environmental, and social-ecological damage that beggar our Western imaginations. The old smokestack industries make things that no one wants to buy; modern management techniques, accounting procedures, and investment practices are largely unknown. The air, water, and soil have been fouled beyond the most lurid imaginings of any Greenpeace pantheist. Even more seriously, the wounds inflicted on the souls of the people in the region by forty-plus years of Communist tyranny, mendacity, and stupidity have yet to heal; indeed, they have been scraped raw more than once by unscrupulous politicians abusing the privileges of freedom.

Under these circumstances, the astonishing thing is not that there has been political and economic turmoil in Poland, Czechoslovakia, Hungary, the former East Germany, Romania, and Bulgaria, and murderous mayhem in the late Yugoslavia. The astonishing thing is that, with the exception of the catastrophe in the Balkans (for which inept U.S. and Western policy bears a measure of responsibility) and, arguably, of Romania, real progress has been made toward the consolidation of political and economic freedom in these countries—the American press (ever more alert to failure than to success) to the contrary notwithstanding.

One cure for analytic myopia in these matters is to reread the works of Timothy Garton Ash, the young British historian who was the finest chronicler (and, in a sense, balladeer) of the Revolution of 1989 as it gestated throughout the 1980s. For Garton Ash grasped the human dynamics of these stunning events with a remarkable combination of insight and enthusiasm that assiduously avoided the perils of romanticizing the people of the revolution or their circumstances.[1] But Garton Ash has not (yet?) given us a comprehensive account of the revolution, its origins, and its immediate aftermath that would cast light on the perils and possibilities of post–Communist reconstruction. Happily, though, a part of that gap has been filled by a young Romanian-American scholar, Vladimir Tismaneanu, whose study entitled *Reinventing Politics: Eastern Europe From Stalin to Havel* was published in the summer of 1992.[2] While Tismaneanu's analysis is not without its own lacunae, he gets the basic story line just right—

Communism was defeated in central and eastern Europe, not by the glittering promise of BMWs, but by the "reinvention of politics": by the reemergence of civil society from under the rubble of the totalitarian state.

But there is no way to grasp that central dynamic of the Revolution of 1989, or the troubles that have followed in its wake, without revisiting the distinctively destructive system that the revolution overthrew.

THE DESTRUCTION OF CIVIL SOCIETY

Tismaneanu has little use for the economistic explanation of the revolution that has dominated both the American press and the American academy. The condition for the possibility of "1989" was not unrequited consumerism, he argues, but rather "universal boredom" and the smoldering resentments caused by year after year of "asphyxiating bureaucratic dictatorship."[3] Undoubtedly the non-violent revolutionaries of 1989 hoped, indeed believed, that the demise of the Yalta imperial system would mean a better life for the people of the region. But the essential prerequisite to any economic reform was toppling the Communist regimes that had created the insane economies of the Warsaw Pact countries in the first place. The revolution, in short, was first and foremost an *anti-totalitarian* revolution.

When Communism came to power in central and eastern Europe, riding on the tanks of the Red Army at the end of World War II, it brought with it an especially stolid and vulgar cadre of party leaders. The intellectually interesting Marxists from an earlier period of revolutionary fervor had all been purged (i.e., shot) during the Moscow "trials" of the mid-1930s. They were replaced by creatures wholly subservient to Stalin and wholly committed to the "leading role" of the Soviet Communist party in the worlds of proletarian internationalism. Bolesław Bierut in Poland, Walter Ulbricht in Soviet-occupied Germany, Klement Gottwald in Czechoslovakia, Gheorghe Gheorghiu-Dej in Romania—these were the kinds of crude, brutal, and unquestioning tribunes that Stalin preferred as procurators for the new imperial provinces. (Yugoslavia's Tito, an equal-opportunity oppressor, was every bit as cruel and brutal; but he had an ego to match Stalin's, and the geography of his country made his declaration of quasi-independence feasible.)

How did these men consolidate their control? There was a lot of breakage, to be sure. Political opponents were ruthlessly suppressed, as were alternative centers of cultural power (like the churches). An enormous secret-police apparatus thrust itself into every nook and cranny of personal and communal life, ferreting out dissidents and poisoning human relationships through the suborning of informers and other collaborators.

But we would miss the point of this Stalinist reign of terror if we were to think of it as simply terror for terror's sake. There was that dimension to it; but it was all in aid of a larger strategic goal, which was the destruction of "civil society." Vladimir Tismaneanu describes this "systematic destructive operation" in these terms:

> . . . [T]he main purpose of totalitarian practice in this century [was] to annihilate the sources of human creativity, to separate individuals from one another by making them mutually inimical, and to replace collective bonds of solidarity and support with the supremacy of the party-state, acclaimed as omnipotent and omniscient. All previous associations and groups had to disappear. The values long held to be sacred—patriotism, family, national traditions—had to be redefined in the light of Communist dogmas. An overhaul of each country's cultural tradition and a revision of the moral postulates, including those derived from the European humanist tradition, were accomplished through the Marxist dogma of the class struggle.[4]

The strategic goal of the Stalinist imposition of Communist power in central and eastern Europe was to turn a living organism, the body politic, into a ventriloquist's dummy. The secret-police apparatus and the machinery of repression severed the bonds of human fraternity that gave society its tensile strength. Relentless propaganda, officially sanctioned atheism, and Communist domination of the public organs of culture eroded society's moral faculties.

In this repressive context, Communist ideology had an instrumental character: its purpose, according to the Polish poet Czesław Miłosz (author of the classic dissident text *The Captive Mind*), was to "neutralize the faculty of doubt." Amidst the chaos of post-war Europe, Communist ideology had an answer for every uncertainty and an explanation for every historical conundrum. Irony, a staple feature of the moral landscape of central and eastern Europe, would be replaced by certitude (if of a particularly crude sort). Miłosz described the process in a terrible image:

> There is a species of insect which injects its venom into a caterpillar; thus inoculated, the caterpillar lives on though it is paralyzed. The poisonous insect then lays its eggs in it, and the body of the caterpillar serves as a living larder for the young brood. Likewise . . . the anaesthetic of dialectical materialism was injected into the mind of an individual in the people's democracies. When the individual's brain was duly paralyzed, the eggs of Stalinism were laid in it. "As soon as you are a Marxist," the party says to the patient, "you *must* be a Stalinist, for there is no Marxism outside of Stalinism."[5]

As the former seminary student Stalin himself once put it, one ran an empire, not by sheer brute force alone (although that would be used as necessary), but by deploying "engineers of souls."

The Failures of Reformism

Stalinism in its most overtly cruel form did not long outlive its sire. For shortly after the Soviet dictator's death in 1953, his heirs came to understand that the system he had perfected (so to speak) would destroy them all, were its madnesses allowed to run on unchecked. Moreover, it was obvious to even the most ideologically besotted Kremlin leaders that their empire was falling further and further behind the West economically (and thus militarily). East Germany vs. West Germany and Hungary vs. Austria provided all too clear examples, all too close to home. Something had to be done. But how could the system be reformed when it was, by ideological definition, irreformable?

A delicate problem indeed. The man who attempted to solve it was not notable for his delicacy of thought or manners. Thus in February 1956, at the Twentieth Congress of the Communist Party of the Soviet Union, Nikita Khrushchev, Stalin's former proconsul in Ukraine, tried to salvage the Communist system by fixing the blame for its excesses and failures on Stalin's psychopathologies. The late leader had simply gone too far, because of his own private demons. The system was not at fault; what was to be deplored was the distortion introduced by Stalin's paranoia.

Khrushchev's denunciation of Stalin's "cult of personality" at the Twentieth Party Congress sent shock waves throughout the Yalta imperial system. It was all too much for Poland's Bierut; he took sick in Moscow and died, to be succeeded at home by a former purgee, Władysław Gomułka, who could appeal to the nationalism that Bierut's thugs had never managed to extinguish. But it was under the leadership of Hungary's Imre Nagy that the reformism set loose by Khrushchev's speech went furthest. For Nagy not only conceded the errors of the Stalinist past but accepted the principle of political pluralism as the guide to Hungary's future.

This was more than Khrushchev could tolerate; mild de-Stalinization was one thing, but a frontal challenge to the "leading role" of the Communist party was something else entirely. And so the immediate result of Nagy's reformism was the Soviet invasion of Hungary in 1956 (Nagy himself was executed in 1958). The boundaries of acceptable "reform" were narrow indeed, even when the reforms were under the control of the party leadership —a point that would be driven home again, forcefully, a decade later.

Khrushchev's erratic behavior (authorizing the publication of Solzhenitsyn's brilliant evocation of the Stalin-era labor camps, *One Day in the Life of Ivan Denisovich*, while concurrently letting loose a vicious persecution of religion), and his international "adventurism" (which led, *inter alia*, to the 1962 Cuban missile crisis), soon proved indigestible, and he was replaced in a bloodless 1964 coup by Leonid Brezhnev. Brezhnev re-tightened the screws of internal Soviet control while making it clear that he would tolerate no deviation from a Moscow-directed line in the outer provinces of Stalin's empire. In 1968 the "Brezhnev Doctrine" on the irreversibility of Communist systems was proclaimed as the ideological justification for repressing another attempt at liberal Communist reformism, the Prague Spring led by Czechoslovakia's Alexander Dubček.

Unlike Nagy, Dubček did not end up dangling from an executioner's rope. But when Marshal Grechko's Red Army tanks halted the Prague Spring, they also put an end to any remaining illusions about the possibilities of reform "from within" existing Communist parties and elites. Even intellectuals of the Left, at least in the countries affected, conceded that the system was irreformable. No amount of liberalization could curb its excesses, for it was now clear, beyond argument, that the "excesses" were of the essence of the system. They were, to borrow from the Marxist catechism, a "historical necessity."

Brezhnev's neo-Stalinism may have lacked the ideological *élan* that sustained an earlier generation of Soviet dictators and *apparatchik* governors of the imperial provinces. But the dead weight of Brezhnevite "inertial authoritarianism" was no lighter for that. It was hard to see a way out. Reform from within the party was impossible. Rescue from the West was not in the cards. Revolution, on the romantic models of East Germany in 1953, Hungary in 1956, and Czechoslovakia in 1968, was hopeless: the bad guys had all the tanks.

What was to be done?

THE RESURRECTION OF CIVIL SOCIETY

A new strategy—one that went far beyond "reformism"—was essential. As Vladimir Tismaneanu writes, this new strategy

> had to take into account the growing obsolescence of the founding mythology of the existing system, the passing of the first generation of Stalinist crusaders, and the rise of political elites interested in the simple preservation of their advantages. The system had lost its initial absolutist drive: stagnation and immobility were its main characteristics. The increasingly routinized mechanization of [Communist] ideology laid open the cracks in the system's edifice for easier exploitation by the opposition.[6]

In other words, the battlefield of the 1970s and 1980s in central and eastern Europe would not be the streets, but rather the hearts, minds, and souls of the people of the region. The key to a more humane future would be found in "the restoration of the hope for social change." And that was a process that would take place, not from the top down, as in Dubček's Prague Spring, but from the bottom up. Workers and intellectuals who had grown resigned to their powerlessness would have to rediscover and reclaim the power that was in fact theirs: the power to be themselves, which meant the power simply to say "No" to the system.

There were, to be sure, external supports for this process of social self-regeneration. One of the most important was the 1975 Helsinki Final Act, the "Helsinki Accords," and here there were many ironies in the fire, indeed. Brezhnev wanted the accords as confirmation of the Yalta imperial system in Europe. Western conservatives and "captive nations" activists opposed the accords for precisely that reason. Henry Kissinger, perhaps thinking that he was arranging another "decent interval" during which the United States would grow accustomed to playing a declining Athens to the ascendant Soviet Sparta, got President Gerald Ford to sign for the United States. Thus the star of the show, the man regarded on all the pundits' form sheets as the real winner at Helsinki, was Leonid Ilyich Brezhnev, who, when he put his signature on the Final Act, probably thought he was securing a hundred years' lease on Stalin's empire.

In fact, as things turned out, he was signing its death warrant.

For the Helsinki Final Act contained something called "Basket Three"—a checklist of human-rights principles that was tacked on, almost as an afterthought, to what the establishments, East and West, regarded as the "real business" of the Helsinki Conference on Security and Cooperation in Europe: the security and trade agreements. But "Basket Three" quickly became the catalyst for an unprecedented eruption of human-rights activism throughout the Warsaw Pact countries. Moreover, for the first time since Yalta, these organizations now had a lifeline to the West, through human-rights groups set up to monitor the Helsinki Final Act. By means of this linkage to Western "Helsinki Watch" groups, activists in the Warsaw Pact countries could, through the periodic "Helsinki review conferences" mandated by the Final Act, help bring the criticism of Western governments to bear, publicly, on the regimes of Stalin's outer empire.

These new human-rights organizations—prominent among which were Poland's "Committee for Social Self-Defense–KOR" and Czechoslovakia's "Charter 77"—became, over time, indispensable agents in fomenting what we have come to know as the Revolution of 1989. The new revolutionaries had learned from the mistakes of "reformisms" past. Communist divide-and-conquer tactics would be firmly resisted: conscious efforts were made to link workers and intellectuals, believers and non-believers, Christians and Jews, leftists, liberals, and conservatives across the traditional chasms of animosity, chasms that the Communists had exploited as part of their strategy of social control.

Challenging the Lie

But the human-rights revolution that eventually gave birth to the political Revolution of 1989 depended upon more than tactical innovation. It also involved a new strategic concept: resistance to the Communist culture of the lie would take the form of "living in the truth" in what the Czech dissident Václav Benda styled a "parallel polis," a zone of self-created freedom, which could not be occupied by the Communist authorities because their writ did not run into the sanctuary of the individual conscience.

The new human-rights revolutionaries had, in other words, seized on two decisive truths: that the Communist system was built on a foundation of lies, and that resistance to the Communist system must be, first and foremost, moral resistance. Recognizing these truths meant taking a hard look in the mirror, which then meant taking seriously the problem of acquiescence to the neo-Stalinist system. Yes, there were "us" and "them," or, as people said in Poland, "the society" and "the power." But the problem was more comprehensive, indeed more critical, than that. As Václav Havel would put it in his penetrating essay "The Power of the Powerless," the fault line in Communist countries did not run only between "us" and "them." Rather, Havel argued, it ran through every person. Bad as "they" were, "they" were not the only ones to blame. Everyone who cooperated with the system of the lie—even by modest gestures of acquiescence, in order simply to be left alone—was responsible for the perpetuation of the system.

Havel and others realized that the only way to weaken the system was to attack it at its roots: enough people had to find enough courage to reject the moral serfdom that was the basis of the system's power. Enough people had to be prepared to resist the "moral numbness" that was, Vladimir Tismaneanu argues, the system's greatest ally.[7]

The Revolution of 1989 began, in sum, with the self-emancipation of individuals who decided to "live in the truth." The first revolutionary act was private, personal, and conscientious. Its aim was not the seizure of power but the reclamation of self-respect. Its goal was to exorcise the dimension of "them" that had invaded the souls of "us."

And yet these personal decisions of conscientious resistance were politically powerful because of the nature of the system in which they were taken. They challenged the system at its maximum point of vulnerability: its supreme confidence in its ability to compel or coerce acquiescence. To "live in the truth" in a neo-Stalinist or Brezhnevite Communist state was necessarily to live as a revolutionary. Or as Havel put it,

> living within the truth has more than a mere existential dimension (returning humanity to its inherent nature), or a noetic dimension (revealing reality as it is), or a moral dimension (setting an example for others). It also has an unambiguous political dimension. If the main pillar of the system is living a lie, then it is not surprising that the fundamental threat to it is living the truth. This is why it must be suppressed more severely than anything else.[8]

This commitment to living "normally," to living "as if" one were free, was the common moral thread that linked dissidents across central and eastern Europe in the 1980s. And that commitment was also crucial to one of the other distinctive characteristics of the Revolution of 1989: its non-violence. True, the bad guys had all the guns, and the good guys knew it. But the choice for non-violence was rooted in richer moral soil than that of mere pragmatic calculation. Poland's Adam Michnik caught the essence of the dissidents' attitude when he said they had chosen non-violence out of the conviction that "people who begin by storming Bastilles end up building their own."

The Dominos Fall

Once "civil society" had achieved a certain critical mass in central and eastern Europe, with the concurrent demoralization of the party elites in the countries involved (an unintended consequence of Gorbachevism), the end of the Yalta imperial system came very fast indeed.

Poland was first. The April 1989 roundtable negotiations led quickly to the overwhelming electoral victory of Solidarity in June of that year. And by September, Tadeusz Mazowiecki had become the first non-Communist prime minister of a Warsaw Pact country.

At about the same time, Hungary, where the old-line leadership had been thrown out and an explosion of democratic organizing was under way, "took the unprecedented step," comments Vladimir Tismaneanu, "of allowing East German tourists to cross into Austria on their way home . . . and thus opened the way for a demographic hemorrhage that would ruin the East German economy."[9] That crack in the façade of the Warsaw Pact had immediate repercussions inside the restive GDR: massive demonstrations took place in East Berlin, Leipzig, and Dresden. By October 18, the neo-Stalinist dinosaur Erich Honecker had been replaced by a younger face, Egon Krenz. But no Communist leader could undo the salient geopolitical fact that "once the logic of the Cold War was recognized as obsolete, the GDR lost its reason to exist."[10] On November 9, the Berlin Wall was breached, and it was only a matter of time before Germany was reunified.

Then, on November 17, Czechoslovak police and internal security troops viciously attacked a group of non-violent student protesters in Prague and triggered the "velvet revolution" that, six weeks later, installed Václav Havel (a political prisoner as recently as the preceding May) as president of the country.

Things were less dramatic in Bulgaria, and, as the world remembers, Romania's anti-Ceauşescu revolution was both violent and truncated. But in central Europe, the heart of the Warsaw Pact, the empire that had seemed a fixed point of reference fell to pieces in the seven brief months between Poland's June elections and Havel's triumphant trip to Prague Castle.

It was, in another irony, a striking confirmation that there may have been something to the "Domino Theory" after all.

THE "FINAL REVOLUTION"

The *sine qua non* of the Revolution of 1989 was the reconstitution of civil society, which was the effective antidote to the poison of Brezhnevite neo-Stalinism. Moreover, as Vladimir Tismaneanu demonstrates, the rebirth of civil society required the rediscovery of "morality as a primary source of political behavior."[11] The Revolution of 1989 restored central and eastern Europe to the great political tradition of the West, in which it has been understood since Aristotle that politics is an extension of ethics; that is what one hears, time and time again, from the people of the revolution themselves.

But then why has there been so much trouble among the heirs of the Revolution of 1989? Doesn't the return of age-old patterns of ethnic and religious strife in some of these countries falsify the claim that a moral revolution preceded and made possible the political revolution that overthrew Communism in central and eastern Europe?

No, it does not.

The societies that emerged from the Revolution of 1989 were not developed and secure democracies. They had undergone, under extreme circumstances, what Tismaneanu calls a "gradual reconstruction of political space." There was room to breathe again. But the air that could be breathed more freely was not without its toxic fumes, moral as well as chemical. Communism had not eradicated the ancient animosities of the region; it had merely frozen them under a thick pack of field ice, whose crackup had freed them once again. A further problem (almost wholly ignored by the Western media) was the persistence of ex-Communists (euphemistically styled "post-Communists") in positions of political and economic power; this led, in short order, to the formation of ex-Communist mafias, to lingering resentments among the population, and to an emerging cynicism about the extent of change that had in fact taken place. And that cynicism was exacerbated by the inevitable dislocations and hardships caused by the transition to a market economy.

Worst of all, though, was the moral hangover: the lack of a work ethic, the mistrust of the motivations of others, the fear of initiative, the longing for security even at the cost of full freedom, the tendency to see everything in conspiratorial terms. Parliamentary democracies and competitive, entrepreneurially oriented market economies are difficult enough to operate for people with a lot of experience (look at us): they require certain carefully cultivated habits of the mind and habits of the heart, as Tocqueville recognized in the early nineteenth century. But these habits of thrift, deferred gratification, trust, imagination, cooperativeness, and satisfaction in the achievements of others are precisely the habits—the virtues—that Communism sought to eradicate.

In sum, the reconstitution of civil society in the countries of the old Warsaw Pact is not complete. It must continue. And the work of political and economic reconstruction is even more difficult than the work of rejection. To succeed, it will require a deepening of civility and a thickening of the bonds of social solidarity.

The Herald of the Revolution

It would seem rather cheeky to think that anything other than the reconstruction of "civil society" in the countries of the Yalta imperial system was the key to the Revolution of 1989, since this is what virtually all the key leaders of the revolution say about their accomplishment. But let's go back for a moment to the "pre-revolution" before the *annus mirabilis*. Everyone agrees that the rise of Solidarity in the summer of 1980 was the beginning of the end of Stalin's empire (even if it took another nine years to finish the job). The "independent, self-governing trade union Solidarity" put the final nail into the coffin of Communist ideological pretension. The negotiations leading up to the proclamation of the union, and the sturdy fellowship exhibited after it was brutally suppressed in December 1981, proved that radicalized workers and dissident intellectuals could form a common front against the Communists.

But whence came Solidarity? Why in Poland and why in 1980? There were antecedents, of course: in the worker-based resistance on the Baltic coast in 1970, in Ursus and Radom in 1976, and in the formation of the Committee for Social Self-Defense–KOR. But the Baltic workers were badly organized, and the Committee was a very small group indeed.

The difference, this time, was the pilgrimage of Pope John Paul II to his homeland in June 1979. That was the moment when "we" and "they" were decisively clarified. That was the moment when the basic human error of Communism was publicly proclaimed, and that proclamation was publicly acclaimed, from one end of the country to the other. That was when unprecedented numbers of Poles decided to live "as if" they were free, and when "living in the truth" became a program as well as a slogan.

If the revolution in Poland (the country that Stalin considered the keystone of the Yalta imperial system) touched off the Revolution of 1989, and if the rise of Solidarity was the essence of the Polish revolution, then the person who lit the flame that ignited the Polish revolution was Pope John Paul II. And he did it, not by advocating the politics of rebellion, but by preaching "the final revolution," the human turn to the good, to the truly human— and, ultimately, to God, who alone can make all things new.[12]

The image of the "final revolution" brings us full circle, to the difficulties of the new democracies of central and eastern Europe in the aftermath of the Revolution of 1989. The "final revolution" is a moral, not temporal, image: an image of depth rather than of length. The "final revolution" does not mean the end of history; it means the restoration of history to human dimensions. Communism tried to accelerate history, to bring on the worldly millennium by a forced march toward utopia. The "final revolution"—the revolution of conscience by which men and women said "No" to the Communist system and its culture of the lie on the basis of a higher and more compelling "Yes"—brought history back to a more human scale: which, unavoidably, means back to sin as well as to the possibility of nobility.

And that is why the future of democracy in central and eastern Europe (no less than in the United States) is, at bottom, a matter of virtue. Democracy is always an experiment. Its success depends on those habits of the mind and heart—those virtues—that make self-governance, in justice, with a care for the common good and a commitment to the defense of the rights of others, possible. Thus what is being tested in central and eastern Europe today is not just the capacity of market economies to produce and distribute wealth; it is, first and foremost, the virtues of the peoples of the new democracies. That there is no escape from such a testing is one of the crucial lessons to be discerned in the "how" and "why" of the great Communist crackup.

2

Death of a Heresy:
The New Russian Revolution

What died in the former Soviet Union on August 21, 1991, was a heresy. For Communism was never just economic foolishness married (in its Leninist form) to draconian forms of social control. Communism was a false doctrine, a congeries of false teachings about human nature, human community, human history, and human destiny. Therein lay its power to attract, and its power to coerce.

Heresy often consists in the exaggeration of one part of a complex truth. Communism was particularly seductive in the West precisely because the taproots of Western civilization, and its distinctive understanding of history as purposeful, are nourished by the stories and images of Jewish and Christian eschatology and apocalyptic. (There was in fact an eerie sense of contemporaneity in perusing Norman Cohn's brilliant study of medieval millenarians, *The Pursuit of the Millennium*, during the New Russian Revolution of 1991.) But Communism was evil, first and foremost, not just because of its view of history, but because it taught falsely about man. And from that falsehood came both the idiocies of a command economy and, far worse, the Gulag.

Simply put, the Communist heresy was the cruelest form of an evil that has beset the West since the intellectual prologue to the French Revolution: the tyranny of the political. This terrible simplification, which taught the perfectibility of man and of human community, was in fact a radically secularized version of the Jewish and Christian hope for a messianic age. For Rousseau and his epigones, though, the messiah was ultramundane: it was, in fact, politics. And the project was to remake flawed humanity —to usher in the messianic new age of justice and righteousness —through the medium of politics. Communism, the ultimate expression of this heretical project, was Jewish and Christian eschatology forced into history, without God or God's messiah. Little wonder that those who got in the way were ruthlessly eliminated or, in one of Lenin's favorite verbs, "exterminated."

Focusing on Communism as a heresy also helps us deepen our grip on the central dynamic of the Revolution of 1989 and its successor, the New Russian Revolution of 1991: that these were, as we saw in the previous chapter, first and foremost revolutions of the spirit, in which people said "No" to Communism on the basis of a higher and more compelling "Yes."

Throughout the Western world, pundits, academics, and reporters have tried hard to fix an explanatory label on these stunning events. "Delayed modernization" seems to be the most popular: the Warsaw Pact countries couldn't sustain themselves in an international economy dominated by the microchip and fiberoptics revolutions, and because of that, their political systems imploded, almost as a matter of course. (It probably tells us something, and something not altogether heartening, that so many Western intellectuals reach for an essentially Marxist answer to the collapse of Marxism.)

But there was nothing new, in 1989, about the economic backwardness of the countries of the Yalta imperial system. Compared to western Europe, central and eastern Europe had been an economic backwater for generations—does anybody recall Ladas, Trabants, and Skodas outselling Volkswagens, Peugeots, and Fords twenty or forty years ago? Even the imperial hegemon was in bad shape, long before it collapsed: the Soviet Union, breadbasket of the region in czarist days, had to buy or beg grain to feed its people and livestock.

This soft economism used as a means of explaining the breakup of the Communist system is, in truth, simply a less odious version of the ultramundane heresy. To accept it is to concede one of the corollaries of Rousseau's false doctrine of human nature and history: that the only real world—the world where issues of real consequence get sorted out—is the world of the political. Such an exalted view of politics is a satisfying fantasy to indulge in if you happen to be a member of the political class. But "politics" (as the term is usually understood today) just doesn't explain the Revolution of 1989 and the New Russian Revolution of 1991.

For the great, distinguishing characteristic of these upheavals—the explanation of their success that is commensurate with the nature of the evil they overthrew and the way in which the overthrow took place—is that they were essentially *pre-political* revolutions. As the Polish authorities put it with unintentional accuracy during the martial-law period of 1981–83, Communism was in a "state of war" against society. Politics was demanding that it be allowed to fill the space previously occupied by society and by culture. The antidote to that tyranny of the political could not be, well, more politics. The antidote had to come from elsewhere.

The tyranny of the political inevitably resulted in the atomization of society. Resistance (and, ultimately, rollback) required that the connective tissue of social life, of human community, be rebuilt. That meant, as Pope John Paul II understood from the outset, rediscovering the virtue of social solidarity, of human fellow-feeling and a sense of mutual moral obligation. Thus solidarity, the virtue, preceded Solidarity, the trade union/political opposition.

Such a process was also under way during the last years of the late Soviet Union. Although it was largely ignored by Western analysts (including, alas, much of the Bush administration), many of whom were in thrall to Gorbophilia, a few others looked at the rising democratic *opposition* to Gorbachev and at the reconstituted elements of civil society from which that opposition grew, and saw the future more clearly than the Gorbophiles.

For several years, S. Frederick Starr of Oberlin College had been urging Western analysts to take more seriously the rapid growth of independent social and cultural organizations across what was then the USSR. Here, Starr argued, was the existential rejection of the tyranny of the political; here was the civic and civil opposition on whose foundations a political opposition might be built.[1] Similarly, James H. Billington, the Librarian of Congress, who is also America's foremost historian of Russian culture, had been writing and speaking throughout the late 1980s about the religious renaissance under way in Great Russia and throughout the Soviet empire. This dynamic revival of Christian conviction not only proved a more powerful stimulus to dramatic change than Gorbachevian reformism—it also helped set an important foundation for future efforts to exorcise the demons of the Leninist past and to construct a more humane future.

Had Billington, Starr, and others like them been taken as seriously as they deserved, and had the lessons of that prior revolution of the spirit that rolled like a cleansing tide across central and eastern Europe in 1989 been absorbed, the West might not have been quite so surprised by the non-violent resistance that checked the Gang That Couldn't Shoot Straight in Moscow in August 1991.

THREE DAYS IN AUGUST

As it happened, James Billington was in Moscow on Library of Congress business when Lenin's Communist imperium finally imploded. For three days in August 1991, Billington wound his way back and forth between the meetings he was scheduled to attend and the revolution he was, in a sense, born to cover. The result, a book called *Russia Transformed*, is a fascinating combination of fast-paced instant history and thoughtful cultural analysis that reinforces the claim that the Communist crackup was not simply a dramatic form of consumer revolt.[2]

The politics of fear in Russia has a long and unhappy history. In a reflection on the continuities of Russian culture that offers a gentle challenge to the great Aleksandr Solzhenitsyn (among others), Billington describes traditional Russian self-consciousness as a "negative nationalism derived from the traditional fears that exposed peoples on the steppe felt toward both external invaders and internal betrayal."[3] The ancient practice of autocracy fed a tradition of fanaticism on the part of the rulers. And this, in turn, generated countercurrents of fanatic resistance: utopian religious dissidents like the apocalyptically oriented "Old Believers" and the often murderous and anarchistic revolutionaries of the Russian intelligentsia, from whose ideological womb were eventually born the Bolsheviks. Could this cyclical pattern, which had trapped the Russian people in a vortex of political violence for centuries, ever be broken?

That was the deeper moral-cultural issue resolved, for the time being at least, by those three stunning days in August 1991. The key date, according to Billington, was August 19, the first day of the attempted coup. For it was on that day that what at first seemed to be the overwhelming power of the coup plotters was countered by three elements: "the image of the leader, a circle of supporters, and the dispatch of messengers."[4]

The *image* was that of Boris Yeltsin proclaiming his defiance of the coup from atop a tank outside the White House, the residence and offices of the president of the Russian Republic. Here, Billington writes, was the "simple icon everyone needed to engage the emotions in a society where words have often been debased and where words alone have never been enough."[5]

The *circle of supporters* was the human wall that the democratic resistance formed around the White House. That spontaneous chain of non-violent physical resistance made it clear that the mere threat of coercion was no longer sufficient to cow the populace. But the human wall did more than protect Yeltsin and those of his people who stood guard within the White House itself. The human wall projected a kind of irresistible moral power: "Like waves rolling outward from a central point, an alternative allegiance seemed to be radiating to the broader society."[6]

Moral power was necessarily reinforced by bargaining, argument, and negotiation: thus the *dispatch of messengers* from Yeltsin's enclave to the army and KGB troops with which the coup plotters planned to crush the democratic resistance. Heated debates took place between the democratic emissaries and two key military units: the Red Army's elite Tamansky division and the KGB's "Alpha" anti-terrorist strike force, which had been assigned to storm the White House. But at the end of the arguments, Billington writes, the calculus of coercion had been reversed: "The age of the Russian Rambos was over. The burden of fear had shifted from the populace at large to the KGB."[7]

How was it possible for the New Russian Revolution to break

the historic and violent cycle of fanaticism and counter-fanaticism that had previously defined the rhythm of Russian political history? Billington suggests that three key influences were at work.

The first influence was the West: particularly Western ideas, and most especially the Western ideal of an open, democratic society. This ideal, Billington argues, and not the attractions of a more open, market economy, was what "brought young Russia to the barricades" in August 1991. Gorbachev had offered the market (or a form of the market) without democracy. And that, as well as a return to the politics of mass coercion, was what the resistance rejected when it defied the coup and supported Yeltsin.

Here, Billington gives considerable credit to Ronald Reagan as the Western leader whose ability to articulate a vision of law-governed democracy was crucial to the transformation of Russian consciences. "The very qualities that annoyed many of President Reagan's critics at home—the simplicity of his message and the use of moralistic language ('evil empire')—found a certain resonance among Russians, who were beginning to cut loose from the sophisticated rationalizations in which Gorbachev was still trying to wrap his reform Communism."[8] Billington also stresses the corrosive impact on the totalitarian system of Western information technology, including radio broadcasts and that grail of the communications revolution, the copying machine.

The second key influence on the events of August 1991 was the transformation of politics in the Russian hinterlands. Long a bastion of reactionary Communist orthodoxy, Siberia had undergone dramatic change: by the early 1990s, writes Billington, it "was no longer the place that received exiles from the authoritarian center. It was sending to that center elected radical democrats from a resurgent periphery."[9] Billington's description of the historical demographics of this crucial reversal is a fascinating exploration of the ways in which, over time, the coercive powers of a state can generate the very antibodies that eventually attack, and destroy, the cancer of repression.

And the third influence was religion. Billington, as noted previously, was acutely aware of the renaissance of Russian Orthodoxy that was taking place at the popular level while Western analysts and politicians focused almost exclusively on the elite processes of *glasnost* and *perestroika*. And thus he found it altogether fitting that the New Russian Revolution took place in a period of time "framed by the Feasts of the Transfiguration and the Assumption."

Due credit is given to Patriarch Alexei II for his "anathema against fraternal bloodletting," issued at 1:30 A.M. on August 21, just before the anticipated "Alpha" assault on the White House. But Billington leaves open the still-unresolved question of the patriarch's initial reaction to the coup, and concentrates instead on the crucial roles played by such modern martyr-confessors as Father Aleksandr Men and Father Gleb Yakunin in the recovery and reconstruction of the national conscience. Here, Billington argues, was born the "realization that overcoming totalitarianism meant breaking with the enslaving passion for revenge that fed into the Communist culture of vengeance and scapegoatism."[10] Thus the non-violence of the democratic resistance was neither an accident nor simply a matter of smart tactics. It was a matter of moral conviction.

GORBACHEV'S REVISED STANDARD VERSION

According to an old saw, history is always written by the winners. But in his May 6, 1992, speech in Fulton, Missouri, delivered from the very podium at which Winston Churchill lamented the descent of an "iron curtain" across Europe, Mikhail Gorbachev, the man whom history overran during those three stunning days in August 1991, tried to effect a comeback by rewriting the story of the Cold War—alas, to the applause of far too many American pundits, reporters, and men of means.

Showing an impressive instinct for the intellectual and moral vulnerabilities of the more tender-minded in his audience, Gorbachev argued that there were no winners and losers in the Cold War. There was, rather, "a shattering of the vicious circle into which we had driven ourselves." Thus the West should avoid "the intellectual, and consequently political, error of interpreting victory in the cold war narrowly as victory for oneself."[11]

And what was the Cold War? It was a bit of a misunderstanding, rooted in the "fateful error" the West made in assuming (imagine!)

that Stalin intended to expand Communist hegemony beyond eastern Europe. According to Gorbachev, this was fantasyland: Stalin and the USSR were simply too exhausted by the exertions of the Great Patriotic War against the Nazis to do much of anything about extending the sway of Soviet power. (This analysis doubtless came as news to the peoples of Poland, Czechoslovakia, Romania, Bulgaria, Hungary, and the old East Germany, as well as to those Greeks who remember the Soviet role in their civil war.)

Moreover, Gorbachev added, the West compounded its analytic error of 1945–47 by the folly of adding the "nuclear component" into world politics. (On a future fund-raising trip to the United States, perhaps Mr. Gorbachev could be taken to the FBI building, where the physical evidence of Soviet penetration of the Manhattan Project is amply displayed. And perhaps the Gorbachev Foundation could sponsor research in ex-Soviet diplomatic and Party files so that we might have a clear picture of just why Stalin rejected the Baruch Plan for the internationalization of atomic power.) Thus, in Gorbachev's telling of the tale, the world entered the "vicious circle" of the arms race, from which it was released, he implied, by his initiatives of *glasnost* and *perestroika*.

One might have expected a man who presided over the greatest collapse of political power in human history to take a more chastened view. One might have thought that a man whose resignation was greeted with yawns of boredom by his countrymen (who had long before concluded that he was an anachronism, and worse, a bumbling anachronism) would be less inclined to suggest that he was responsible for breaking the "vicious circle" of "the arms race." One might even have hoped that a man once noted for his call to "new thinking" might engage in a bit of that very thing on the question of the origins of the Cold War.

But genuinely, radically new thinking is not something of which Mikhail Gorbachev was, or apparently is, capable. Instead, at Fulton, Yuri Andropov's protégé trotted out a slightly revamped version of the revisionism that was hot stuff on American campuses twenty-five years ago. He thereby systematically distorted the history of the immediate post–World War II period, demeaned the memory of Churchill, and retroactively laundered Stalin's dirty linen in a thoroughly reprehensible fashion. Then, by the use of the "vicious circle" imagery, Gorbachev appealed to the persistent fantasies of those who insisted that an irrational "enemy mind-set" led to an "arms race" in which the antagonists were, in Paul Warnke's famous (or infamous) phrase, "two apes on a treadmill." At the end of World War II, Gorbachev said,

> the USSR and the United States missed . . . the chance to establish their relationship on a new basis of principle, and thereby to initiate a world order different from that which existed before the war. . . . If the United States and the Soviet Union had been capable of comprehending their responsibility and sensibly correlating their national interests and strivings with the rights and interests of other states and peoples, the planet today would be a much more suitable and favorable place for human life.[12]

Indeed, it would be. But how can any serious person, in the wake of the crackup of the USSR, think of it as a partner capable of the kind of world-order building that Gorbachev suggested was possible in 1946? How could an empire that was itself a prison house of nations contribute to the pursuit of peace through freedom among nations? And what about Communism? What about Stalinism? On what "basis of principle" was the West supposed to do business with the greatest mass murderer in human history? How could the West have "correlated" its "national interests and strivings" with those of this pathological monster and the aggressive police state he ruthlessly controlled and exploited? (Ask the people of central and eastern Europe, and indeed of what was once Stalin's internal empire, about the late dictator's sense of their "interests and strivings.") The whole thing would be laughable, if it did not debase the witness of those who stood firm against Stalinist aggression and terror—and if Gorbachev had not been applauded for speaking such arrant nonsense by Americans who ought to know better (including, it is sad to recall, Ronald Reagan).

Thus Mikhail Gorbachev remained, in his Fulton speech, what he has always been: a reform Communist, unwilling (or unable) to grapple in an intellectually or morally serious way with the crimes of the totalitarian system in which he rose to power and from which he benefited enormously. That he had the gall to stand where the greatest political leader of the West in the twentieth century once stood and proclaim that the last phase of the fifty-five-year struggle against totalitarianism was based on a Western misunderstanding—this gives *chutzpah* a wholly new dimension.

Gorbachev, interestingly enough, was never viewed with adulation by the leaders of the Revolution of 1989 in central and eastern Europe. They were grateful that he was not Leonid Brezhnev, and that the tanks did not roll westward into Poland in June 1989—which most assuredly would have happened under Brezhnev. The more favorably inclined among those we once called dissidents saw Gorbachev on the local analogy of an enlightened czar: as a man who operated within a very narrow band of reforming possibilities. But Gorbachev could never seem to grasp the truly revolutionary concept that animated and sustained the successful human-rights activists of the 1980s: the re-creation of civil society as the social embodiment of the transcendent moral dimension of the human person.

And thus, in a supremely ironic way, Gorbachev manifested, not the resurgence of Communist self-confidence in a new, post-Brezhnevite generation of leaders, but the utter moral and intellectual bankruptcy of the Communist project. Rather then representing what had long been sought on the Western left, a self-reforming Communism shorn of its more odious crudities, Gorbachev embodied the inability of even an enlightened leader to salvage a system that was false at the deepest level. Communism was wrong about the nature of the human person, human community, human history, and human destiny. Gorbachev's failure to grasp that was the ultimate cause of his political failure. And thus, as Leszek Kołakowski had discerned years before, the last act of Communism was farce.[13]

THE COMMUNIST HANGOVER

Mikhail Gorbachev's blatant Cold War revisionism did more than distort the past: it also contributed to further Western misunderstanding of the multiple dilemmas of post–Cold War reconstruction in central and eastern Europe.

No small part of the West's confusion and consternation over the tribulations of post-Communist societies is the result of a residual, debilitating misconception of Communism. That misunderstanding, married to the historical myopia too often found among Western elites, has fueled Western incomprehension about the sources and dynamics of the extreme nationalism, ethnic violence, and barbarism that have broken out in several parts of Stalin's old regime.

It seems that it has to be said again, and again, and again: Communism was not just another form of political tyranny. Communism was a form of *totalitarianism*: it sought the transformation, not just of men's politics, but of their souls, their relationships, and their identities. Even under the "bureaucratic totalitarianism" of the post-Khrushchev era, during which the fires of Marxist-Leninist ideological conviction burned less brightly than in the old days, the very nature of Communist social control mitigated against social normality and human decency. And the results are too much with us.

A Damaged Moral Ecology

In a 1993 lecture at George Washington University, President Václav Havel of the Czech Republic made this point in attempting to analyze the "root causes" of the difficulties of post-Communist societies:

> Communism was far from being simply the dictatorship of one group of people over another. It was a genuinely totalitarian system, that is, it permeated every aspect of life and deformed everything it touched, including all the natural ways people had evolved of living together. . . . It was a perverted structure . . . but society nevertheless internalized it, or rather was forced to internalize it.[14]

That "perverted structure," the Communist culture of the lie, collapsed with Communist power in 1989. But, Havel argued, "people couldn't simply absorb and internalize a new structure immediately, one that would correspond to the elementary principles of civic society and democracy. . . . [T]o build a new system of living values and to identify with them takes time."[15]

Thus the old system and its anti-values had collapsed; but the new values necessary to sustain civil society and comity after the overthrow of Communist regimes had not yet been internalized in a durable way throughout central and eastern Europe. And into this vacuum came "radicalism of all kinds," the "hunt for scapegoats," and the "need to hide behind the anonymity of a group, be it socially or ethnically based." The net result was an "unparalleled flourishing of selfishness," itself an expression of the moral-ecological damage that Communism left in its wake.[16]

Havel also reminded his audience that Communism had imposed a "vast shroud of uniformity, stifling all national, intellectual, spiritual, social, cultural, and religious variety." That, in turn, led to "the monstrous illusion that we were all the same." When Communism collapsed, so did that shroud of uniformity —and from beneath it there emerged all those differences that "proletarian internationalism" was supposed to have smoothed out. After the long, dark night of enforced sameness, each of these traits, Havel argued, "felt a natural need to draw attention to itself, to emphasize its uniqueness and its difference from others. This is the reason for the eruption of so many different kinds of old-fashioned patriotism, revivalist messianism, conservatism, and expressions of hatred toward all those who appeared to be betraying their roots or identifying with different ones."[17]

And that dynamic has played itself out in particularly bloody ways in the former Yugoslavia, where the understandable (and ancient) urge to emphasize ethnic and religious uniqueness was welded to nationalism and then exploited by the demagoguery of unscrupulous politicians.

The Return of History

As I argued above, the "final revolution"—the revolution of conscience that shaped the non-violent political revolution in the lands of Stalin's evil empire—was not the end of history but rather the return of history to its normal patterns and rhythms. President Havel takes that analysis a step further, arguing that Communism not only stopped history but thereby forestalled, in parts of eastern Europe, the development of the attitudes and understandings that sustain democracy and pluralism—social traits that had evolved in the West over a long period of time. Moreover, "national and cultural differences were driven into the subterranean areas of social life, where they were . . . prevented from developing freely, from taking on modern form in the fresh air, from creating, over time, the free space of unity in variety."[18]

To compound these difficulties, several countries that had fallen under Communist rule had not, before the fall, resolved some of the crucial questions—especially about pluralism—involved in their very nationhood. These issues lay trapped under the ice of the Communist system. Then, when the icecap broke up, Havel writes, "thousands of unresolved problems suddenly burst forth":

> It is truly astonishing to discover how, after decades of falsified history and ideological manipulation, *nothing has ever been forgotten*. Nations are now remembering their ancient achievements and their ancient suffering, their ancient suppressors and their allies, their ancient animosities and affinities—in short, they are suddenly recalling a history that, until recently, has been carefully concealed or misrepresented [emphasis added].[19]

The turmoil in post-Communist central and eastern Europe is not, therefore, simply the result of the Yalta imperial system; it also involves the long-term residue of the treaties of Versailles and St. Germain–Trianon at the end of World War I. Similarly, the turmoil in the post-Communist ex-USSR is a reflection of the historical impact of Great Russian imperialism on dozens of ancient nations and peoples. Some of these dissaffected people, Havel observes, want to go "even farther back into history [than the Cold War period] and exploit the greatest freedom some of them have ever had to make further amends" for even more ancient grievances.[20] Thus among the ironic "accomplishments" of the Communist empire was that, even as it consolidated the gains of the Romanov imperialism it brutally overthrew, it spared the West, for some forty-five years, the results of Western folly in 1919. We are to be spared no longer, it appears.

Questions of Scale

Finally, Václav Havel asks us to remember the magnitude of the historical change that is now under way. People who never knew how to think about Communism imagine that the problems of post-Communism are roughly analogous to those of any political transition: one set of rascals gets thrown out, another bunch gets in. But the post-Communist world is not to be understood on the analogy of Spain after Franco, or France after Napoleon, much less America between presidents. Rather, Havel argues, "the fall of the communist empire is an event on the same scale of historical importance as the fall of the Roman empire."[21] A vast, continental system of social control has collapsed, leaving behind a jumble of peoples, races, and nations in varying degrees of economic, political, and cultural chaos.

Some of them will recover rather quickly, meaning that in ten or fifteen years they will have established stable democratic polities, well-functioning market economies, and the vibrant moral culture necessary to sustain and discipline free political and economic institutions. The Poles, the Hungarians, and the Czechs are three good bets, if they stay the present economic course and if no mass refugee wave washes over them from an imploding Great Russia. Others—and here we come back to the unhappy southern Slavs—haven't even entered the recovery ward. Still others, including most of the states that emerged from the former Soviet Union, are in an intermediate position; the future of the modest political and economic reforms they have undertaken is very uncertain. Thus it seems prudent to see the wisdom in Havel's judgment that building decent societies "on the ruins of communism might be as extended and complex a process as the creation of a Christian Europe—after the great migrations—once was."[22]

THE POST-POLITICAL FUTURE

If the first, great symbolic reference point for the revolution of the spirit that made possible the political revolution against Communism was the pilgrimage of John Paul II to his native Poland in June 1979, the end of the line may be taken to have come in August 1991 when, as James Billington has noted, Father Aleksandr Borisov, an Orthodox priest and member of the Moscow City Council, distributed some 2,000 Bibles to the soldiers in the tanks outside the Russian parliament (only one soldier refused) and another 2,000 to those on the barricades protecting Yeltsin's White House. Borisov then helped convince Patriarch Alexei to intervene, and the patriarch issued a prayer that, as Billington put it, anathematized fratricide.[23]

And that, as we might say in another context, was the ballgame.

That most of the policy apparatus of Western governments, and much of the fraternity of Western pundits, simply missed this revolution of the spirit (or dismissed it as mere froth on the kettle of economic frustration) is an indication of just how deeply what Jacques Ellul called "the illusion of politics" has infected the West. To decry the tyranny of the political is not, of course, to say that politics is unimportant: but it is to put politics in its place. In the great tradition of the West (the tradition deliberately rejected by Rousseau and Marx, not to mention Vladimir Ilich Ulyanov), politics is not primarily about getting and keeping power. Rather, politics, properly construed, is the ongoing and public deliberation about the good man and the good society. Politics is, inescapably, a function of culture. And the heart of culture is cult, religion.

The pre-political Revolution of 1989 and its child, the pre-political New Russian Revolution, may give birth to the era of the post-political, and sooner rather than later. Delusions about a politically driven messianic age will survive, but their devotees will be increasingly viewed as living anachronisms. New heresies will emerge (some already have: take a close look at the New Age section at your local bookstore). But their driving passion is unlikely to be politics-the-contest-for-power.

The remarkable events of 1989–91 revealed two great truths about contemporary history: that the ultramundane heresy of Marxism-Leninism is finished as a world-historical force, and that the primary struggle in the West will now be at the level of culture. The new *Kulturkampf* in the developed democracies will touch, at points, on the world of politics; like the poor, the Joycelyn Elders of this world will, alas, always be with us. But it is altogether possible, and perhaps even likely, that the men and women of the twenty-first century will look far less to the order of politics as the focus of their energies, and far more to the order of culture. We may even see the revival of a true Judeo-Christian humanism, in place of the sundry false humanisms that have beset us these past two centuries.

That would, in fact, be a wholly fitting wrapup to the Revolution of 1989 and the New Russian Revolution. For it was the humanism whose true roots lie in Jewish and Christian concepts of the human person, human society, human history, and human destiny that finally toppled the modern Moloch, the false and anti-human "humanism" of Marxism-Leninism. Today's springtime of nations, for all its troubles, was born from a springtime of the human spirit. We would do well to remember that, as the hard realities of post-Communist democratic consolidation become ever more pressing in central and eastern Europe.

3

Who Won the Cold War?
How? So What?

Put as baldly as that, the questions seem to answer themselves, and in a commonsense fashion. The West, led by the United States, won the Cold War, whose endgame was defined by the collapse of Communist regimes in central and eastern Europe. The West won by successfully implementing the strategy of containment first enunciated in the late 1940s. And because the West won, the peoples of central and eastern Europe have a new opportunity to build free societies; moreover, the world can breathe a little easier, given the demise of that nuclear-armed superpower once known as the "Union of Soviet Socialist Republics." Amidst all the contentions and confusions of the post–Cold War world, surely this much, at least, could be agreed upon.

Alas, it was not to be. In part because of the pressures of the 1992 presidential campaign, in part because of the aftereffects of some bad ideas that were in broad circulation *during* the Cold War, the very notion of a Cold War "victory" has been challenged by prominent Western analysts as well as by the aforementioned Mikhail Gorbachev. In Gorbachev's case, the challenge was predictable: losing is never easy, and admitting defeat can be even more painful to proud spirits than suffering it. It should hardly come as a surprise that the last general secretary of the Communist Party of the Soviet Union deplores the notion that the West won the Cold War; Field Marshall Jodl wasn't smiling at Reims on May 7, 1945, either. But what are we to make of the *Western* deprecation of what seems to be the West's victory in the Cold War?

The Dean's Nonsense

Take, for example, George F. Kennan, author of the doctrine of "containment" and the man usually considered the "dean of American Sovietologists." Writing in the *New York Times* in the heat of the 1992 presidential campaign, Kennan opined that any claims of Western "victory" in the Cold War were "intrinsically silly."[1]

Why? Because "no great country has that sort of influence on the internal developments of any other one." Moreover, there was never that much to the Cold War anyway: "As early as the late 1940s, some of us . . . saw that the regime was becoming dangerously remote from the concerns and hopes of the Russian people." (In the late 1940s? Prescient, indeed.) Moreover, it was clear, in 1952, "that the [Soviet] regime as we had known it would not last for all time." (A remarkable insight, perhaps influenced by an undergraduate reading of Gibbon.) Evidence of this capacity for growth appeared when Nikita Khrushchev "took the lead in . . . [offering] internal political liberalization and relaxation of international tensions." (As in the forced closure of some 15,000 Orthodox churches, the sundry Berlin crises, and the Cuban missile crisis?)

But these efforts were derailed by the "extreme militarization of American discussion and policy," which led Moscow to "tighten the controls by both party and police" and to abandon many "liberalizing tendencies in the regime." (So much for the West's lack of influence on Soviet policy.) Thus "pretending that the end of [the Cold War] was a great triumph for anyone" is simply a reprise of the "unnecessarily belligerent and threatening tone" that the West adopted too often in its dealings with the Soviet Union. "Nobody—no country, no party, no person—'won' the Cold War," insisted Kennan.

It is sad to read such self-demeaning foolishness from so distinguished a scholar and public servant as George F. Kennan. (Sad, but not wholly surprising; this was, after all, the man who at the height of the Soviet nuclear buildup in the early 1980s argued that we should worry about strengthening the Western deterrent only after we had organized to defend ourselves from the pornography merchants on Fourteenth Street in Washington.[2]) But for all its historical misreadings and internal contradictions, Kennan's article neatly summarized the new revisionist historiography of the Cold War, which turns out, on closer examination, to resemble nothing so much as the Vietnam-inspired Cold War revisionism of the late 1960s:

- the Soviet Union ceased to be an ideologically driven power shortly after the death of Lenin;
- Stalin-era horrors like the Ukrainian terror famine and the Moscow purge trials were expressions of the maximum leader's own pathologies, not the system's;
- the creation of a Soviet-controlled "external empire" was the result of historic Great Russian imperial ambitions exacerbated by a threatening West, the "iron curtain" being, in the final analysis, the fault of Winston Churchill and Harry Truman;
- the inexorable liberalization of the Soviet regime was forestalled, on many occasions, by aggressive Western policies, including weapons developments and human-rights advocacy;
- the only military-industrial complex of consequence was in the West, and specifically in the United States;
- Ronald Reagan was an ignorant cowboy who, by sheer dumb luck, happened to be president when Mikhail Gorbachev, the ultimate liberalizer, came to power in the USSR;
- it was Gorbachev whose initiatives and vision drove the politics of the late 1980s;
- the Warsaw Pact and the Soviet Union unraveled because they could not compete economically with the West.

Therefore, there were no "winners" and "losers" in the Cold War. Q.E.D.

WEAPONS AND POLITICS: REVISING THE REVISIONISTS

Happily, far more persuasive interpretations of the political and military dynamics of the recent past are available. Perhaps the most comprehensive and elegantly argued effort to revise the revisionists is Patrick Glynn's 1992 study, *Closing Pandora's Box: Arms Races, Arms Control, and the History of the Cold War.*[3] Indeed, Glynn's book is intellectually invigorating precisely because he

challenges virtually every one of the principal foreign-policy orthodoxies currently regnant in the American academy, in the
prestige press, and on the port side of the political spectrum.

But Glynn's work cannot be dismissed as mere ideological
fencing. *Closing Pandora's Box* is a serious, scholarly attempt to
grasp the dynamics of the relation between military power and
political power in the era of weapons of mass destruction. As
such, it has relevance for the post–Cold War world as well as for
our understanding of the past.

The "Sarajevo Fallacy"

Patrick Glynn begins his study by revisiting the central doctrinal
orthodoxy that dominated most Western strategic thinking during
the Cold War, and the contradictory policy impulses to which this
orthodoxy gave rise:

> For most of the twentieth century, the hope for peace and the
> fear of war converged on the phenomenon of the arms race. At
> the root of this hope and fear lay a widely shared conviction
> that arms races were inherently dangerous and ultimately desta-
> bilizing. So firmly established was this belief in western political
> discourse that statesmen came to take it for granted. As a result
> of this conviction, western strategy of the postwar era remained
> torn between two fundamentally opposing premises: the notion
> that military strength deters aggression and the competing
> belief that the arms race itself could be a cause of war. Through-
> out the Cold War era, the view that the arms race could lead to
> catastrophe continually challenged and unsettled the western
> faith in nuclear deterrence. Though understanding the need to
> guarantee peace through military power, western governments
> and peoples remained wary of the means at their disposal,
> haunted by the fear that the very measures they took to secure
> their safety could be driving them to oblivion.[4]

One crucial source of this conviction was the interpretation of
World War I adumbrated after the war by, among many others,
Britain's Edward Grey, who had been foreign secretary in the
Liberal government of H. H. Asquith when war broke out in
1914. "Great armaments lead inevitably to war," Lord Grey wrote
in 1925, and that judgment would soon be amplified by a moral
indictment: it was the arms manufacturers, the "merchants of

death," who drove Europe into the slaughter pens of the Somme, the Marne, Passchendaele, Ypres, and Verdun.[5]

On this reading of the history of the late nineteenth and early twentieth centuries, the naval arms race between Britain and Germany and the arms race in land forces conducted by France and Germany had made Europe into a tinderbox by 1914. The only thing needed for the conflagration to begin was a match— even one thrown accidentally. "Arms racing," in other words, created a virtually inexorable drift toward war that no political power, whatever its inclinations, could reverse.

Thus on this analysis, World War I was "caused" by the pre-World War I "arms race." The match thrown into the tinderbox was the assassination of the Austro-Hungarian Archduke Franz Ferdinand by a Serbian nationalist, Gavrilo Princip, in the Bosnian capital of Sarajevo on June 28, 1914. After this, war was inevitable, given the dynamics created by the arms race. This was the interpretation popularized by Barbara Tuchman in her 1962 book *The Guns of August*, a book said to have deeply impressed President Kennedy in his thinking about the nuclear-arms competition between the United States and the USSR. Indeed, the "guns of August" imagery and analysis have become so deeply ingrained that the "arms race" explanation for World War I has seemed virtually incontestable.

Patrick Glynn, however, wishes to contest it. He labels the Grey/Tuchman interpretation the "Sarajevo Fallacy," and argues that it

> gives a completely distorted picture of the events that culmi-nated in war in 1914. It obscures the source both of the arms race and of the war itself, which lay in German ambitions and conscious decisions made by the German Reich. . . . The key question was always whether Germany wanted war and was willing to risk it, and whether the Entente powers, Britain in particular, could take actions that would render such risks unacceptable. World War I did not result from any "accident"; war came in 1914 for the relatively simple reason that a hege-monic state sought to expand its influence in the world and was persuaded by the apparent momentary weakness and indecision of its opponents to do so by violent means.[6]

World War I, in other words, need not have happened, had the Entente powers effectively resisted Kaiser Wilhelm's efforts to expand Germany's sphere of influence *prior* to the outbreak of military hostilities. There was nothing inevitable about the "guns of August." The slaughter commenced because one great power's ambitions were met by weakness and indecisiveness on the part of the other great powers. The "answer" to the puzzle of World War I does not lie in odd notions of historical inexorability linked to a totemic understanding of the power of weapons; the answer lies in the human dynamics of politics and political decision-making.

Glynn's identification of the Sarajevo Fallacy is an important attempt to restore human intentionality to the politics of a technological age. Things need not have been the way they were. Men could have decided differently. The weapons don't control us; we control them, if we have the will and the wisdom to do so.

More Heresy

As Patrick Glynn would readily acknowledge, the Sarajevo Fallacy image does not explain everything about the dynamics of international politics in the twentieth century. But the analysis does provide a sharp scalpel for cutting through some of the fustian that surrounds the historiography of the Cold War.

Glynn makes several other heretical assertions that challenge the regnant orthodoxies. First, he claims (and illustrates through detailed research) that military capability remained a crucial determinant of political power throughout the Cold War. When the Soviet Union believed it was on the front end of the curve in its military competition with the West, its efforts to increase its international influence increased accordingly. But in the face of demonstrated U.S. military capability and the threat to use it, Soviet leaders backed off.

Running radically against the grain of the conventional wisdom, Glynn even defends the political utility of John Foster Dulles's doctrine of "massive retaliation," which has been sharply attacked from virtually all ideological quarters since it was first enunciated in the early days of the Eisenhower administration. Glynn cites an interesting witness in his case for the defense: Nikita Khrushchev himself. "Dulles," Khrushchev wrote in his memoirs, "was a worthy and interesting adversary who forced us to either lay down our arms or marshall some good reasons to continue the struggle. . . . It always kept us on our toes to match wits with him." The former Soviet leader was not enamored of Dulles's bellicose approach; the policy of threatened "massive retaliation" was, Khrushchev argued, "barefaced atomic blackmail." But "it had to be reckoned with at the time."[7] Thus Glynn, while reminding his readers that there are gentler callings than leadership at the higher altitudes of international politics, frontally challenges the notion that the nuclear age rendered military power essentially useless—and on the evidence of a crucial Soviet witness.

Another of Glynn's heresies is his argument that ideology— and specifically the conviction that the USSR was in a moral struggle with the West, a struggle that was not an accident but a necessary byproduct of the fundamental clash of convictions between Communism and liberal democracy—was a decisive factor in Soviet decision-making well into the Brezhnev era. Yes, the white heat of ideological conviction had cooled after the first generation of Bolshevik leaders; the Communist millennium was clearly not at hand. But the argument that post-Lenin (and even post-Stalin) Soviet leaders remained dedicated Communists, de-termined to secure their own power and to expand its sway in world politics, seems a far more plausible explanation of actual Soviet behavior than others bruited over the past generation.

An "Arms Race"?

Glynn dismisses as historically ignorant and politically naïve the "two apes on a treadmill" image used by Paul Warnke (nominated by Jimmy Carter to be director of the U.S. Arms Control and Disarmament Agency and chief SALT II negotiator) to describe the U.S./Soviet nuclear "arms race." Of even less consequence was the psychobabble notion, popularized by Sam Keen in the early 1980s, that the West's bewitchment by an "enemy mind-set" drove it to misperceive the intentions of its adversary. Indeed, the implication of Glynn's historical analysis is that the very image of the "arms race" was itself a misapprehension that, by reviving the Sarajevo Fallacy under new and more ominous circumstances, almost inevitably produced vulgarizations like Warnke's "apes."

Whatever else was going on, what was usually described as the "arms race" was not, according to Glynn, an action-reaction cycle initiated by the West (and those new "merchants of death," the "military-industrial complex"). Rather, and throughout the ebbs and flows of the Cold War, the *Soviet* military-industrial complex (the only such phenomenon worthy of the name) ground steadily on, with one aim in mind: victory, meaning the triumph of its system over the rival system of capitalist democracy.[8] Given that bottom-line reality, when the history of the attempt to reverse the "arms race" by "arms control" is conceived (as it usually is) as a series of "lost opportunities," a grave misconception of Soviet decision-making is at work.

Glynn is particularly adept in his critique of "arms control," a phrase that, like "arms race," obscured far more than it clarified. In fact, the two idioms reinforced each other in a kind of mirror-imaging. Who could be *for* the "arms race"? And who could be *against* "arms control," a phrase so reasonable-sounding that its critics could easily by dismissed as warmongers and simpletons. Yet the truth about "arms control" was far more complex, and far more interesting.

Out of Control

"Arms control theory" was born, not so much from a moral revulsion against weapons of mass destruction, as from the concern for rational and cost-effective defense management that emerged when Western strategists abandoned any hope of achieving meaningful disarmament as long as the Cold War endured. Arms "control" was about precisely that: it was a tool for managing the ongoing competition in conventional and especially nuclear weaponry between the United States and the Soviet Union. It was not about massive reductions in nuclear weapons; indeed, one of the things that the "arms control process" seemed to foster (or at least did virtually nothing to stop) was the evolution of ever more destructive nuclear weapons. But "arms control" had to be sold to the public as a form of disarmament, if only because "arms control theory" contained some very counterintuitive notions that its proponents suspected (and not without reason) the American people would find incredible.

The intellectual architecture of "arms control" was itself dependent on the arcana of game theory, that form of probability mathematics in which seemingly rational choices can sometimes lead to undesirable conclusions—as in the famous "Prisoner's Dilemma" game. Thus "arms control" gave birth to several curious doctrines that, for all their intellectual elegance, seemed somewhat detached from the grubby realities of politics—and even from common sense. Perhaps the most famous of these formulations was Mutual Assured Destruction (MAD), by which it was argued, first, that it was a Good Thing for the United States and the Soviet Union to have achieved the capacity to destroy each other many times over, and second, that the two superpowers ought to remain vulnerable to each other's nuclear weapons.

According to MAD doctrine, the "arms race" could not be won. Moreover, the very notion of "winning" was a bit medieval, a hangover from the days before nuclear weapons and ICBMs. And, as winning was bad, so was defending yourself: for defense threatened the balance of nuclear terror that, according to the theoreticians, was the regulatory mechanism in superpower relations. Thus, according to "arms control" doctrine, a "rational" nuclear "actor" would understand that any attempt to defend his society from devastating destruction would be regarded as a gravely threatening breach of the protocols of deterrence by the adversary, who would then be tempted either to build similar defenses (thus creating the illusion of a "winnable" nuclear war) or to strike preemptively before the proposed defenses were in place (thus vitiating the whole purpose of defense).

But for all its intellectual debt to game theory, "arms control theory"—and what might be called the "arms control sensibility"—was most profoundly shaped by the liberal dogma of the "arms race": "arms races" were, self-evidently, Bad Things; unchecked "arms races" inevitably led to war. Perhaps disarmament couldn't be achieved (for now). But surely the "arms race" could be managed, and even tempered, by rational men seeking the rational ends of politics, as those have been understood in the West for centuries.

Below the SALT

The quintessential expression of this "arms control" theory and sensibility in the 1970s was the SALT (Strategic Arms Limitations

Talks) process, initiated by Richard Nixon and carried through to its logical (or illogical) end by Jimmy Carter. SALT was sold to the American public as a brake on nuclear-arms competition and as an essential element in a détente between the superpowers (détente being assumed to be a Good Thing). But, as Glynn points out, the "SALT process" produced more nuclear weapons, particularly more *Soviet* nuclear weapons. Why? Why were real cuts in nuclear weapons so difficult to achieve?

The standard explanation from "arms controllers" like Paul Warnke was that the United States wasn't putting enough on the table. And thus the Carter administration,[9] as Glynn puts it, "proved tireless in devising . . . new concessions to sweeten relations with Moscow." But the hard truth of the matter, illustrated in painstaking detail in *Closing Pandora's Box*, is that "arms control" didn't produce real cuts because the Soviet Union didn't want real cuts. Indeed, one of the great services of Glynn's book is its powerful demonstration that the Soviet leadership never adopted the dogmas of "arms control theory." By Soviet lights, one could never have too much offense or too much defense. And by the late 1970s, even the Carter administration's defense secretary, Harold Brown, had conceded that "when we build, they build. When we stop, they nevertheless continue to build."

"Arms control" did function as a restraint: but only on the side that accepted "arms control theory." And this, in turn, led to a general pattern of Western strategic and political deterioration. Indeed, as Glynn argues,

> the most harrowing periods of the Cold War [were] always those in which the apparent balance of power . . . shifted in favor of the Soviet Union. In 1949, the Soviet explosion of an atomic bomb had prepared the way for actual "hot" war in Korea. In 1957, the launching of the *Sputnik* satellite had inaugurated five years of crisis, culminating in the Cuban missile showdown. In 1979, the Soviet invasion of Afghanistan marked the beginning of yet a third period of protracted confrontation.[10]

This time, of course, the confrontation ended with the decisive victory of the West and the collapse of the Soviet Union, shortly after the demise of its external empire. The cycle had been broken, not by "arms control," but by a president who thought that more was better, that defense was good, and that ideological confrontation should be vigorously engaged in. All this seemed the most dangerous simplemindedness to the cultured despisers of Ronald Reagan (including virtually the entire "arms control" guild). But Reagan intuitively grasped the enduring dynamics of the politics of nations in a way that had eluded the "arms control" sophisticates.

The result was the goal that the arms controllers sought but that "arms control" was inherently incapable of delivering: the end of the "arms race," and the dramatic reduction of the threat of nuclear war.

KISSINGER REVISITED

The degree to which the "arms control" sensibility continues to shape (and distort) certain construals of the recent past is amply shown by a comparison of Glynn's analysis in *Closing Pandora's Box* with Walter Isaacson's in his 1992 mega-biography *Kissinger*.[11] Isaacson, an assistant managing editor of *Time*, not only argues that Henry Kissinger's détente policies were a Good Thing at the time but implies that they helped pave the way for the new era of Soviet-American relations inaugurated by Gorbachev. Glynn, an official in the Arms Control and Disarmament Agency during the Reagan years, argues that Kissinger's détente was a major factor in the deteriorated strategic position in which the United States found itself by the late 1970s.

Isaacson's is the quintessential liberal interpretation of Kissinger: a not-so-admirable figure personally—grasping, ambitious, mendacious, and vain—whose strategy and diplomacy nonetheless did very good things for U.S.-Soviet relations. Glynn offers a rather different interpretation. Kissinger's pessimism about the inexorable decline of the West led him to adopt a policy of strategic retreat, which would be transformed in the early (i.e., pre-Afghanistan) Carter years into a variant on the old appeasement strategy of Neville Chamberlain and Sir Horace Wilson in the 1930s. In Glynn's view, it was precisely the rejection of this declinism by Ronald Reagan, and the embodiment of that rejection in policy (the deployment of Pershing II and cruise missiles in western Europe, the MX, the Strategic Defense Initiative, the Reagan Doctrine of support for anti-Communist insurgencies, the creation of the National Endowment for Democracy) that brought the Cold War successfully to a close. Isaacson's "good Kissinger" is, in sum, Glynn's "bad Kissinger."

The Ultimate Heretics

The sharp contrast between the Isaacson and Glynn interpretations of the last two decades of the Cold War is also illustrated by the authors' dramatically divergent analyses of the phenomenon of anti-Communist neoconservatism, and of the role played throughout the détente years and beyond by a man who best embodied the neoconservative perspective in high national politics, Senator Henry M. Jackson of Washington.

Despite his evident admiration for Kissinger's skills as a negotiator, Walter Isaacson charges that his subject was an amoralist whose "brutal actions betrayed a callous attitude toward what Americans like to believe is the historic foundation of their foreign policy: a respect for human rights, international law, democracy, and other idealistic values." Indeed, Isaacson goes farther and turns his critique of Kissinger's Realpolitik into a more comprehensive filter for understanding the Cold War: ". . . the main reason that the United States triumphed in the Cold War was not because it won a competition for military power and influence. It was because the values offered by its system—among them a foreign policy that could draw its strength from the ideals of its people—eventually proved more attractive."[12]

But who was it, in the mid-1970s, who urged a foreign policy based, not on Spenglerian gloom, but on a renewed confidence that the "party of liberty" in world politics had the resources to bend history in its preferred direction? Who kept the democratic faith when both realists and liberals expressed the deepest skepticism about its prospects? Who offered the most sophisticated criticism of détente? Who recovered human rights as a major theme in America's address to the world?

There is ample credit to be distributed, as one seeks to identify the sources of intellect and energy that helped America recover its nerve in the 1980s. But any just distribution of credit will take serious account of the role played by those chastened liberals who came to be called "neoconservatives." Allied with traditional conservatives who had transcended the isolationism of their grandfathers and fathers, and who had come to a Burkean appreciation of the democratic possibility, the neoconservatives provided much of the ideological energy, and more than a few of the key policy initiatives, of the Reagan years, the years in which the Cold War was won. And no serious analysis of the neoconservatives' approach to foreign policy can ignore the central role played in its formulation by Senator Jackson.

Yet this is what Walter Isaacson cannot admit. In his rendering, Senator Jackson was a man devoid of sophistication about the world; it was his desire for the presidency that led him to an ideological "crusade" against détente.[13] The key initiative in this crusade was the Jackson-Vanik Amendment linking Most Favored Nation trading status for the USSR to a liberalization of Soviet emigration policies, particularly for Jews. According to Isaacson, "the idea of making such a demand on another sovereign nation was beyond Kissinger's ken," and Isaacson appears to share Kissinger's view that Jackson was "willing to sacrifice true American interests—such as more trade, the future of détente, the ability to use economic ties as leverage on issues such as arms control or Vietnam—in order to further the moral sentiment of championing Soviet Jewry" and in service of the senator's presidential "yearning."[14]

But in fact Jackson-Vanik was an attempt to hold the Soviets accountable to international human-rights standards to which they had committed themselves in a host of treaties, declarations, and U.N. covenants. Moreover, Jackson-Vanik was a test of Soviet seriousness about a genuine détente—as distinguished from a détente in which Soviet demands were always the occasion for further American concessions. Isaacson also dismisses those who supported Senator Jackson in his human-rights enterprise as a "self-appointed clique" who were willing to put the national interest on the back burner while they pursued their own ethnic or political agendas.[15]

But why does Isaacson, given his critique of Kissinger's Realpolitik, then attack Jackson's effort to restore the moral dimension to U.S. foreign policy? Isaacson's anti-Jackson animus is explicable only when one understands that, for liberal analysts, the heresiarchs of the Cold War were (and are) the neoconservatives.

Why? Because the neoconservatives denied what Isaacson claims is "the most important insight of the nuclear age: that an unconstrained arms race was futile, costly, and dangerous."[16] Which is to say, because the neoconservatives challenged the Sarajevo Fallacy.

According to the neoconservatives (and Senator Jackson), this one-eyed obsession with the "arms race" was emphatically *not* the "most important insight of the nuclear age." It was, to begin with, empirically wrong. The "arms race" was not bilaterally "unconstrained"; it was unilaterally unconstrained on the part of the Soviet Union. Yes, the "arms race" was costly, but the costs were radically asymmetrical: at the height of the Cold War, the Soviet Union was spending twice, thrice, or on occasion perhaps even five times the percentage of GNP on its military that the United States spent. And, yes, the "arms race" was dangerous: but precisely because Kissingerian and Carteresque détente had led to a deterioration of America's military forces and strategic position.

A Clash of Moralities

Moreover, the neoconservatives denied this central "insight" because it seemed to them morally craven. The most important thing was not simply to grasp the "danger of nuclear war"; anyone not certifiably insane could understand that. The important thing was to grasp the nature of the totalitarian adversary and the totalitarian project. The Cold War was a clash of worldviews and moralities, not just of great powers. Once that was understood, a wide-ranging menu of policy options could be considered: military and non-military, diplomatic, humanitarian, and ideological. And that was what happened in the Reagan administration: a commitment to restoring the military balance of power was married to non-military initiatives, the entire package being aimed at reversing the process of strategic deterioration.

The neoconservatives also knew that "strategic deterioration" involved the deliquescence of the democratic idea as well as the diminishment of America's military capability. Thus it was the neoconservatives who led the way in the articulation of the Reagan administration's defense of basic human rights, and in the formulation of Reagan's democracy initiative. The neocons, in other words, wedded what had been traditional liberal Democratic concerns (prior to the liberal self-flagellations of the Vietnam and post-Vietnam eras) to the unrepentant anti-Communism that had become confined almost exclusively to the starboard side of the political spectrum.

And this, one suspects, is what Walter Isaacson and those of his ideological persuasion cannot forgive. The neoconservatives were more faithful to core elements of the traditional liberal Democratic heritage than were many post-McGovern liberals. The neoconservatives were a mirror into which liberals were compelled to gaze: and what they saw, they didn't like. But being unable to admit their own complicity in the failed politics of the new appeasement, they are now reduced to demeaning the reputations of those who were in fact vindicated by events.

More Than Hardware

While *Closing Pandora's Box* is a far more trustworthy guide to understanding the military-political dynamics of the Cold War than *Kissinger*, it is not (and does not pretend to be) the whole story. As its subtitle announces, Patrick Glynn's focus is on "arms races, arms control, and the history of the Cold War." He barely mentions the "software" side of the period 1975–1991: the Helsinki Final Act and the subsequent eruption of human-rights monitoring organizations in central and eastern Europe—organizations that became the backbone of the democratic resistance to Communism in the 1980s; the democracy initiative of the Reagan administration, which provided crucial moral, political, technical, and logistical support to the people and organizations that led to the Revolution of 1989 and the New Russian Revolution of August 1991; the resistance churches in the old Warsaw Pact nations, which were instrumental in the moral revolution against Communism. As man does not live by bread alone, neither is "politics" reducible to hardball—or military hardware—alone.

The Cold War was won—and, yes, the correct verb is "won" —because of a complex of factors. The great merit of Glynn's analysis is that he reminds liberals, and those conservatives given to a too radical interpretation of the notion that "ideas have consequences," that even after Alamogordo, military power is not a negligible aspect of the politics of nations. It made a great deal of difference indeed, in the endgame of the Cold War, that the "hardware" side of the strategic deterioration of the 1970s had been reversed.

Yes, the deepest values of the American people proved more resilient and more attractive than the debased and inhuman anti-morality of Marxism-Leninsm. But that victory of the human spirit was made possible by the fact that containment—hardware, and hardball—had created circumstances in which an effective, non-violent moral resistance could succeed.

4

Settling Accounts:
A Post-Communist
Political and Moral Reckoning

When Hitler's Germany was defeated in 1945, there was little doubt in anyone's mind that if a democratic regime was to be established in that country, a period of "denazification" would be necessary. Thus with broad support in the United States, a process began of prosecuting the major Nazi criminals and rooting out lesser functionaries who had served the Nazi regime, even if they had not actually committed crimes themselves.

Compare what has happened since the defeat of European Communism, the other great totalitarian system of our time. What Zbigniew Brzezinski pointed out in 1990 remains true: "To this day, though we have been saturated with revelation after revelation of the monumental scale of Stalinist crimes, literally not one, not even one Stalinist murderer has been punished for Stalinist crimes anywhere by anyone!"[1] Even much milder efforts of "decommunization" not only have been sharply resisted within the former Communist countries themselves but also have been denounced in the United States, where the denazification efforts were so widely applauded.

In Russia, when President Boris Yeltsin did to the Communist party what had been done to the Nazi party in post-war Germany—ban it as a criminal organization—a group of Communists challenged the action in court as unconstitutional. As the trial opened, a well-known American specialist in Soviet affairs

59

and the court Sovietologist at CBS, Professor Stephen F. Cohen of Princeton, speaking from Moscow, told the *New York Times*, "This country has had too many political trials already, and this one will have a chilling effect on the development of democracy here." Would an American professor have said anything like this in Berlin in 1946?

In Poland and the former German Democratic Republic, decommunization efforts have focused on exposing people listed in secret-police files as informers or collaborators. In Ukraine, the relationship between leaders of the Orthodox Church and the KGB has become an especially neuralgic point. But the case that generated the most American attention was the "lustrace" (or vetting) law passed by the federal parliament of the late republic of Czechoslovakia in October 1991. This law and the debate it provoked illuminate the argument over post-Communist accountability both in eastern Europe and in the United States.

THE CASE FOR A RECKONING

Given the revolution of conscience that had preceded and made possible Czechoslovakia's Velvet Revolution of 1989, a moral reckoning with the past might have been expected to happen quickly and naturally. But the corruption was too deep and too pervasive for that. The managers and principal beneficiaries of the *ancien régime* did not go gracefully; most, in fact, did not go at all. As the new president of Czechoslovakia, Václav Havel, put it in October 1991:

> Those involved in one way or another with the totalitarian system were given a magnanimous opportunity. They could leave their posts quietly and inconspicuously. Nothing would have happened to them. They could have reflected on the roles they had played. They had enough opportunities to do so. They have not made use of this opportunity. They have just perked up. They have settled down in various new posts and positions and have even started to laugh at us. . . . This has aroused general dissatisfaction, nervousness, when people see the self-same people who were humiliating and persecuting them in various ways for years still sitting in various offices, occupying leading posts in farm cooperatives, district authorities, local and

municipal administration, ministries, and the like, and they are working using the selfsame methods to which they had become accustomed. They behave toward people in the same arrogant way as they did before.[2]

And again, several months later:

I am very concerned by something that I have been hearing for two years: that various *nomenklatura* clans—including members of the former State Security—still control many enterprises and offices, continue to enrich themselves illegally, continue to invest stolen money, and continue happily to rule over those who have always lived honest lives. Those people take advantage of the fact that we have not managed early enough and with enough emphasis to part ways with the past and to restrict the influence of all those who actively co-created that past.[3]

Clearly something had to be done. To do nothing would have meant consigning the new Czechoslovak democracy to the death of a thousand cuts, with the dull blade of cynicism slicing away at the body politic until it bled to death, morally and politically.

The Lustrace Law

The aim of the lustrace law passed in October 1991 was not revenge; its aim was to secure and consolidate the transition to democracy and the free economy that had begun with the Velvet Revolution. The new law proposed to do this by restoring public confidence in the basic fairness of the machinery of governance, and by preventing former Communist officials, state-security (StB) agents, and their collaborators from sabotaging democratic and market reforms.

In light of the subsequent charges of "witch hunt" (with the inevitable overtones of McCarthyism that such charges carry in America), it is important to clarify what the lustrace law did *not* do. It did not exile anyone. It did not ban former Communists and collaborators from employment, or remove pension claims or rights. It did not impose criminal sanctions for past actions. It did not prevent anyone from running for the federal parliament. It did not forbid anyone to publish, or to speak, or to organize.

What did the lustrace law do, then?

By requiring a "clean" certification from the federal Ministry of the Interior (which controlled the old party and StB files), the law banned former high-ranking Communists, and former StB members and collaborators, from employment in key public positions for a period of five years. These include senior jobs in the federal police and internal-security forces, the higher courts, and the upper levels of the state administration, the armed services, state-owned enterprises, and state radio and television. Occupants of these posts who failed to provide such a certification had to leave their jobs within fifteen days; applicants for the posts who lacked certification were not hired. (But two levels of appeal, administrative and then judicial, were available.)

The law was remarkably lenient. It laid down none of the civil penalties involved in the denazification program in post-war Germany; nor were there to be any criminal trials of the sort held at Nuremberg. (The law was also far less severe than the measures taken during the occupation of Japan, by which the United States "purged" some 220,000 public figures, banning them from public office at any level and also from important private-sector positions.)

Moreover, many of the state-owned enterprises in Czechoslovakia were privatizing in late 1991, and employment in senior positions in these did not fall under the ban. Even within the state-run enterprises, the uncertified in high-ranking positions did not have to leave; they could accept lower positions instead. Similarly, an army colonel could accept a demotion to major and remain in the service.

Critics of the law (such as former dissident and quondam Czechoslovak foreign minister Jiři Dienstbier) said it was based on the notion of "collective guilt." This is a particularly provocative charge in the central European context, given recent history and the depredations of both Nazi and Communist regimes in the region. But it is not so easy to find a morally persuasive kernel within the husk of this particular bit of rhetoric. After all, people prospered in the higher echelons of the Communist party and the StB, and collaborated with the latter, not by accident of birth or race but by choice. The guilt in question is individual, not "collective."

Critics also charged that the lustrace law violated a fundamental "democratic norm," the presumption of innocence. But since the law did not involve a criminal proceeding, it is not clear why the canons appropriate to criminal law should apply. (Furthermore, at least one established democracy, France, does not include a "presumption of innocence" in its criminal law.)

Nor is it easy to see what procedure would have more satisfactorily removed from power, during the crucial period of democratic and free-market consolidation, people who had been the prime beneficiaries, and in many cases the active agents, of the old regime's crimes and persecutions. Some have suggested that a case-by-case review process, involving what would amount to a criminal charge against an officeholder or applicant for a post, would have been less problematic. But Pavel Bratinka, a former dissident who led the parliamentary struggle for the lustrace law, argued the opposite. A host of inquisitorial tribunals investigating and passing judgment on every senior job-holder or applicant would have been more humiliating for the individuals in question, Bratinka said, and more susceptible to corruption, since "charges" would presumably have been brought to such tribunals by people with various axes to grind. It would also have taken an extraordinary amount of time, during which the problems (uncovered in July 1991 by a parliamentary investigative commission) of Mafia-like *nomenklatura* conspiracies, racketeering, and theft would have continued unabated, and public cynicism about the democratic prospect would no doubt have sunk to new depths.

At first glance, the Czechoslovak lustrace law may appear vulnerable to the criticism that it did not differentiate between levels of guilt, and therefore levels of accountability, for former senior party members and for StB operatives and collaborators. Yet the law did distinguish between party "big fish" (who were banned) and party "little fish" (who were not). As for StB collaborators, the ban applied to those who participated in the most odious activities, which required deliberate choices to persecute or to collaborate in persecution.

A more serious problem was that the law did not provide adequately for former Communist officials who made a clean break with the party after the Prague Spring of 1968. There were also major questions about the reliability of StB files—although file-rigging could presumably be caught, and mistaken decisions based on rigged files then reversed in the appeals process.

That the lustrace law, mild though it was, should have provoked a heated debate within Czechoslovakia, where so many people—some of them perhaps innocent of any real wrongdoing—were in danger of being hurt by it, is easy enough to understand. One could also understand why even some former dissidents came out against it: they would like to put the painful past behind them and move on. Less understandable is why the law was consistently attacked in the United States.

Rumors of Witch Hunts

According to Stephen Engelberg of the *New York Times*, for example, the entire issue of post-Communist accountability had been "fanned and perpetuated by self-serving politicians." Czechoslovakia and the other countries of the old Warsaw Pact were, Engelberg wrote, "in the midst of a painful economic transition, so politicians are strongly tempted to divert attention from the grim reality to 'decommunization.' If they cannot deliver bread, why not the heads of a few supposedly fat Communists?"[4]

Even Jeri Laber of Helsinki Watch, who diligently and forcefully chronicled the depredations of the StB for years, joined in the denunciation of the lustrace law. Writing in the *New York Review of Books*, she declared that the law had led to a "witch hunt" and a public atmosphere of rumor-mongering, revenge, and fear. "Rather than judge," she added elsewhere, "they [the Czechs and Slovaks] should seek a general healing."[5] But as Havel, himself a critic of certain aspects of the lustrace law, once put it: "We cannot proceed indefinitely from the idea, 'Let bygones be bygones,' and 'You scratch my back and I will scratch yours.' This has cost us dearly, on more than one occasion in history."[6]

As for Laber's charge of a "witch hunt," her colleagues in the British Helsinki Human Rights Group had this to say:

> Unlike witches and unlike the subversives who, in Senator McCarthy's febrile imagination, peopled the State Department, members of the Politburo and secret policemen did exist in Czechoslovakia between 1948 and 1989. Czechs and Slovaks at every level know that the StB and its informers distorted their

lives and preserved a totalitarian regime in power [for] four decades.[7]

THE MORAL BLINDNESS OF THE WEST

The October 1991 lustrace legislation in Czechoslovakia was soon overrun by events, not least the division of the country into the Czech Republic and Slovakia. And there is no doubt that, in the Czech lands and elsewhere (Poland, for example), the attempt to come to grips with the past through the use of old secret-police files was subject to corruption by unscrupulous politicians and journalists. But one detected, even in 1991, a different motive for some of the criticism of these attempts to determine accountability and responsibility for the sufferings of the Cold War: to be blunt, one detected, especially in the Western academy and media, an extreme reluctance to revisit the recent past for reasons of contemporary self-preservation.

And indeed it is not McCarthyism but simple intellectual honesty to note, with chagrin, that many of the key culture-forming institutions of American public life did rather badly in the post-Vietnam phase of the Cold War.

There were, to begin with, the churches. Against the counsel of brave dissidents among their own co-religionists behind the iron curtain, mainline/oldline Protestantism and its chief ecumenical agencies, the National and World Councils of Churches, taught the morality of accommodation, condemned Western attempts to revivify containment, wildly exaggerated the dangers of nuclear holocaust, largely ignored the suffering of the persecuted Church in central and eastern Europe, debased the theology of peace, demeaned the just war tradition, promoted a form of pacifism that frequently smacked of ecopantheism, and participated in the propaganda activities of crude Communist-front organizations like the Christian Peace Conference. Nor have the churches of what Richard Neuhaus has called the Protestant Descendancy shown the slightest inclination to come to grips with their dereliction of Christian duty.

The Catholic Church's American leadership was only marginally better during the 1980s. Pope John Paul II was, as noted, a great influence on the moral revolution that helped cement the foundations of the political revolution of 1989; but the Catholic bishops of the United States can make no similar claim on their own behalf. Like their Protestant confreres, the bishops, in their famous 1983 pastoral letter "The Challenge of Peace," succumbed to the Sarajevo Fallacy and largely accepted the political logic of the nuclear-freeze movement, with its one-eyed focus on weapons, not regimes. Two years later, the bishops (whose policy statements persistently reflected the orthodoxies of the "arms control" mandarins) expressed grave reservations about the Strategic Defense Initiative—which most leaders of the new democracies in central and eastern Europe regard today as a crucial factor in resolving the Cold War in their favor.

It was not only on matters of nuclear weapons and U.S.-Soviet relations that the churches proved to be deficient moral mentors. Throughout the 1980s, domestic resistance to the application of the anti-Communist/pro-democracy Reagan Doctrine in Central America was primarily based in the churches—despite the persecution of the Catholic Church in Nicaragua by the Sandinista regime.

The philanthropic community, one of the distinctive ornaments of American democracy, also has cause to examine its conscience in the aftermath of the Cold War. For it, too, in the early 1980s, listened to the siren songs of "nuclear winter" as sung by the likes of Jonathan Schell and Carl Sagan, and poured tens (perhaps even hundreds) of millions of dollars into "preventing nuclear war." Probably a few interesting books got written thereby; but would anyone argue seriously that the anti-nuclear agitations paid for by the MacArthur Foundation, the Ford Foundation, and the Carnegie Corporation had any real impact on the collapse of Communism—which was, indisputably, the *sine qua non* for the end of the nuclear-arms race? Have any of the grant-makers who insisted that the issue was weapons, not regimes, felt any remorse over their expenditure of vast sums of money on a chimera?

A Lament for the Academy

In an excessively conciliatory mood, one might consider the extenuating argument that American religious leaders and grant-makers were really not professionally equipped to grasp the dynamics of the endgame of the Cold War. But what are we to make of the dismal performance of so many Sovietologists and international-relations experts during the 1980s? What explains the colossal failure of insight on the part of those whose professional business it was to know what was going on, and why?

The problem is not (as sometimes asserted) that Western scholars of central and eastern Europe and the USSR failed to anticipate the rapidity of the Communist crackup. No one, not even the people on the ground, predicted that. The problem is that many, perhaps most, of our academic scriveners were then, and remain today, sublimely oblivious to the ways in which their secularist-positivist assumptions about man and society, their soft-Marxist notions of the relationship between economics and politics, and their enthrallment to "methodology" (as understood by empiricist social science) blinded them to the deeper realities of the phenomena they analyzed.

The 1992 *Columbia History of Eastern Europe in the Twentieth Century* is a case in point.[8] In its 400 pages, there is virtually no grappling with Communism as an ideology, indeed an ersatz religion. The authors (all doubtless distinguished scholars in their fields) do not describe in any detail the effects of Communism on the moral-cultural texture of central and eastern European societies. Nor do they analyze the complex patterns of acquiescence and resistance that formed the dialectic of political life in the Communist culture of the lie. Major dissident texts, including seminal works by Adam Michnik and Václav Havel that decisively shaped the politics of 1989, are strikingly absent from the book's bibliography, which "represents those sources the contributors to this collection have relied on most heavily." Little wonder, then, that these scholars barely mention the widespread conviction among the people who made the Revolution of 1989 that a moral revolution—the reconstruction of civil society—was the necessary antecedent to the political overthrow of the Yalta imperial system.

Among the analytic flaws most characteristic of this kind of political "science" is its misconstrual of "neutrality" and "objectivity" in dealing with the linguistic ecology of Communist societies. The pervasive use of euphemism in the culture of the lie in Communist central and eastern Europe has been widely noted: almost everybody remembers *Animal Farm* and *1984*. But little serious attention has been paid to the extent to which distortive and euphemistic language seeped into the *lingua franca* of Western political science and international-relations theory.

Thus in the *Columbia History* Professor Sharon Wolchik of George Washington University describes the correlation of forces in post-war Czechoslovakia in these gelded terms: "From the beginning of the post–World War II period, however, the Communist party enjoyed certain advantages over its democratic opponents. These included the . . . presence of the Red Army." (An "advantage" indeed!) Czechoslovakia's Communist rulers, after seizing power, "stepped up" their "efforts to discredit and reduce the power bases of non-Communist actors. . . . This process . . . included the political use of judicial and propaganda campaigns against leaders of other parties." (Among the refinements of those "efforts" and "campaigns" were a ubiquitous and fearsome secret-police apparatus; judicial murders under trumped-up charges of treason; and the widespread use of concentration camps, prison camps, and slave-labor camps, including the notorious uranium mine pits in Bohemia to which numerous Catholic clergy and lay activists were consigned.) Professor Wolchik does report that the Czechoslovak Communists "mounted a concerted campaign against religion" and that the number of priests in the country was "reduced"; but the brutal means used to effect these "reductions" go wholly unremarked.

Why did the Prague Spring of 1968 and its attempts at reform Communism fail? Because Alexander Dubček couldn't reassure Czechoslovakia's "external allies" that things wouldn't get out of hand. Did everybody in Bohemia, Moravia, and Slovakia sign on to the post-Dubček program of Communist "normalization" enforced by Gustáv Husák? We are told that "many groups in the population continued to hold values at odds with those of the leadership." What about the mass purge that followed the collapse of the Prague Spring? Well, the universities suffered because of the "personnel changes made at this time." And on and on it goes.[9] Moreover, Professor Wolchik is no exception in her guild, but rather a capable representative of the political-science mainstream.

Whether deliberate or unwitting, the adoption of the Communist language of euphemism by Western social scientists—in the name of a scholarly "objectivity" that supposedly transcended the "Cold War mentality"—masked the full squalor of life within the Communist web of mendacity; it also obscured (or just plain missed) the heroism and the political impact of those who steadfastly chose to "live in the truth," as Havel described the moral resistance movement that ultimately made possible the political overthrow of Communism. In these intellectually debased circumstances, it is little wonder that the professoriate was caught off guard by the dramatic events of the Revolution of 1989 and the New Russian Revolution of 1991, and has had such a tough time grasping their internal logic ever since.

The Contagion Spreads

Moreover, the impact of the follies of the academics was not limited to the universities. Doctors and lawyers, regurgitating themes from the campuses and the anti–American-nuclear-weapons movement, soon discovered that they had a similar responsibility for "preventing nuclear war," primarily by inveighing against Western security policy.

The mindset that dominated two typically accommodationist groups in the 1980s, Physicians for Social Responsibility and Nobel Peace Prize–winning International Physicians for the Prevention of Nuclear War (IPPNW), was nicely (if crudely) captured at Stanford in 1987, where one IPPNW founder, Dr. Herbert Abrams, dismissed the recently released Soviet dissident Yuri Orlov as an "arrogant son of a bitch." Orlov's offense was to raise cautions about the relationship between regime-approved international exchanges (like those conducted by IPPNW) and the machinery of totalitarian control in the USSR.

The 1985 exchange agreement between the American Bar Association and the Association of Soviet Lawyers was another exercise in immoral accommodationism. The Soviet "association" was a well-known propaganda organ, led at the time by Samuel Zivs, a notorious anti-Semite whose secondary specialization was the defamation of Andrei Sakharov. But when a small band of ABA dissenters challenged the propriety of the exchange agreement, they were dismissed as "noisy . . . insignificant . . . [and] misguided" by a leading light of the American bar. Another legal worthy pronounced the exchange agreement "extremely successful." At what?

Finally, there was the fourth estate. It, too, had drunk deeply from the wells of anti–anti-Communism in the wake of Vietnam. And that draught led to a pattern of coverage and commentary whose apogee (or perigee) was the description of the Soviet Union by NBC's John Chancellor in a broadcast from Moscow on the day after the coup failed in August 1991:

> It's short of soap, so there are lice in hospitals. It's short of pantyhose, so women's legs go bare. It's short of snowsuits, so babies stay home in winter. . . . The problem isn't Communism; nobody even talked about Communism this week. The problem is shortages.[10]

(Imagine Edward R. Murrow standing in the rubble of Berlin in May 1945 and saying, "The problem isn't Nazism; nobody even talked about Nazism this week. The problem is shortages.")

Anti–anti-Communism in the media was also exacerbated by a new concept of the press's function in American society. The Watergate experience (and its subsequent cinematic romanticization) had moved "investigative reporting" (once known as "muckraking") from a specialty to the heart of the reportorial enterprise. The assumption was that the government was always lying, and that the task of the journalist was to expose its habitual fraud and mendacity. Thus the press could spend an inordinate amount of time ferreting around in the Iran-Contra imbroglio while paying scant attention to a story of infinitely greater consequence—the beginnings of the unraveling of the Soviet imperial system.

But even the probes that were made into that drama were discolored by the evident preference in many media circles for Mikhail Gorbachev over Ronald Reagan. The *Seattle Post-Intelligencer*, for instance, a paper that had once supported Senator Henry M. Jackson, editorialized in these terms after the 1988 Moscow summit: "Reagan's insistence on making the abuse of human rights in the Soviet Union and the mistreatment of Soviet dissidents a major summit issue could have wrecked the summit, but Gorbachev to his credit wouldn't let it."[11]

Truths and Consequences

The common thread linking these phenomena—the sentimentalism of the churches, the foolishness of the great foundations, the myopia of the academics, the corruption of the professions, the incomprehension of the media—was a failure of moral imagination and nerve in which fear of nuclear holocaust, and fear of a democratically elected Reagan administration, played large roles. The survivalism of the early 1980s was, to be sure, only a long-winded variant on the old slogan "Better Red than Dead." But where an earlier generation of the cultural elite, faced with the threat of Soviet totalitarianism, had produced Dean Acheson, containment, and NATO, this generation produced *The Fate of the Earth*, the nuclear-freeze movement, and Physicians for Social Responsibility—all three of which it vigorously promoted as exemplars of moral sensitivity and political courage.

The great irony, of course, is that much of the American intellectual and cultural elite lost its moral nerve just when central and eastern European dissident intellectuals were regaining theirs. While American academics and columnists were teaching that Harry Truman had started the Cold War and that Ronald Reagan was needlessly prolonging it, Václav Havel was emphasizing the necessity of "living in the truth" as the antidote to Czechoslovak Communism. While the churches of the mainline/oldline urged the morality of accommodation, Adam Michnik (a secularized Jewish intellectual) was stressing the importance for Poland of a recovery of the Christian notion of self-sacrifice. (That Havel and Michnik were men of the Left only intensified the irony.) While participation in the anti-nuclear agitations of the 1980s was considered, among many American intellectuals, a moral imperative, one of the most devastating moral critiques of the appeasement mentality of Western "peace" activists was written by none other than Havel.

The central and eastern European intellectuals had grasped, in other words, a moral truth that many American intellectuals and professionals had forgotten: that only a life lived "in the truth," even if that meant a life at risk, was worthy of a human being. The central and eastern Europeans, under the pressure of a stultifying public atheism, had also grasped something that their more genteelly secularized American colleagues seemed to have forgotten: that "living in the truth" means holding oneself accountable to transcendent moral norms. And, finally, the dissident intellectuals had grasped a practical truth that eluded many American tastemakers: that it was better to be neither Red nor dead, and that the odds on avoiding both slavery and incineration improved if one took account of the totalitarian nature of the adversary, and worked to change that.

We are unlikely to think clearly about the future if we remain bedazzled by mendacious renderings of the past. The Cold War was not the result of a misunderstanding; it was the result of Stalin's imperial-ideological ambitions and their continuation in the Brezhnev Doctrine. The stakes involved in the Cold War were not simply political and economic; they were moral—for the Cold War was, at bottom, a struggle between two radically different conceptions of the human person, human society, human history, and human destiny. It made a great deal of difference that the Cold War ended, not in some sort of draw, but in a clear victory for human rights, democracy, and the free economy. It would make a great difference to the renewal of American society after the Cold War if that home truth were recognized by those responsible for our major institutions of culture, moral formation, and learning.

PART TWO

The Elements of Strategy

"The only way a man can remain consistent amid
changing circumstances is to change with them
while preserving the same dominating purpose."
WINSTON S. CHURCHILL

5

Lessons From the Fifty-Five Years' War: Ideas, Passions, and History

In early 1992, the columnist Charles Krauthammer wrote movingly of a letter he had received from a former professor of his who had begun his career in Germany in the 1930s and emigrated to the United States to escape the Nazis. The professor, just back from a trip to Berlin with his wife, described his feelings in these words: "It is hard to believe. The two tyrannies dominating the affairs and lives of hundreds of millions of people everywhere are no longer. We are grateful for having lived long enough to witness the events of the last three years."[1]

Jeane J. Kirkpatrick, the former U.S. ambassador to the United Nations, gave a historically concise formulation to a similar intuition, shortly after the New Russian Revolution of August 1991: "For the first time since the Spring of 1936," she said, "we are not facing mortal danger."[2]

Both Krauthammer's teacher and Ambassador Kirkpatrick were, I think, saying this: that what ended with the collapse of the Union of Soviet Socialist Republics was a Fifty-Five Years' War between the forces of freedom and the forces of totalitarian tyranny—a war between imperfect democracies (and their allies) and pluperfect despotisms (and their epigones).

News of this victory has occasionally breached a few of the ramparts of the academy and the prestige press. The category of "totalitarianism," once dismissed as McCarthyite by revisionist

Western historians and political scientists, has been revived as the only possible analytic model for understanding the Soviet experience from Lenin through Gorbachev—not least because of the insistence on this point by reformist Russian scholars and publicists. Perhaps even more surprisingly, in a 1992 review of Alan Bullock's *Hitler and Stalin: Parallel Lives* for the *New York Times Book Review*, British historian Norman Davies was permitted to suggest what had been hitherto unthinkable in some circles: that Nazi totalitarianism and Marxist-Leninist totalitarianism were two variants on the same evil deconstruction of politics.[3]

Lord Bullock himself couldn't quite make the leap beyond the standard historical account—i.e., that Nazism was obviously beyond the pale, but that Communism was a bit less odious and somehow reformable. Bullock's failure to make a clean break with the received wisdom may have had something to do, according to Davies, with a too rigid adherence to the familiar right/left taxonomy of Nazism and Stalinism, which misses the socialist elements of the former, the xenophobia and nationalism of the latter, and the totalitarian intention common to both. In any event, Davies suggested, "parallel lives" (which, like parallel lines, do not meet) is no longer the appropriate image for thinking about Hitler and Stalin—if it ever was. What with the collapse of the USSR and the Cold War, and the possibility of seeing the past through lenses other than those befogged by Cold War political struggles in the West, the way has been cleared, wrote Davies, for "the definitive history of European tyranny in our time"—which is to say, a history that will describe the Fifty-Five Years' War, the war that began when Hitler re-militarized the Rhineland and that ended with the failure of the August 1991 coup attempt in Moscow, as one great struggle against the totalitarians.

One might even go a step further, as I suggested above, and argue that what ended in the New Russian Revolution of 1991, and in the Revolution of 1989 in central and eastern Europe, was a period of history that began with Rousseau and those other heralds of the French Revolution who taught the perfectibility of man through politics. Thus the end of the Fifty-Five Years' War means that politics has been put back into its proper—which is to say, important but not all-important—place. On the cusp of the third millennium of the common era, and as a result of the crackup of totalitarianism, the West may once again have grasped a truth central to its ancient tradition about the right-ordering of societies: that the apotheosis of the political means the end of the *polis*, and indeed the end of man.

THREE LESSONS FROM THE 1980S

What other valuable lessons might be drawn from the recent past? Here are three that I would take from the 1980s, the endgame of the Cold War:

1. Regimes, not weapons, are the basic threat to peace and security.

Think back on the symbolic apogee of the Revolution of 1989: the breaching of the Berlin Wall. Then, through the prism of that memory, think back on the anti-nuclear agitations of the early 1980s: the nuclear-freeze movement; Physicians for Social Responsibility; Helen Caldicott; Msgr. Bruce Kent; the women of Greenham Common; Petra Kelly and the Greens; "The Day After"; Bishop Gumbleton and Archbishop Hunthausen (". . . the Trident submarine is the Auschwitz of Puget Sound"); the awarding of the Nobel Peace Prize to International Physicians for the Prevention of Nuclear War; Vladimir Pozner.

It seems almost surrealistic. And yet for almost seven years, from the late 1970s through 1985 or thereabouts, these people and their movements played an enormous role in the domestic politics of Western countries. The activists in question had different intentions, some honorable, others not. But they had a common analysis: the gravest threat to world peace and security was the *fact*, the sheer fact, of nuclear weapons.

They were wrong, not only about nuclear weapons, but, as we have seen, about the relation between weapons of any sort and peace.

The Revolution of 1989—and the Gulf crisis of 1990–91—ought to have driven this message home with irresistible force: the instabilities and aggression that lead to wars are caused not by weapons but by regimes (or by individuals whose regimes are expressions of their personal demons). Change the regime (cf. the

Warsaw Pact) and the threat of war dramatically declines; fail to change the regime (cf. post–Gulf War Iraq) and the threat to peace and security remains.

This is not to say that weapons don't count. They do. Indeed, a persuasive argument can be made that the emplacement of Pershing II and cruise missiles in western Europe, in tandem with the Strategic Defense Initiative, helped break the will of the Soviet Union to maintain the Yalta imperial system by force of arms.

Nor did the end of the Cold War mean it was no longer necessary to maintain significant military assets. American and Western military capability spared the world a disaster in the Persian Gulf. Moreover, given the global proliferation of ballistic-missile capability, defensive weapons are going to take on even greater significance in the post–Cold War world. The swords will not be entirely beaten into plowshares in the near future.

But those basic facts of life shouldn't obscure one crucial lesson: the basic threat to peace and security lies not in military hardware but in regimes and their intentions.

2. *Ideas and values count in the affairs and fates of men and nations.*
The human-rights revolution that has swept through much of the world in the past fifteen years has been, first and foremost, a revolution of ideas and expectations. Latin America is making progress (admittedly slow, and not yet irreversible) toward democracy and prosperity because of ideas. East Asia has taken off economically, and is making strides democratically, because of ideas. The Revolution of 1989 in central and eastern Europe was, first and foremost, a revolution of the spirit, a revolution of moral ideas. The contest between the democratic opposition in the Soviet Union and Mikhail Gorbachev's stale brand of reform Communism was about ideas. The revolutionary change that is transforming South Africa is a revolution of ideas (most of them F. W. de Klerk's).

Ideas have consequences for ill as well as for good, of course. The concept of "self-determination," and the ideas and passions that make up historic ethnic memory in central and eastern Europe, are leading to bloodshed today; three years ago, they were leading to the largely non-violent overthrow of Communism. There are no guarantees in history. Bad ideas have bad consequences. And the ability to distinguish good from bad ideas —which involves the delicate art of assessing the impact of ideas according to historical circumstance—is as crucial a talent in international affairs as it is in, say, marketing.

But the word is out, in the Third World but also in the underdeveloped nations of what we used to call the Second World, that things don't have to be the way they are. Any "new world order" that does not come to grips with that widespread understanding will fail. And any attempt to build a "new world order" that measures "power" solely in terms of military capabilities and economic performance will be dangerous, because it will ignore the most potent motive force in the world today—the desire, indeed the demand, for change.

3. American leadership works.

Although we are regularly accused of braggadocio (even by the French!), the United States is not only the reluctant superpower but also the modest superpower.

I get around the country a fair amount and spend my share of time on the talk-shows; my travels and conversations give me little sense of a people that thinks of itself in grand terms—as the leader of a great coalition that has won one of the titanic struggles of human history. Americans seem glad that the Cold War is over. But are they smugly basking in the glow of victory? Hardly.

This may have less to do with modesty than with the fact that the American people were told by their media for well over five years (and also by the Norwegian Nobel Committee) that the real winner of the Cold War was . . . Mikhail Gorbachev, the last dictator in Europe! But let's not lay all the blame on the fourth estate. Americans' unwillingness to seize the lion's share of the credit for having won World War III, the Cold War, also reflects the isolationist temperament that runs so deep in the national character. (A current version is the subject of chapter 8.) We prefer to be left alone. We fought World War III as we fought World War II: much less as an ideological crusade than as a necessary piece of unpleasant business.

That venerable isolationist current has its uses; it is, among other things, a pretty solid barrier against the "imperial over-stretch" about which the *cognoscenti* regularly fret. But the isolationist impulse is also problematic. Because we do not, as a people, feel like victors in a world war, we have not fully grasped the fact that this is a unipolar world in which the reluctant superpower is the only superpower.

And yet surely one of the lessons of the 1980s is that American leadership not only is necessary but can be very effective indeed. Absent American leadership, would the West have held fast against the provocations of the Soviet Union in the matter of INF modernization in Europe? (And had that not happened, would there have been a Revolution of 1989?) Absent American leadership, would the Soviet Union have come to understand, however reluctantly, that it could not win an arms race with the West? (And had that not happened, would the USSR have taken a turn toward amiability in the arms-reduction field?) Absent American leadership, however fumbling at times, wouldn't Central America now be like Cuba, an impoverished historical backwater? Absent American leadership, wouldn't Saddam Hussein now control almost half of the world's proven oil reserves?

And given American leadership, might economically booming China now be making at least modest progress away from neo-Sino-Stalinism in its politics?

Awareness of the importance of ideas and moral passions in the world should not blind us to another truth: often things don't happen merely because they are *supposed* to happen; they happen because they are *made* to happen. We are neither omnipotent nor omniscient. There are some things that we cannot do much about, and we often see as through a glass, darkly. But what we want to happen certainly won't happen if we don't exert ourselves. American leadership works.

DISORIENTATIONS

It would be rank hubris to imply, though, that there is wide agreement on these "lessons" in the United States. Indeed, American debate on world politics since the end of the Cold War suggests that our countrymen are in a position not unlike Shakespeare's bloody and wearied Henry V in the first moments after his great battle with the French on October 25, 1415:

> *King*:   I tell thee truly, herald,
> I know not if the day be ours or no,
> For yet a many of your horsemen peer
> And gallop o'er the field.
> *Herald*:   The day is yours.
> *King*:   Praised be God, and not our strength, for it!
> What is this castle called that stands hard by?
> *Herald*:   They call it Agincourt.
> *King*:   Then call we this the field of Agincourt,
> Fought on the day of Crispin Crispianus.[4]

We, too, seem unsure of our victory and of what to call it. The real and present danger of totalitarianism had one clear advantage for the analyst, the policymaker, and the citizen: it clarified our circumstances and set rational and broadly accepted boundaries for the policy debate. But with the collapse of the totalitarian project, a case of hypoxia, with its attendant erratic behaviors, seems to have set into the body politic. Since that startling day when Boris Yeltsin climbed atop a tank in front of Moscow's White House, the threats to our (and the world's) well-being have not come into clear focus; neither have our responsibilities as one of the chieftains of the victorious party of freedom.

That disorientation has been exacerbated by certain domestic political currents. There are some on the Right who wish to make victory in the Fifty-Five Years' War the occasion for a new form of "rollback"—this time, of modernity and all its works and pomps. There are some on the Left who, having drastically minimized the Communist threat, are now busily rewriting recent history so that their own gigantic failures of analysis (and nerve) might be explained away. Moreover, our political leaders in the months following the end of the Cold War seemed more like followers. They appeared to take their cues, not from an appreciation of the democratic and capitalist revolutions that seem to be sweeping the globe, but from videotapes of "focus groups"—as if these were high-tech tarot cards from which the future (understood as next month's opinion polls) could be read. Their successors in the Clinton administration seem similarly disinclined to challenge a fractious and emotionally isolationist public to a larger view of the nation's interests, and its purpose, in the world.

Then there is the foreign-policy establishment. It is, in the main, intellectually exhausted. But that is not all that hinders its post–Cold War analysis. Just as the academy has largely become, in Paul Mankowski's pungent image, the playground of the vandals (whose tenure now allows them comfortably to pursue politics first brewed in the ideological cauldron of the Sixties), so has the foreign-policy establishment been reshaped by the long march through the institutions now led by the soft Left tribunes of race-class-and-gender. Too many of the names on the ballot for election to the board of the Council on Foreign Relations in 1992 were there, in all charity, for one reason: "sensitivity" to gender and racial quotas. But nothing seems too odd for the Council these days. In early 1992, the emblematic elite institution of American internationalism published an isolationist tract, *The Imperial Temptation*, by Robert W. Tucker and David C. Hendrickson—sophisticated isolationism, to be sure, but still isolationism.[5]

The Quest for a Master Concept

Amid the turmoil and rapid change have come frequent calls for a "new strategic framework," a new master concept to replace "containment of Communism" and do the job that "containment" did for almost forty years: provide an intellectual template against which we can measure and cut our responsibilities and our policies. Sundry intellectual and political architects have already drawn up their blueprints:

1. The America Firstism of the new/old isolationists. Their resounding defeat in the 1992 Republican primaries seems to have put little dent in the new isolationists' conviction that they represent the broad mainstream of American opinion. (More on these folks in chapter 8.)

2. The school of National Interest/Home Repairs. According to this analysis, any foreign involvements ought to be measured strictly by their capacity to help us renovate our ramshackle republican domicile. This proposal, reflected somewhat in the Tucker/Hendrickson tome, has been most vigorously argued by libertarian publicists like Ted Galen Carpenter and Doug Bandow, and by Alan Tonelson of the Economic Strategy Institute.

3. Democratic Internationalism. Its proponents urge that the advance of the democratic revolution in world politics should be the "norming norm" in U.S. foreign policy because it is both the right and the prudent thing to do. Charles Krauthammer, Joshua Muravchik, Gregory Fossedal, and Larry Diamond have played distinctive variations on this theme in recent years.

4. Collective Security/Power Realism. As displayed by the Bush administration, this position was profoundly skeptical of ideology and a bit thin in terms of the "vision thing." It showed itself largely incapable of reading the signs of the times in the collapsing Soviet Union, admirably suited to assembling a coalition against Saddam Hussein, vulnerable to internal coalition pressures in failing to finish the Gulf War, and utterly befuddled when its bluff was called by Slobodan Milosevic of Serbia/Yugoslavia.

The interaction among these various schools of thought has not been uninteresting. As hammer hits anvil, sparks sometimes fly, followed by the occasional flash of insight. But the calls for a new "master concept" may be premature. And the attempt to create such a framework may, in the unsettled circumstances of the present, contribute to the disorientation we are feeling at the end of the Fifty-Five Years' War.

First, Building Blocks

The grand design may come later. For now, our primary task is to clear our minds on some very tough prior questions:

- The possibilities and limits of U.S. leadership in world politics after the collapse of "bipolarity";
- The meaning and limits of sovereignty and self-determination;
- The exigencies of democratic consolidation in the new democracies of the formerly Communist world and Latin America;
- The role of collective security and international organizations in the post–Cold War world.

And, as ever, there are basic questions of the dialectic of might and right in the politics of nations to be pondered. No grand design is possible until there is more clarity—and more agreement—on these fundamental issues.

But while seeking clarification and a measure of consensus, we ought to keep our minds open to the possibility that something of truly world-historical consequence may be happening right under our noses. Christopher Dawson, the great medievalist, wrote of one great shift in the tectonic plates of history in words that ought to command the respectful attention of any serious student of world politics today:

> When St. Paul, in obedience to the warning in a dream, set sail from Troy in A.D. 49 and came to Philippi in Macedonia he did more to change the course of history than the great battle that had decided the fate of the Roman Empire on the same spot nearly a century earlier, for he brought to Europe the seed of a new life which was ultimately destined to create a new world. All this took place beneath the surface of history, so that it was unrecognized by the leaders of contemporary culture, like Gallio the brother of Seneca, who actually saw it taking place beneath their eyes.[6]

Thus we cannot know the long-term significance of the restoration of the Slavic peoples to "Europe"; or of decisions taken by Hamas activists in a house in Ramallah; or of the introduction of the microchip to the ancient cultures of the Asian subcontinent; or of the below-replacement-level birthrates of western Europe and the fecundity of Muslims in the Maghreb; or of CNN and the phenomenon of crisis-watching in "real time." Things are going on, inexorably, "beneath the surface of history." And that those things will have much to do with the shaping of the twenty-first century is quite probably the one certainty in the whole business. That realization should not paralyze us. But it might well humble us—and remind us that prudence is the chief of political virtues.

Before we set off in search of clarity on some of the crucial problems that will shape the debate over international life after the Fifty-Five Years' War, a further reflection on truths (which is to say, ideas) and consequences is in order.

THE IGNITION OF HISTORY

Although the conservative historian Richard Weaver popularized the notion that "ideas have consequences," the principle is not a private preserve of conservatives. John Maynard Keynes, for example, had this to say about the role of ideas in history:

> Both when they are right and when they are wrong, ideas are more powerful than is commonly understood. In fact, the world is ruled by little else. Practical men, who believe themselves to be quite exempt from any intellectual influences, are usually the slaves of some defunct economist. Madmen in authority, who hear voices in the air, are distilling their frenzy from some academic scribbler of a few years back. . . . Soon or late, it is ideas, not vested interests, which are dangerous for good or evil.[7]

Nor is the claim that ideas—and the moral norms and moral passions they generate—are among the principal motors of history just a bit of guild propaganda created in their own self-interest by those whose job it is to think and write. Indeed, the twentieth century, for good and for evil, has been the exemplar of the claim that "ideas have consequences":

- Lenin's ideas—about the dynamics of history, about vanguardism and the organization of revolutionary politics—set in motion the greatest tyranny in human history, killed well over a hundred million people, and ruined the social ecology of half of Europe.
- Hitler's ideas—about race, about Germany, and about his own messianic role in the working-out of history—destroyed European Jewry, launched World War II, and brought his other great nemesis, the "Slavic hordes" from the east, to Berlin, Prague, and the gates of Vienna.
- Churchill's ideas—about freedom, about Britain, about the special relationship between Britain and the United States—steeled the West at the moment when it was on the verge of cutting a deal with the evils of Nazism.
- David Ben Gurion's ideas—and those of Herzl, Weizmann, Jabotinsky, and other Zionist leaders—led to the restoration of a Jewish state for the first time since Titus destroyed Jerusalem in A.D. 70.
- The Fabian socialist ideas of the professoriate at the London School of Economics in the 1930s and 1940s—insufficiently informed by the democratic idea and transformed into policy by the

leaders of the newly independent nations of Africa and Asia in the 1950s and 1960s—were influential in creating a "fourth world" of human misery that sometimes seems in danger of dropping off the edge of history.

■ Gamal Abd al-Nasser's ideas about the "Arab nation" shaped the politics of the world's most volatile region for almost forty years and were an important factor in the wars of 1956 and 1967.

■ Mohandas K. Gandhi's ideas about non-violence pulled the linchpin from the world's greatest empire, informed a civil-rights movement on the other side of the world, and eventually came to influence the social teaching of the Roman Catholic Church— thereby hastening the demise of the Yalta imperial system through the Solidarity revolution in Poland.

■ Aleksandr Solzhenitsyn's ideas—about the nature of Soviet totalitarianism, about Russian-ness, and about the moral responsibilities (and moral failures) of the West—helped break the psychological impasse of the Cold War by deconstructing the myth of Communist irreversibility, whose political expression was the Brezhnev Doctrine.

■ Karol Wojtyła's ideas about Christian humanism, the unity of European culture, and the moral unacceptability of the Yalta arrangement, and Václav Havel's ideas about the Communist culture of the lie and the need to resist it through a strategy of "living in the truth," helped ignite the revolution of conscience that made possible the political Revolution of 1989 in central and eastern Europe.

Francis Fukuyama, the author of that famous essay on "the end of history," may be a suspect witness in these matters, given his high-octane Hegelianism and his commitment to the priority of Mind in history. But in light of the list above (which could, of course, be expanded greatly), one need not share Fukuyama's Hegelian worldview to recognize the justice of his challenge to the realist school: "Those who believe in the primacy of power should consider that the greatest shift in the balance of power in world history was brought about by the spread of democratic ideas throughout the former Soviet bloc."[8]

The Unsecularization of the World

If the foreign-policy establishment and the academic political-science and international-relations guilds have usually had trouble with the role of ideas in shaping modern history, they become utterly numb when the ideas in question are religious in character. The point was nicely illustrated in April 1992 by Harvard's Stanley Hoffmann, writing on "Delusions of World Order" in the *New York Review of Books*.[9]

Professor Hoffmann is not completely tone-deaf to the music of ideas in history. As a fervent admirer of Le Grand Charles (de Gaulle, of course, not Wojtyła), Hoffmann certainly appreciates how a great idea carried by a forceful personality (in this instance, that "certain idea of France" with which DeGaulle began his memoirs) is capable of bending events in its preferred direction. But in a long essay on the prospects for an orderly international system in the aftermath of the Cold War—during which he discusses nationalism, "self-determination," constitutionalism, human rights, and other powerful ideas behind the politics of the twentieth century—Professor Hoffmann is mute on the matter of religion.

He says nary a word about Islam, in either its militant or more pacific forms—which is to say, Professor Hoffmann says nothing about a body of religious thought that is shaping the daily lives and political destinies of some 800 million human beings.

Nor does he discuss one of the most important moral-cultural dynamics in the world in the aftermath of the Fifty-Five Years' War: the growth of evangelical, fundamentalist, and charismatic Protestantism in the Third World, which in many cases seems linked to the emergence of what was long thought impossible in those precincts, namely, a middle class.

Nor does he analyze the role of Roman Catholicism in central and eastern Europe, despite the fact that virtually all the major figures in the Revolution of 1989 give the Church high marks for its role in the non-violent overthrow of Communism.

Nor does he assay a view on the role of Orthodoxy in the period of turmoil that has broken out as the nations of Stalin's old empire move into a post-Soviet future; he simply doesn't mention the subject.

Thus the unsuspecting or unwary reader can finish Professor Hoffmann's essay with little sense of just how dramatically different the ideas and passions that move large parts of the world today are from the secular ideas and passions that move the worlds of Harvard's graduate departments and its Kennedy School of Government. It would be a mildly charming conceit, this "we are the world" attitude characteristic of our academic elites, if it were not so dangerous.

Perhaps this stubborn and myopic secularism, which is so typical of the scholarly confraternities in which Professor Hoffmann is a respected leader, will appear simply bizarre to historians of ideas fifty or a hundred years from now. At a time when religious ideas and religious movements are shaping (and shaking) history from Sri Lanka to Novosibirsk, from the favellas of São Paulo to the Dome of the Rock on Jerusalem's Temple Mount, a long, detailed essay on the future of world politics (by a man who is, among other things, and at one remove, a major intellectual influence on the foreign-policy pronouncements of the National Conference of Catholic Bishops) says not a word about religion.

Hoffmann is, of course, not alone in his secular cocoon. At the level of self-parody, the index of the aforementioned *Columbia History of Eastern Europe in the Twentieth Century* has nine references to King Zog of Albania and one to Pope John Paul II.

What Is Going On Here?

Some of this confusion can be attributed to that hostility shown to the worlds of faith since the days of the French Enlightenment by the "cultured despisers of religion," as Friedrich Schleiermacher described the breed in 1799. And, as previously noted, one also has to look to the reigning methodological orthodoxies in political science and international-relations theory for explanations of this systematic misapprehension of reality. There, where scholars have long been vulnerable to the claim that the mathematizable hypotheses and empirical/experimental methods of the natural sciences provide the only sure approach to advancing human knowledge, anything not quantifiable and measurable is, all too frequently, off the analytic board. But how can the evolution of a people's conscience be measured? How does one mathematically describe the sources of moral conviction that led people to say "No" to Communism on the basis of a higher and more compelling "Yes"?

In the world of the policymakers (which overlaps extensively with the world of the academics), it can also be argued that the myopia on these matters reflects the continuing and baneful influence of the late Hans Morgenthau. Whatever his own intentions, Morgenthau's bifurcation of "politics" and "morality" came to mean that policymakers were to be "tough-minded," "realistic," and "hard-nosed" about the things that moved the gears of history—things like military power and economic power. This was a useful corrective to the liberal romanticism and moralism that characterized a competing school of thought in American foreign-policy circles. But as a master concept in its own right, Morgenthauian realism has shown itself to be strikingly inept at a realistic assessment of the dynamics of recent history—and by "realistic" I mean accurate. Slobodan Milosevic understood something that George Bush and James A. Baker III didn't. And because of that, Sarajevo is in ruins today.

Any probings toward a new grand design for American foreign policy after the Fifty-Five Years' War will have to take ideas, moral norms, and moral-political passions far more seriously than has been done by the past several generations of academics and policymakers. And, at a time when religion is waxing in world-shaping influence (for good and for ill), it is long past time for the scholarly guilds and the foreign-policy establishment to abandon their secularist prejudices and get in touch with the real world—where, at the end of the twentieth century, knowing about Islam and about the sundry forms of Christian millennialism is at least as important as knowing about the negotiating mechanisms of the GATT and the "side agreements" of NAFTA.[10]

6

Beyond Moralism and Realpolitik: Notes Toward Redefining "America's Purpose"

The initial draft of a 1992 Pentagon planning study suggested —rather boldly, as things turned out—that there was something to be said for unipolarity in world politics as long as the United States was the sole great power in question. "Our first objective" in the post–Cold War world, the document asserted, "is to prevent the re-emergence of a new rival, either on the territory of the former Soviet Union or elsewhere, that poses a threat on the order of that posed by the Soviet Union. This . . . requires that we endeavor to prevent any hostile power from dominating a region whose resources would, under consolidated control, be sufficient to generate global power."

Sounds reasonable enough, right? Well, to judge from the firestorm of criticism that ensued on the editorial and op-ed pages, you'd think the Pentagon had proposed a strategy based on boiling babies in oil. From sea to shining sea, the cry of "imperial overstretch" was heard once again. Dark warnings about the corrupting dangers of "global empire" rumbled forth from the caves of the paleoconservatives. And what might have been an occasion to think seriously about the responsibilities and dangers of American leadership in a unipolar world quickly degenerated into sound-bite sniping and political posturing. A few months later, the revised draft of the planning document listed deterring aggression and strengthening defense alliances as the principal business of post–Cold War U.S. grand strategy, and the editors of the *New York Times* and the *Washington Post* heaved great sighs of relief.

Despite all the hyperventilation in the press and in the halls of Congress, there have been occasional signs of interest in a more serious public debate about the obligations and limitations of America's role in the post–Cold War world. One welcome indicator is that the theme of a "national purpose" seems to be catching on. A 1991 symposium on "America's Purpose" in the distinguished foreign-policy quarterly *The National Interest* was later transmuted into a book by the same title.[1] Even the 1992 isolationist tract by Robert W. Tucker and David C. Hendrickson, *The Imperial Temptation,* was subtitled "The New World Order and America's Purpose."[2]

The notion of a "national purpose" sets off alarm bells in some minds. It may seem to connote an affinity for a form of "global messianism" that is often attributed, rightly or wrongly, to Woodrow Wilson. "American purpose" could also be construed as a curious form of American exceptionalism. Can a nation have a "purpose"? No one would think of starting a journal called "British Purpose" or "French Purpose" these days; something called "German Purpose" or "Japanese Purpose" would probably be greeted with considerable coolness; "Canadian Purpose" would be a candidate for "Saturday Night Live."

But the widening use of the phrase "national purpose," however variously it may be understood, suggests that the concept of the "national interest" is increasingly seen as insufficient for defining the ends and means of U.S. foreign policy. Serving and advancing the interests of the American people is surely one of the primary responsibilities of American statesmen. But the historical record suggests that Americans are most likely to support a vigorous engagement in world politics when they sense that larger issues are at stake than their own interests, narrowly construed. Some may regard this curious idealism as a kind of low-grade national fever. For others, it reflects the fact that ours is a proposition country: a nation founded, not on the tribal elements of blood, race, and soil, but on adherence to certain "self-evident truths" understood to be universal in character.

Moreover, with the phrase now part of the common vocabulary of the foreign-policy debate, it should become ever clearer that there is no contradiction between the pursuit of the "national interest" and an enlivening sense of "American purpose." "Interest," even "self-interest," is not in itself an immoral or amoral concept. It simply reflects the fact that, in a democracy, those in public authority stand in a position of fiduciary responsibility toward those in whose name, and by whose sufferance, they govern.

Indeed, the truth of the matter may be that no definition of "national purpose" will be tethered to political reality unless it includes a commitment to the defense of the "national interest." And conceptions of "national interest" that savor of moral autarky are unlikely to draw the support of an American electorate that has long shown its distaste for the cruder tactics of Realpolitik as traditionally practiced in Europe and elsewhere.

Understanding the relationship between "interest" and "purpose" in U.S. foreign policy is an exercise at the intersection of political thinking and moral reasoning. A correct understanding of how "interest" and "purpose" are related could help us overcome one of the primary obstacles to wise American statecraft in the 1990s and beyond: the logjammed debate between "realists" and "idealists" over America's role in the world. By deepening our concept of politics while tempering our historic national tendency to collapse morality into moralism, a fresh reflection on the age-old dialectic between the way things are and the way things ought to be might help us avoid the temptations of both messianism and cynicism.

National Interest and National Purpose: Ten Theses

The complex relationship between "interest" and "purpose" is at the heart of any serious effort to grapple with America's role in the post–Cold War world. I believe that a proper understanding of that relationship can be outlined in the following ten theses. Taken together, these theses do not yield a new master strategic concept for U.S. foreign policy. But they may help set the right intellectual and moral framework for the debate over grand strategy in the 1990s and beyond.

1. There is no escape from moral reasoning in politics.

Politics—even international politics—is an irreducibly moral enterprise, because politics is a human activity and human beings are distinguished from other animals precisely by their capacity to reflect and to choose. Politics is, as Aristotle affirmed and Hans Morgenthau denied, an extension of ethics. To attempt to subtract the moral element from politics is to debase public life and to disfigure public policy.

2. History can be bent to our wills.

Those who deny the possibility of purposefulness in this kind of world—for reasons of "complexity," or because of the "impersonal forces of history"—have not reflected very deeply on recent history. The twentieth century is replete with examples of men and women whose "purposeful" policies bent events to their wills. Lenin, Hitler, Mao, Churchill, and the founders of the State of Israel are among the obvious examples. In the more morally admirable of these cases as well as in the more odious, concepts of "purpose" were informed and tempered by concepts of "interest." "Interest" and "purpose" seem, empirically, to be linked. And the linkage has the appearance of a dialectic, in which interest and purpose reciprocally interact and are thus mutually refined.

3. Moralism is of no use in statecraft.

There is a traditional form of American morality—call it "cultural Protestantism"—that identifies "political morality" with the injunctions of the Sermon on the Mount. It is a morality of intentions, deeply suspicious of the very concept of "interest," uncomfortable with the exercise of power, and tending towards literalism in its appropriation of the Bible. This species of moral*ism* is inadequate to the tasks of moral reasoning and practical action required of statesmen.

4. Realism's critique of moralism remains essential to wise statecraft today.

The older American morality (or moral*ism*) was the object of the critique of the realist school in the foreign-policy debates of the 1930s and 1940s. The realist critique, particularly as articulated by Reinhold Niebuhr, remains a necessary corrective to the many flaws of "cultural Protestantism" and its secular heirs.

To put the matter more positively: understanding the inevitable irony, pathos, and tragedy of history, being alert to the problem of unintended consequences, maintaining a robust skepticism about all schemes of human perfection (especially those in which politics is the instrument of salvation), cherishing democracy without worshipping it—all these elements of Reinhold Niebuhr's moral sensibility are essential intellectual furnishings for anyone who would think wisely about "interest" and "purpose" in U.S. foreign policy.

Thus realism today is less a comprehensive framework for thinking about foreign policy than a crucial set of cautions essential to the exercise of practical reasoning about America's role in the world.

5. Realism must be completed by a concept of human creativity in history.

Realism, and especially Christian realism, must guard against premature closure in its thinking about the possibilities of human action in this world. As Niebuhr put it, we must never forget "the important residual creative factor in human rationality." Things can change—things can be *made* to change—for the better: sometimes.

6. Social ethics is a distinctive moral discipline.

As we think about America's responsibilities and duties in the world, the moral reasoning we need will reflect the morally distinctive nature of political action. It will not confuse politics with interpersonal relationships. Thus "social ethics"—moral reasoning about common, public action through politics—will be understood as a discipline with its own canons and its own methods of assessment: which are related to, but not identical with, the canons and methods of moral reasoning appropriate to the question, "But what should *I* do?" The moral reasoning we need will demonstrate to the policymaker that his choice is not between an immoral or amoral Realpolitik, on the one hand, and naïveté (dealing with international outlaws as if they were refractory children or difficult relatives), on the other.

7. *The "national interest" includes prudent efforts to bring a measure of order to international public life.*

The irreducible core of the "national interest" is composed of those basic security concerns to which any responsible democratic statesman must attend. But those security concerns are not unrelated to a larger sense of national purpose: we defend America because America is worth defending, on its own terms and because of what it means for the world. Thus those security concerns that make up the core of the "national interest" should be understood as the necessary inner dynamic of the pursuit of the "national purpose."

And the larger American purpose in world affairs is to contribute, as best we can, to the long, hard, never-to-be-finally-accomplished "domestication" of international public life: to the quest for ordered liberty in an evolving structure of international public life capable of advancing the classic goals of politics—justice, freedom, order, the general welfare, and peace. Empirically and morally, the United States cannot adequately defend its "national interest" without concurrently seeking to advance these goals in the world. Empirically and morally, those goals will not be advanced when they are pursued in ways that gravely threaten the basic security of the United States.

8. *"National purpose" is not national messianism.*

The "national purpose" should be seen as a horizon toward which our policy (and our polity) should strive. That horizon of purpose helps us measure the gap between where we are and where we ought to be. But it is not something that we shall achieve in any final sense. Understanding the national purpose this way is a barrier against the dangers of a simpler (and more dangerous) notion of national "mission," which implies a far shorter timeline.

9. *Casuistry, informed by the virtue of prudence, is the moral art appropriate to international statecraft.*

The practical relationship between national interest and national purpose is defined, for both the moral analyst and the policymaker, through casuistry: through the moral art of applying principles to world politics by means of the mediating virtue of prudence. Prudence does not necessarily guarantee wise policy. It does reduce the danger of stupid policy based on moralistic or Realpolitik confusions.

10. *The argument over the relationship between "interest" and "purpose" is perennial, but not necessarily circular.*

The dialectic of national interest and national purpose will remain unresolved. Pursuing a narrow concept of "interest" without reference to purpose risks crackpot realism. Pursuing grand and noble purposes without regard for the responsibilities of safeguarding the national interest risks utopianism. These two temptations—crackpot realism and utopianism—may be unavoidable, the world being what it is. But succumbing to those temptations is not unavoidable, given a clear understanding of both the inherently moral nature of politics and the distinctive canons and methods of social ethics.

Thus the debate over the right relationship between the national interest and the national purpose will be a perennial one, given the very nature of politics, as well as the historical character of the American people and their democratic experiment. But if it is informed by a proper understanding of the distinctive character of social ethics, the argument will not be circular and may yield a measure of wisdom from time to time.

Self-Determination and Sovereignty

Reconfiguring the debate about the relationship between interest and purpose in U.S. foreign policy is an ongoing exercise in reflection about *us*. But other basic questions, equally as complex and almost certainly as perennial, exist "out there," in the world with which our foreign policy must deal. Two of these questions have to do with the controverted terms "self-determination" and "sovereignty." Some clarity on what these terms mean—and don't mean—is the essential, real-world corollary to our ongoing moral and political reflection about how our ideals, our obligations, and the limits of our statecraft are related.

The twentieth century has seen three great experiments in social-political transformation on a mass scale: Leninism, Wilsonianism, and British colonialism. Their common thread was that they all tried (for very different reasons, of course) to make "normal" nation-states—of the sort that had emerged in Europe after the 1648 Peace of Westphalia—out of vastly complex jigsaw puzzles of ethnicity, race, and religion.

None of these experiments succeeded. The embodiment of the Leninist experiment, the Union of Soviet Socialist Republics, no longer exists. Yugoslavia, one incarnation of the Wilsonian impulse after World War I, is another fatality; and a second expression of Wilsonianism, Czechoslovakia, also came apart, albeit in a civilized fashion. The jewel in the crown of British colonialism was "India," understood as the entire Asian subcontinent; it has been subdivided twice already (with Pakistan and Bangladesh the results), and there is no guarantee that further divisions (perhaps followed by brutal reunifications) will not take place.

Leninism is over and done with, and so, very likely, is British colonialism. But what about Wilsonianism? Something has in fact endured as a legacy of the Wilsonian experiment: the notion that peoples have a "right to self-determination," a right that other peoples are obliged to respect. Moreover, it is usually (though not always) understood that the "right to self-determination" carries with it the right to an independent, sovereign nation-state.

The assertion of this right, and the attempt to embody it in the forms and trappings of national statehood, is now the single most volatile element in world politics. In recent years, the "right to self-determination" has been asserted, at various levels of passion and with various degrees of political success, by Abkhazians, Basques, Berbers, Bosnians, Bretons, Croatians, Eritreans, Estonians, Inuits, Kurds, Latvians, Lithuanians, Macedonians, Osetians, Palestinians, Québecois, Scots, Sikhs, Slovaks, Slovenes, Tamils, and Volga Germans. There are even separatist grumblings from northern Italians (the Lombardy League) who are tired of associating with southern Italians and Sicilians.

The volatility of these claims, the passion with which they are pursued, and the means adopted by some states to meet these challenges have raised questions about another claim: "sovereignty," and the attendant notion that a state's "internal affairs" are not subject to interference from other states, coalitions of states, or the "international community."

The principle of state sovereignty was devised in the seventeenth century to end the bloodletting that had been going on in Europe for a hundred years, ever since the Reformation shattered what was once assumed to be the unity of European Christendom. Europe was, quite literally, killing itself in the wars of religion; and the principle of state sovereignty (and immunity from external interference) was devised to stop the killing. Recalling that history, one is reminded not to tamper blithely with the principle of state sovereignty, for fear of unloosing seven devils worse than the first.

But is there simply nothing to be done while Dubrovnik and Sarajevo are destroyed, or while Kurds and south Sudanese Christians are being slaughtered, or while Haiti sinks deeper into primeval anarchy? How do we adjudicate various peoples' sometimes conflicting claims to a "right to self-determination" without creating conditions of chaos in which no one's interests are served? Is it possible to modify the principle of state sovereignty without committing different crimes of injustice, and without turning the world into a kind of free-fire zone?

In the aftermath of the Fifty-Five Years' War, questions like these are at or near the top of the international agenda and certain to recur time and time again. The way America thinks about these questions will have much to do with the way the "international community" thinks about them and acts on them. Here are three considerations that may help to frame the debate:

1. The Limits of Sovereignty

State sovereignty, and the consequent immunity of states from interference in their "internal affairs," is not an exceptionless norm. By agreeing to certain international human-rights agreements, for example, states have voluntarily limited their sovereign claims to non-interference in their internal practices. The nature of international public life today has also "internationalized" questions that would, in an earlier era, have been regarded as a state's domestic affairs. When innocent citizens of European and North American states are put at risk in European airports because of disputes over "self-determination" in the Middle East, those disputes (and the involvement of other states and terrorist organizations in them) cannot be considered the "internal affairs" of the states (and the organizations) involved.

Moral reasoning, too, leads us to conclude that the principle of state sovereignty must not be considered exceptionless. Suppose that Nazi Germany had forsworn aggression after recovering the Rhineland and the Sudetenland, and had proceeded to implement the "Final Solution" to the *Jüdenfrage* within its own internationally recognized borders. Would the principle of state sovereignty have meant that other states were forbidden to interfere in this German "internal affair"?

Most reasonable people today would regard a positive answer to that question as morally absurd. But suppose an Indian government, controlled by militant Hindu nationalists and capable of deploying nuclear weapons, decided to settle the "Pakistan problem" and redress what it considered the fundamental injustice of the 1947 partition of the subcontinent, using its claims to sovereignty in Kashmir as the opening wedge for military action. Or, at a somewhat less apocalyptic level, suppose the government of Turkey decided to rid itself of the Kurds in the manner in which it once decided to rid itself of the Armenians. Does the principle of state sovereignty mean that these affairs would be no one else's business? Would it constitute a fundamental breach of the principle of sovereignty if an international force—or an individual state, for that matter—intervened to stop the genocide of Christian tribesmen in the south of Sudan?

Put that way, the question seems to answer itself: whatever else it might mean, the principle of state sovereignty cannot mean that states are free to engage in the indiscriminate slaughter of religious, racial, or ethnic minorities within their borders. When that is taking place, others have a right—perhaps even a duty—to intervene to stop the killing.

The more difficult cases arise from the crackup of older sovereignties. How can we tell the difference between a civil war and a war between newly minted and legitimate sovereign states? The moral revulsion most people feel at the catastrophe that has befallen the former Yugoslavia suggests a grave deficiency in the argument that the principle of non-interference precludes intervention to stop this carnage, whether one considers the conflict a civil war or a regional war among micro-states. (Whether such an intervention could be justified on prudential grounds is another, second-order question.)

2. The Limits of "Self-Determination"

If state sovereignty and the attendant immunity from interference in one's internal affairs do not constitute an exceptionless norm, then neither does the "right to self-determination" trump all other claims.

Why? Because claims to be exercising the right to self-determination are not made in a historical or political vacuum. They inevitably abut other claims, some of which may be prior claims. They take place within an existing state system, whose stability is not without moral and political value. They are made in a world in which economic autarky is impossible, and in which adjudication of the claim to self-determination almost inevitably affects lives far beyond the claimant's boundaries. If the right to self-determination could trump all other rights claims, the world would no doubt exemplify Thomas Hobbes's famous "war of all against all."

So there are limits to the exercise of the right to self-determination. The blunt fact of the matter is that, as long as the world is organized (and disorganized) the way it is today, some nations cannot be states. And yet other nations clearly have a claim to self-determination that cannot reasonably be denied. How do we distinguish between the two?

History helps to sort these things out. The claims to self-determination advanced by the Lithuanians, Latvians, and Estonians carried considerable weight because within the living memory of many persons these nations had lost their independent statehood through brutal invasion and subjugation. (This raises another issue in other contexts, of course: is there a reasonable statute of limitations on national grievances?) Considerations of internal and regional stability will also figure in these determinations. Take the Baltic states again: the recovery of their independence seemed unlikely to lead to a general unraveling of public order, nor did these states seem likely to start making irredentist territorial claims on their neighbors. The same cannot be said, alas, about various other peoples who are now pressing claims to self-determination.

Questions of economic viability also need to be raised. If it is true that no nation-state today can be an economic island, it is also true that economic stability and progress are more likely for some regions and nations if they are part of a larger political construct.

"Self-determination" cannot, then, trump all other claims. In some instances, this claim ought to be accepted, and a new nation-state recognized. But in others, because of historical, regional, or economic factors, nationhood cannot lead to statehood.

Then what?

3. The Necessity of Intermediate Arrangements

The European world evolved the Westphalian system of sovereign, independent states to meet an emergency that was unmanageable through the political processes and institutions in place prior to the crisis of the Reformation. We may be living in a similar time of emergency, when new forms of political association are required in a world that is both increasingly interconnected and increasingly fissiparous. We may need, in other words, intermediate arrangements that fall short of full independence and yet allow a considerable measure of national/cultural autonomy.

A friend used to say that humankind's two greatest discoveries were the "two f's," fire and federalism. He may have been on to something.

If by "federalism" we mean, not a point-for-point replication of the American system, but a mode of association in which some limited powers are conceded to a national political authority while others are reserved to local, regional, or, conceivably, ethnic authorities, then various "federal" or "confederal" arrangements may be the intermediate path down which the passions for independence that often lead to mass violence ought to be channeled. Very likely the Russian Republic will either discover the virtues of federal arrangements or revert to more traditional forms of authoritarianism as a means of maintaining a minimum of public order and national unity. The same can be said about the Balkans and indeed the entire Danube basin.

There are also lessons in the recent history of western Europe about the ability of joint economic and political arrangements, even among sovereign states, to temper ancient passions. The Franco-German conflict, for centuries the cockpit of European rivalry, now seems considerably ameliorated. Have the French and Germans become altogether nobler and more instinctively cooperative? No. Institutional economic innovation created conditions that made a more peaceful relationship possible, because they rewarded cooperation and punished xenophobia. How much better off would the states of the late "Yugoslavia" have been had they been able (or compelled) to agree on national independence combined with a common market, a common foreign and defense establishment, and a human-rights compact subject to the oversight of the European Community and its human-rights court?

The issue, then, need not be conceived as sovereignty vs. subjugation. There must be ways to allow a plentiful expression of ethnic, religious, and/or national identity without the full trappings of sovereign statehood. (Paul Johnson's related call for a "new colonialism," a new trusteeship system, will be examined in the next chapter.) Those intermediate arrangements will loom larger in importance as the world becomes at once more internationalized and more localized.

DEMOCRACY, "COLLECTIVE SECURITY," AND AMERICAN LEADERSHIP

In 1991–92 a democratic revolution seemed well on its way to sweeping the globe. Today, while there is still considerable reason for satisfaction, the picture looks far more complicated. The consolidation of democratic regimes is by no means secure in the new democracies of central and eastern Europe and Latin America. One billion Chinese remain under the heel of the world's last Marxist-Leninist despotism. Elections in the Arab Middle East, where they are permitted, frequently return profoundly antidemocratic legislators to office. Sub-Saharan Africa is an economic and political disaster area (although South Africa continues to inspire hope that a peaceful and democratic transition to a post-apartheid society is possible). History is not quite over yet. But the successful playing out of the democratic revolution will have a lot to do with whether the continuation of history moves the world closer to order, or to chaos. How should the lonely superpower be thinking about the problems of democratic consolidation in the formerly Communist world, and in the countries of Latin America once ruled by authoritarian military regimes?

The key to democratic consolidation would seem to be the same as the key to the overthrow of the old despotisms: the reconstitution of a civil society in which the habits of mind and of heart necessary to sustain self-governance are nurtured and transmitted. To put it another way, we have to think about democracy culturally as well as structurally.

"Democracy" cannot be equated merely with the presence of certain political structures and processes. Those mechanisms— elections, legislatures, independent judiciaries, rotating executive authority—are not self-sustaining; they must rest on moral-cultural foundations. Even under Peter Berger's winsomely minimalist definition of democracy—"Democracy means that you can throw the bastards out every now and then, and that there are limits to what they can do when they're in"—the hard fact remains: you cannot have a democracy without a sufficient critical mass of democrats. Civil society is essential for democratic consolidation. Thus the former president of Argentina, Raul Alfonsin, was putting the matter rather too simply when he wrote, in the wake of Alberto Fujimori's 1992 auto-coup in Peru, that "the only thing democracy needs, aside from its basic institutions, are democratic subjects: men and women who have internalized the values of freedom, solidarity, tolerance and public commitment and justice and will not break the rules to gain their ends."[3] Democracies need citizens (not, by the way, "subjects"). And the virtues required for democratic citizenship are not easily developed—as any thoughtful citizen in an established democracy will attest.

Moreover, and as we saw earlier, the task of democratic consolidation in the formerly Communist world has been immensely complicated by the fact that Marxism-Leninism ruined more than the economies of the countries it ruled: it shattered their cultures, their social ecologies, as well. The 36-year-old prime minister of Bulgaria, Philip Dimitrov, stated the problem eloquently in a

March 1992 address at Washington's Woodrow Wilson International Center for Scholars. His analysis is well worth a lengthy quotation:

> The most serious challenge that Bulgaria is facing today is how to become a normal country again. As a state objective, this may sound a little odd, to those familiar with the urgent need for fundamental political and economic change in eastern Europe. But I believe that a return to normalcy is the essential precondition for all the other changes that need to occur. And by normalcy I understand not only consensual politics and a rational economic system, but a civil society functioning on the basis of shared moral values. . . .
>
> The Communist frame of reference . . . left a deep and lasting imprint. There were countless mechanisms within this frame of reference that enhanced its impact. The Communist authorities had indoctrinated people to feel vulnerable and dependent on the state, and not only in the sense that it could violate their rights. By imposing a great number of impractical and often illogical restrictions and limitations that were inevitably and routinely breached or disregarded, they also cultivated in the individual a feeling of being an offender in any case. This served to blur the line between the permitted and the forbidden, the acceptable and the unacceptable. It also negatively affected the moral standards of society, by stripping cheating, theft, and dishonesty of their moral repulsiveness.
>
> This moral confusion was accompanied by an utter confusion of values and their meaning at the level of societal activity, ranging from the glorification of betrayal, in the story of Pavlik Morozov, a "hero-child" who had betrayed his parents to the authorities, to the bizarre fact that throughout the communist period in Bulgaria, a square meter of linoleum cost more than a square meter of land.
>
> Honest and moral people would think nothing of stealing from the state or cheating the authorities. Liberty and love were defined through their opposites. The pursuit of happiness was discredited by the Communist perversion of the Hegelian concept that one should never feel contented. There was no faith to lean on, since religion and belief in God were subjected to such suppression and brainwashing that even those who did feel the inner need of God would express it only in a shy and perplexed manner, as if feeling vaguely ashamed of being involved in something so "outdated" and "unscientific."
>
> All this left little room for what one would call normal behavior by members of a civil society.[4]

The moral-cultural wreckage left by Communism was particularly severe. But democrats in formerly authoritarian states, and, truth to tell, democrats in established democracies, will recognize many of their own problems of social ecology in Prime Minister Dimitrov's remarks. The mechanisms of democracy are not all that hard to set up; the really tough job is the creation of a democratic and civil citizenry.

Amid all the difficulties of democratic transition and consolidation, two truths stand out, one old and the other newer. The old truth is that no polity can last without a minimum of acquiescence and legitimacy. The new truth is that in much of the world today, legitimacy comes through democracy. Why? Because the democratic revolution has been the political expression of an older and deeper revolutionary impulse, the human-rights revolution. In an impressively transcultural fashion, human beings across the world have decided that life under repression and political disempowerment is not simply in the nature of things. Freedom may have been the exception, rather than the rule, in most of human history. But that vast numbers of people today expect to live in a considerable measure of political freedom is one of the principal story lines of our time.

The United States was the first modern polity to claim political legitimacy on the basis of its recognition of certain truths about human freedom. It would be unworthy of us not to take that history seriously as we think about our responsibilities in the world in the twenty-first century.

No Escapes From History

We have been hearing a lot more, in recent years, about "collective security." The 1992 "Pentagon paper" on the future of U.S. strategic planning seemed to bend over backwards to demonstrate America's commitment to a world in which "collective security" arrangements predominate, operating under the authority of the "international community."

But there is no such thing, in real, functional terms, as an "international community." Secretary General Boutros-Ghali's colossal ambitions notwithstanding, the United Nations remains today, in its address to security issues, what it has been since 1945:

a stage on which a script written elsewhere is played out. If it is better able to act in a peacekeeping or peacemaking role in the 1990s, that is largely because there is no longer a Soviet Union to write an alternative script to that proposed by the West. The prospects for an effective U.N. have indeed been enhanced by the end of the Cold War. But that does not mean the U.N. is capable of acting without strong leadership from the United States, as the cases of the Gulf War and the debacle of Yugoslavia have proved, in very different ways.

Neither can we look to "Europe" to act as an agent of "collective security," even in its own precincts. The U.S. State Department's lethal fumbling of the Yugoslav crackup since 1991 has been matched, misstep for bumbling misstep, by the European Community. This does not bode well at all, given the possibility of more Yugoslavia-type conflicts in the lands of the former USSR.

In sum, "collective security" does not exist, in and of itself. Collective action, leading to an enhancement of "collective security," is more likely in the post–Cold War world—but only with the leadership of the United States or, less probable, of regional powers backed by the full, public assurance of U.S. support.

This is not the news that candidates for public office are eager to bring before the American electorate these days, because they think it is not the news the people want to hear. My hunch, however, is that the American people are eager, not for followership and not for pandering, but for a leadership that is commensurate with the realities of the West's recent victory in the Fifty-Five Years' War and the responsibilities that victory has laid upon us. So far, an extraordinary opportunity to shape a world order more reflective of humankind's nobler instincts is being botched, in part because of sheer inattention.

It is time for the return of "the vision thing."

7

The New Colonialism, and Other Political Incorrectnesses

R onald Reagan, the eternal optimist, liked to tell about a man who, assigned to sweep out a stable chock-full of manure, cheerfully went about his malodorous task convinced that "there's a pony in here somewhere." It is a parable that President Clinton and his people might well keep in mind, for the list of extant and impending crises that confronted them during the early months of the administration was daunting to say the least:

■ The new administration had to determine when the goals of the U.S. mission in Somalia had been achieved, and how a reversion to anarchy and auto-genocide was to be avoided in that unhappy land. Moreover, another half-dozen Somali-style disasters were impending in sub-Saharan Africa: was some form of crisis-prevention possible?

■ Then there was the continuing torture of what used to be Yugoslavia. The Bush administration's ineffectual hand-wringing over a catastrophe it helped make more likely presented the Clinton administration with some bitter choices. But the initial decision, after Secretary of State Warren Christopher's feckless foray through the paralyzed capitals of western Europe, was, in truth, not to decide. The initiative was thus left in the hands of various ethnic-nationalist aggressors—with little hope that long-term stability in the region, much less a minimum of justice, had been secured.

■ Boris Yeltsin's high-wire act continued, as the divisions within Russia over the nature, scope, and pace of economic and

109

political reform widened. Could Russia hold together and stay on course toward marketization amidst political chaos? What would the U.S. response be to some form of relatively benign authoritarianism that presented itself as an interim, stabilizing administration? Moreover, there was unrest in the Baltic states (over ethnicity and citizenship, economic and energy dislocation, and the continuing presence of Russian troops); Ukraine was hedging its commitment to de-nuclearizing its military; and bloodshed continued in the trans-Caucasian republics of Armenia and Azerbaijan. Attention had to be paid, and soon, to the Commonwealth of Independent States, lest it metamorphose into the Cauldron of Warring States and Tribes.

■ Parts of Central Europe seemed in reasonable shape, with Poland set to turn the corner economically and the Czech lands poised for take-off. But would ethnic violence break out between Hungary and Slovakia after the Slovak Republic was established? The conflict over the Slovak damming of the Danube (which had immediate ill effects on the ground water across the border in Hungary), the presence in Slovakia of a large Hungarian minority, and bitter Slovak memories of forced "Magyarization" during the last decades of the Austro-Hungarian Empire made for an explosive ethnic mix that, if it were ignited, could set off further ethnic-nationalist warfare within the late Warsaw Pact.

■ The final act of the Fidel Castro story remained to be played in Cuba, and there were reports that the last caudillo yearned for a Wagnerian climax to his career (introducing biological toxins into the water supply of Miami was one of the less lurid suggestions being bruited). No matter how one assessed the likelihood of such a finish, though, nothing in Fidel's script to date suggested that he was going to go gently into that good night.

■ Haiti remained a miserable debacle in our own Caribbean backyard. The U.S.-led OAS boycott had intensified the suffering of the people and created a major refugee problem while failing to bring a sustainable political solution any closer. Meanwhile, the cause of the exiled Haitian president, Jean-Bertrand Aristide, had been taken up by the very same people who once told you what splendid fellows the Sandinistas were; Father Aristide's fondness for the Haitian version of the South African "necklace" as a means of consolidating power went unremarked in these quarters. Haiti (like Somalia) posed an urgent question in stark terms: Are some Third World countries simply incapable of making the transition to democracy in their present low state of political culture?

■ The fuse on Hindu-Muslim antipathy on the subcontinent of Asia had gotten alarmingly shorter in the late 1980s. Here were two very large states—two civilizations, really—that had already gone to war three times since 1947. Ancient and modern grievances remained unresolved (and perhaps unresolvable), and the result was an intensification of religiously sanctioned political fanaticism. Meanwhile, India had a nuclear capability and Pakistan was working overtime to get one.

■ Iran was reportedly shopping for both stolen nuclear weapons and weapons-grade fissile material, throughout the old USSR and in the murky bazaars where terrorists and international weapons-brokers gather.

■ Saddam Hussein was still in power in Iraq, and while his quest for weapons of mass destruction and reliable ballistic-missile delivery systems had been set back, it had not been halted. Then there was Saddam's attempted assassination of former President Bush—a crime that could not be ignored.

■ North Korea, perhaps the most heavily militarized and regimented country on the planet, was ruled by an increasingly erratic octogenarian who seemed to retain fantasies about reunification through force. Meanwhile, America's new/old isolationists had settled on South Korea as the first target of their campaign to withdraw U.S. forces from foreign arenas, regardless of whether they serve a crucial deterrent function.

■ And, as if all that were not enough, the thirty-year-old problem of Cyprus started heating up again. The basic political stalemate remained, while weary contributor states began withdrawing peacekeeping forces from the U.N. mission on the island. The Turks and Greeks could yet go at it in the grand manner once again on Cyprus, and at precisely the time when their other sphere of confrontation, the Balkans, is near explosion.

The end of the Cold War has not meant the end of international conflict; nor, despite the fervent wishes of isolationists old and new, has it rendered U.S. foreign policy unnecessary. But the crises are not all there is. The crackup of the old bipolarity has given rise to both crises and opportunities.

To see opportunities amidst the impending chaos is neither an act of wishful thinking ("there's a pony in here somewhere") nor a facile assertion that a problem seen from the other side is an opportunity. The opportunities have been cast up by the plasticity and dynamics of post–Cold War international public life. If we have trouble getting them into as clear a focus as the crises, it may be because of the strategic myopia fostered by the Bush administration's disdain for "the vision thing."[1]

History—and, for those of us who read history through distinctive lenses, Providence—has put before us a great opportunity to take a significant step forward in what Churchill called "the hard march of man." In this case, the step forward would be progress toward a world that is increasingly characterized by the rule of law rather than the rule of brute force. Such a "domestication" of international politics is unlikely ever to be accomplished with any finality. But progress toward it—which is to say, progress out of the Hobbesian jungle where all are at war with all—is possible.

And it is possible now because of a rare confluence of events.

There is only one great power in the world today, and it is one that has retained significant elements of altruism in its general outlook. Yes, there is ritual grumbling about "American hegemony." But we now have an unprecedented chance to exercise enlightened leadership in the world. Further, the technological and communications revolutions that have shrunk the globe dramatically have sensitized our consciences and heightened others' sense of the possible. Aspects of the human condition that have long been considered inevitable—famine, rampant disease, tribal and ethnic warfare—become intolerable when broadcast into our living rooms in color day after day after day. In addition, much of the world knows that things don't have to be the way they are, and that conviction can be the source of useful political action, if it is properly channeled.

But to what ends? And by what means? Here is where the "vision thing" becomes crucial.

THE VISION THING: THE JOHNSONIAN EDITION

As we ponder what we can and ought to do in the closing years of this century, few commentators have a stronger claim to our respectful attention than the English historian-journalist Paul Johnson, whose *Modern Times* remains the single best overview of the rhythms of history over the past ninety years. In late 1992, Paul Johnson turned his formidable intelligence toward the future, in a striking article published in *National Review*.[2] The results were, to put it mildly, thought-provoking.

Johnson's reputation as a devout Thatcherite, and the venue of his essay, should not deter liberals from considering his dramatic proposals for the future of world politics and economics, many of which are likely to be the source of considerable distress among both Old Right conservatives and libertarian isolationists. For Paul Johnson—whose *Modern Times* nailed down, historically, the indictment of statism and utopian ideology as the sources of most of the century's pain—has proposed that our goal in the twenty-first century should be nothing less than a new world order: an order characterized by collective security arrangements, the increasing sway of international law, a global free-trading zone, and . . . the "new colonialism."

Paul Johnson is no Panglossian naïf: indeed, he begins his essay by noting the forty regional conflicts in the world in the early 1990s, the remaining 30,000 nuclear warheads in the old Soviet Union, the recrudescence of nationalist and ethnic violence, and the world's worst recession since the 1930s. And yet, Johnson suggests, our attitude toward the future should be one of "cautious optimism."

Why? In no small part because "we have survived the twentieth century, perhaps the most dangerous century in the history of humanity." International public life, which collapsed in 1914 and remained abnormally fissiparous until the late 1980s, has been "at least partially restored and with good prospects of a complete recovery." Even more importantly, we have learned—or at least we have begun to learn—the lessons of this awful period. The march toward the utopian future imagined by Communism (on the basis of class) and Nazism (on the basis of race) has been abandoned. Democracy and the market are the systems of choice throughout much of the world.

So why not simply bask in the afterglow of a job well done? Because, Johnson argues, the "solidity of the international peace we all enjoy" depends upon our success in making it possible for "this comparative and unprecedented felicity to be spread progressively to the rest of the world." Forging the first global society is thus not simply a possibility; effective work toward that end is a responsibility, on both pragmatic and altruistic grounds.

Paul Johnson's "new world order" (the phrase has been debased, but it will have to do for now) is built on two liberal pillars, collective security and a global free-trade system, to be erected by predominantly conservative means.

First, the pillars.

Bolstering Collective Security

While the United States took the diplomatic lead and bore the brunt of the military burden, Desert Shield and Desert Storm were, in Johnson's judgment, "classic exercise(s) in collective security" that brought the U.N. Security Council back to "ardent life" after the gridlock caused by Cold War bipolarity. Moreover, the great international coalition assembled to resist Saddam Hussein's aggression in Kuwait was a sign that the world had indeed learned the lesson of the 1930s: appeasing dictators doesn't work, and the legitimate use of force can contribute to the building of a measure of order in world affairs.

The next step, Johnson suggests, is to transform "an ineffectual and hypocritical" U.N. centered on the General Assembly into a "realistic and forceful" U.N. centered on the Security Council. This will require a new secretary general (Dr. Boutros-Ghali being "out of date"), a trimmed down and sharpened up U.N. staff, and the addition of Germany, Japan, and India to the permanent membership of the Security Council. In this arrangement, Johnson foresees that the permanent membership of the Council will, despite its ideological differences, become used to acting as the "inner cabinet" of the world community, whose primary task will be policing the global neighborhood and enforcing the U.N. Charter's strictures against aggression.

But what if there is no classic cross-border aggression (as there was not in Somalia)? What is the revamped Security Council–led U.N. system to do when countries implode, or degenerate into chaos and anarchy? Is "preventive maintenance" possible in world affairs? Johnson hints at the necessity of Charter revision, to permit the U.N. to enter conflict arenas where it has not been invited and where traditional aggression hasn't yet occurred (a point that was finessed in Somalia). But he seems even more interested in the evolution of ongoing and extensive "international contingency planning." This would involve the creation of a Security Council–led international military and intelligence force that would maintain a global "Disaster Survey." Constantly updated information and regularly revised options for intervention (diplomatic, economic, and/or military) would allow the Security Council to "move in swiftly when action will be most effective," rather than waiting (as in Kuwait, Somalia, and Yugoslavia) until disaster had fully struck. This monitoring/contingency-planning function would be staffed by diplomats and military officers of "all the major powers and many minor ones"—which would have the additional benefit of helping to make "the spirit and technology of collective security . . . an integral part of their training and experience."

The net result, Johnson believes, is that "we will cease to think of the U.N. as well-meaning but contemptible, and regard it increasingly as a formidable and professional instrument of world crisis-management."

A Global Free-Trade System

Johnson, like others, foresees the evolution, over the next decade or so, of a trilateral system of international trading blocs: Europe, the Americas (with the North American Free Trade Agreement eventually extending to the major Latin American economies), and East Asia. The crucial question is whether these blocs turn inward, becoming, in effect, transnational "protectionist superpower(s) with high external tariffs," or whether their "ultimate destiny and common purpose is to merge in one global system."

Johnson is, of course, a convinced exponent of the latter approach, not least because of his study of the lethal part protectionism played in setting the stage for the Great Depression of the 1930s. One key test of the future prospects of global free trade will come, he believes, in sorting out the European Community's Maastricht Treaty, which, as originally designed, would set up a "deep vertical structure" of integration-plus-protectionism that could throw a monkey wrench into the works in the Americas. For if the EC becomes Fortress Europe, Fortress America will not be far behind. And if that happens, then with two gigantic high-tariff blocs in play within the global trading system, East Asia will be sure to follow suit. This is a catastrophic prospect, says Johnson, for "history shows that trade wars have a depressing tendency to erupt into fighting wars." Much depends, therefore, on whether the EC goes down the "vertical integration" route preferred by France and the Brussels bureaucracy, or opts for the "horizontal integration" of new members (the Scandinavians, the central Europeans, and eventually eastern Europe), coupled with less centralized bureaucratic management, preferred by the United Kingdom.

In thinking about the future of the world economy, Johnson also argues for taking not just Japan but all of Asia far more seriously. Here, he suggests, the sheer magnitude of the demographics involved requires a change of perception. For if population is destiny, then the *axis mundi* is shifting inexorably eastward. Six Asian nations—China, India, Pakistan, Bangladesh, Indonesia, and Vietnam—will be home to 5.25 billion human beings by the mid-twenty-first century. Their colossal numbers, coupled with the rapid advance of capitalism and the economic dynamism characteristic of the region, virtually guarantee the development of "enormous markets" that will, in turn, prompt the formation of regional trading arrangements such as we already find in embryonic form in Southeast Asia.

Regional economic integration, then, is a fact. The trick is to integrate regional economies in ways that make the eventual creation of a truly global free-trade zone more, not less, likely. For the danger Johnson foresees is that the ideological bipolarity of the Cold War could be succeeded in the twenty-first century by a protectionist trilateralism. Not only would this be bad for the global economy and for the individual countries involved; it would also make the evolution of an effective and truly global collective-security system virtually impossible. The two go together: international collective security and global free trade.

Interestingly enough, Paul Johnson then offers a quartet of essentially conservative means to these liberal ends.

A New Colonialism

The first is a benign new form of colonialism, in a revival of the trusteeship system first devised by the League of Nations after World War I. On this point Johnson is at his anti-utopian sharpest. He regards as "illusory" the notion that all peoples are ready for independence—a claim that achieved the status of unchallengeable orthodoxy in the years immediately following World War II. The result of this illusion has been an "incalculable cost in human misery."

The historical record is truly sobering here. Some of the post-colonial entities we now call "states" cannot function as such: "government cannot discharge its elementary functions of maintaining external defense, internal order, and an honest currency." Moreover, there is little reason to think that many of these states are "countries" in any recognizable sense of the term; many of their borders were fixed, not by the evolution of history, but by colonial adventurers, military officers, and European diplomats. "Zaire" is a country in its present form, not of its own accord, but by ukase of King Leopold II of the Belgians.

And the sorry prospect is that things are going to get worse, rather than better, in these less-than-states, particularly in Africa. (Indeed, one of the colonial hangovers from which we must recover, and quickly, is the notion that it is "racist" to discuss the political and economic incapacities of many "states" in sub-Saharan Africa. The true racism is to suggest that African countries are to be excused from observing the standards of civilized behavior we expect from everyone else.) Unlike Asia, Africa is not taking off economically; most of it is stuck in reverse. Political succession is too often determined by bullet, not ballot. There is far too much military ironmongery lying around, and far too little of the infrastructure of modern civilization. An AIDS plague of truly pandemic proportions could further dissolve what fragile bonds of community exist within and among African nations in the 1990s and into the next century. Thus a dramatic collapse of social order on a continental scale—the result of famine, disease, corruption, and gross militarization—is not beyond the realm of possibility.

Johnson believes that the root cause of these multiple disasters in Africa is not "colonialism or demographics or shortage of credit." Rather, it is government: "bad, incompetent, or corrupt government—usually all three—or no government at all." The result is an vast ocean of human degradation and misery, and "a threat to stability and peace, as well as an affront to our consciences."

If the problem is bad government, then perhaps the solution is better government, through a return to the "trustee-mandate" system pioneered by the League of Nations under the Treaty of Versailles. This time around, though, the trusteeship function would be exercised, not under the authority of a great power, but under the aegis of the Security Council: on humanitarian grounds, but also as another form of international "preventive maintenance." Rather than applying palliatives after disaster had struck (as in Somalia), the revamped Security Council would try to interdict disaster.

The difference between the new trusteeship system and the old colonialism would lie in the fact that in these new circumstances the mandatory power would not be engaged in extracting wealth for itself from the "colony" or trustee. Instead, one of its primary objectives would be to develop a governmental infrastructure that would permit the country in trusteeship to assume a place at the international economic table.

There could be "several levels or models of trusteeship," says Johnson, "ranging from the provision of basic government almost from scratch to the provision of internal-security systems and mandatory currency and economic management." If such a system proved capable of functioning properly, one could even imagine circumstances in which a country might actually ask to be taken into trusteeship, as a dying corporation tries to revivify itself by going into a court-supervised receivership and reorganization. Functioning in this way, the Security Council would thus "become the last, most altruistic and positive of the imperial powers, restoring to the word colonialism the good name it once enjoyed—in Mediterranean antiquity no less than the nineteenth century."

Taming the Chinese Dragon

The second means to the end of the international collective-security/global-free-trade order that Johnson proposes is the "redirection into positive and constructive channels of China's power to disrupt and menace the Far East."

Here, I fear, Johnson is overly optimistic. He is under no illusions about "the savagery of the regime" in the PRC: it is "Saddam Hussein multiplied by forty." Yet he suggests that Deng and his neo-Sino-Stalinist gerontocrats might better be viewed on the model of Franco or Gorbachev, as autocratic "reformers" who paved the way, wittingly or otherwise, toward a constitutional future.

Johnson also reminds us that China is a great civilization on the verge of becoming a world-class economic power: a " 'have' nation, with more to lose than to gain from regional instability." Thus Johnson's realist "solution" to the problem of the PRC lies in "involving its rulers more and more in the new Security Council system," on the assumption that giving Beijing more responsibilities in the world will encourage it to act more responsibly. "By enmeshing China in the network of duties and privileges of great power status, we will gradually convert her from an international anomaly in a post–cold war world into a central pillar of the new global structure of order."

Perhaps. Still, the odds seem rather prohibitive. And why should we think that the "inclusion" strategy that Franklin Roosevelt tried on Uncle Joe Stalin will bear any better fruit with Stalin's last legatees? China will certainly play an enormous role in the world of the twenty-first century: its combination of population and economic vitality will ensure that. But little in China's current policy (especially on arms transfers) gives hope that it could become a stabilizing power in the foreseeable future, under anyone's tutelage.

Reforming Education and Environmentalism

Back on firmer ground, Johnson suggests that an educational revolution must accompany the ever-expanding thrust of "universal education." Whatever the latter's accomplishments over the past century in the developed world, the system is clearly in crisis:

> All over Eastern Europe, and increasingly in Western Europe, mobs of young people, who have been right through the universal education mill, are ranging through the complete gamut of primitive and irrational behavior—racism, ethnic triumphalism, xenophobia, hatred of refugees. There is a universal complaint in Europe and North America that the young emerge from high school (and often from university) with only tolerable literacy, unable to write their own language well, ignorant of other languages, knowing little of their country's history, literature, and culture—fitter candidates for a mob than for a citizenry.[3]

This educational shipwreck threatens any progress toward a more humane world system, because only an educated electorate will be able to support the transition to "a positive system of international law and the spread of a pattern of world free trade." Johnson believes that the consciousness of this educational failure is so "general and profound" that a "true cultural revolution" is on the horizon, one that will take back the schools and universities from those who have largely destroyed them.

Finally, Johnson believes that a sane environmentalism, stripped of its bogus metaphysics and New Age piety, will facilitate the evolution of his new world order. But it will do so only if it is a bit less frenzied about trees, and more understanding of the fact that "improvement in the use of our human resources" is the environmental key to the future.

Here is one of the great lessons of the twentieth century: that "inanimate resources, important though they are, are not the raw material of the higher wisdom"—or the higher productivity, or the higher rates of economic growth, or the higher rates of material wealth. Human capital—creativity, imagination, discipline, intelligence, willpower—is the key to economic and political development. And here is yet another dimension of the moral scandal of famine and chaos, of the sort now being televised from the Balkans and East Africa: the profligate waste of the "energies and talents . . . the brains, the creativity and imagination, the sensibilities and taste" of the victims of governmental idiocy, human wickedness, and ineffectual international organization.

TOWARD A MORE CAPACIOUS REALISM?

What shall we make of Paul Johnson's bold vision, and his even bolder proposals for translating vision into reality?

Let's begin with the problems.

Whether the U.N. system is as reformable as Johnson suggests is surely an open question. The U.N. bureaucracy is both enormous and resilient, and can be relied on to resist any further efforts to shift the institutional balance of power from the General Assembly to the Security Council. Moreover, the clout of the General Assembly today rests in no small part on a polite fiction that will be difficult to dislodge: the notion of the "equality" of sovereign states in the U.N. context. Were the Security Council to emerge as the "inner cabinet" of a new international crisis-prevention and crisis-management system, the blunt truth of the matter would become undeniable: that some sovereign states count for more, in shaping world politics, than other sovereign states. The states whose only purchase on U.N. power is their equal vote in the Assembly are therefore likely to resist that development strenuously.

The counterargument would be that, should the permanent members of the Security Council decide to go down the road Johnson proposes, the rest of the U.N. would have little choice but to follow along. But could the current permanent members agree? The veto provision requires unanimity, and China (ideologically) and France (by habit) remain prickly characters on the Council, even under post–Cold War circumstances. Even if they fell in line, what would happen if, as Johnson proposes, Germany, Japan, and India were added to the mix? (And if these were added —which would require Charter reform, itself a potential mare's nest—wouldn't the pressure to include Nigeria and Brazil, and possibly Indonesia, be formidable? Then where would we be?)

Such serious institutional problems are likely to be resolved only if there is Western leadership toward that end. But this may be too much to hope for. A general lassitude hangs over what ought to be the most politically dynamic part of the world. "Europe" does not exist in collective-security terms, as the ruins in southeastern Europe mutely attest. The United States is divided on its post–Cold War purposes; some even argue that there are no such purposes. Perhaps the West will break out of its current funk. Until it does, serious international institutional change of the sort Johnson envisions seems unlikely. These things don't happen by themselves.

Johnson also seems to assume that the confrontation between modernity and tradition that is so volatile a force in the Islamic world will be fairly easily resolved, in favor of a reasonably peaceful process of modernization. Perhaps so, in Indonesia and Malaysia, over a longish period of time. But what about the cauldron of the Middle East? What about North Africa? What about the Islamic-Christian confrontation across black Africa? The kind of Islamic theological revolution suggested in chapter 11 of this book would seem to be a prerequisite for the fulfillment of Johnson's vision.

There are also what might be called, for want of a better term, grave psychological problems to be resolved in the evolution of a genuine international security system. Johnson's vision may assume that the "pacifying" aspects of the market revolution and the global communications village will rub away the rough edges of distinctive cultures and identities. But in fact the opposite seems to be happening: globalization seems to be accompanied by dramatically intensified localization or tribalization throughout the world. Could any progress toward a new international security system occur without some assurance to the proposed beneficiaries that they will not be utterly homogenized, culturally, in the process?

On the other, other hand, Paul Johnson's new-world-order proposal is intellectually stimulating precisely because it asks us to jump out of our intellectual ruts and think creatively, rather than defensively, for a change. The difficulties abound (and there are far more than I have sketched here). But that was true in 1947 also, when bold thinking produced the policies and institutions that won the ultimate battle in the Fifty-Five Years' War against totalitarianism.

In the wake of that victory, the American people are being counseled to avoid trouble: and exerting forceful American leadership in developing a post–Cold War international political and economic order certainly runs the risk of trouble. But we are now at the high-water mark of U.S. influence and power. If we do not take the prudent risks of leadership now, while we have the power to bend at least some events to our will, we are virtually certain to get into even deeper trouble later.

8
Why the New Isolationists Are Wrong

The fiftieth anniversary of Pearl Harbor was a mere seventy-two hours past. And less than two days before, Russia's Boris Yeltsin, Ukraine's Leonid Kravchuk, and Byelorussia's Stanislav Shushkevich had put the final nails into the coffin of the Union of Soviet Socialist Republics: an event comparable in geographic and demographic scope to the demise of the Roman Empire (one important difference being that the legions didn't leave 30,000 nuclear warheads behind).

But marching, as he has so often done, to the beat of his own idiosyncratic drummer, Patrick J. Buchanan chose that day, December 10, 1991, to announce the first self-consciously traditional-isolationist campaign for the presidency in two generations.

Only in America.

His curious sense of timing notwithstanding, though, even those who disagreed with the "America First" message had reason to be grateful to Pat Buchanan. For whatever else his campaign managed to accomplish, it brought into the open an argument that had been lurking just below the surface of our public life, in both left- and right-wing forms, since the late 1960s. The argument is about America and the world, and it is an argument down to first principles. Moreover, it is an argument with a singularly ecumenical cast of characters, in which people usually thought to be at opposite ends of the ideological spectrum end up in a common cause.

The revival of isolationism had been brewing for a while. Old-fashioned America Firstism of the sort associated with Senators Gerald Nye and Burton K. Wheeler during the Lend-Lease debate of 1941 never really died, although it was consigned to the more fevered swamplands of American politics after Japanese carrier planes swept over Oahu and left Battleship Row in ruins. But the old isolationism gradually regathered its energies during the Reagan years (curiously enough, since it disdained Ronald Reagan's sweeping defense of the democratic revolution in the world); and it has now been amplified by a renascent and principled libertarian isolationism.

Then there was the neo-isolationism of the Vietnam-era New Left. Reversing the myth of American innocence and inverting the fears of the traditionalist isolationists, it taught that a racist, imperialist, militarist United States was too dangerous and too corrupt to act in the world. In softened form this strain of neo-isolationism dominated the national Democratic Party for twenty years: from the days of the McGovern insurgency to the nomination of Bill Clinton in 1992 (and, some would argue, beyond).

The 1980s Cold War endgame—led in the United States by Old Right conservatives who had learned the lesson of Pearl Harbor, neoconservatives who had read their Koestler, their Sidney Hook, and their Solzhenitsyn, and the occasional liberal internationalist who hadn't bought the notion that Stalin's imperialism was really Harry Truman's fault—kept these sundry isolationist currents more or less below the waterline of national politics. The bipartisan and trans-ideological consensus first forged by Dean Acheson and Arthur Vandenberg held: as it turns out, just long enough to win.

But the crackup of the Soviet Union recast the American debate over America and the world. Reform Communist Mikhail Gorbachev as Lord North to Pat Buchanan's Patrick Henry: you never know, do you?

There are many factions in the new isolationist camp. Among the fresh recruits are the aforementioned libertarians, and those New Left–influenced Democrats whose revivified nationalism—primarily expressed in a vociferous opposition to free trade—is in part an attempt to exorcise their party's twenty-year record of international pusillanimity. The libertarians merit attention, even if their devotion to theory in the face of complex human reality reminds one of the bright student in Philosophy 101 who, having discovered the intoxicating pleasures of abstract reasoning, thinks he has the world by the tail. As for the Democratic refugees from radicalisms past: they, alas, will be with us for a while longer, and their leadership roles in Congress mean that their arguments will have to be engaged.

Nevertheless, it was Patrick Buchanan who focused the country's attention on the resurgence of isolationism. And so it is on his formulation of "America First" that I will focus here.

BUCHANAN'S BRIEF

What, in 1992, did Pat Buchanan and his campaign want? According to an essay Buchanan published in September 1991, he wanted "a more traditionalist, interest-oriented U.S. foreign policy."[1]

I take it that the key term here is "traditionalist." Few would deny that U.S. foreign policy has to be "interest-oriented"; as we saw in chapter 6, the serious arguments have to do with the content of that "interest" and its relationship to a sense of national purpose. But one cannot get at the psychological and ideological roots of Buchananite isolationism unless one grasps its nostalgia —its gut conviction that internationalism is the foreign-policy expression of the moral-cultural deracination of America that, in this view, began with the New Deal and eventually led to the spectacle of Howard Metzenbaum, Patrick Leahy, and Edward M. Kennedy sitting in judgment on Robert Bork and Clarence Thomas. The mental image that Pat Buchanan and his friends have of the "Old Republic" may seem odd, even a tad unhinged, to those with a different reading of the past. But that is their image of what was lost over the past sixty years; and it drives their isolationism today.

Moreover, Buchanan was, to my mind, quite right in several of the judgments that buttressed his America Firstism. He was right that things have changed, that we no longer live in a world defined by the Yalta imperial system, and that it was the old cold warriors who were vindicated by the Revolution of 1989 and the New Russian Revolution of 1991. Buchanan was also right in his claim that President Bush failed to define the content of his "new world order," and in his charge that Bush and his foreign-policy team dithered at key moments (Tiananmen Square, the beginnings of the crackup in Yugoslavia) when we might have made a difference in mopping up the detritus of Communist rule. A foreign policy that stood for self-determination in Kuwait but fretted nervously (and publicly) about self-determination in Lithuania and Ukraine was a foreign policy deserving of criticism.

In place of a vague Bushite internationalism (so redolent to Buchananites of the Eastcoastestablishmentrepublicanism they once thought they had conquered), and with the Communist threat no longer dominating the international horizon, Pat Buchanan offered what he termed "a foreign policy for the rest of us." It was built on four moral, cultural, and historical convictions:

1. Take care of your own.

"America First" wrote Buchanan, "is an idea that engages the heart, and the mind." Why? Because it is a call to tribal loyalty and mutual responsibility. America First "says we will put our family first, our people first, our country first. It invokes tradition; it appeals to patriotism; it is rooted in the Founding Fathers' idea that Americans are to be sent abroad to fight only when Americans—or their vital interests—are at risk."[2]

2. America is falling for geopolitical and economic rope-a-dope.

The United States has played the benign sucker long enough. The intellectualoids "at AEI, Brookings, and Heritage Foundation seminars" may laugh at phrases like "America First" while settling "the fate of the Punjab," says Buchanan; but "the rest of us" are asking questions: "What are we getting for $15 billion in foreign aid? Why, forty-six years after World War II, are we still defending Germany and Japan while they steal our markets?"[3]

3. Imperial overstretch has led to a free-fall in the republic's character and prestige.

"Why must we pacify the Persian Gulf when women walking their dogs in Central Park are being slashed to death by bums?" asked Pat Buchanan. "How come we can seal the border of Saudi Arabia but cannot close our own to illegal aliens flooding California? . . . The incivility and brutality of our cities, the fading of the Reagan Boom, the rise of ethnic hatred, are concentrating the minds of Americans on their own society, their own country. What doth it profit a nation if it gain the whole world, and lose its own soul?"[4]

4. *Admiral Mahan was right, and Woodrow Wilson was wrong.*

American foreign policy should reflect the unique position of the United States, geographically and economically. "Situated on an island continent, the greatest trading republic in history, America has a vital interest in freedom of the seas—the Atlantic, Pacific, Caribbean. We must maintain the world's greatest Navy and Air Force. Because of [the] missile threat, the United States should be first in space. Nor can we let our supremacy in technology be lost. But it is time to review all treaty obligations dating from Iron Curtain days, and recommit ourselves to defend only those regions that are critical to our own security."[5]

These four convictions then yielded seven specific proposals for an "America First" foreign policy:

#1. Contract the boundaries of the Monroe Doctrine. Abrogate the Rio Treaty. Define America's hemispheric security interests as limited to "the north coast of South America, the Caribbean, Mexico, [and] Central America."

#2. Get out of South Korea. Withdraw all our ground forces from the peninsula. "If North Korea, with 10 percent of the GNP [and] half the population of the south, strikes across the DMZ, why should boys from Anacostia and Idaho be first to die?"

#3. Bid "sayonara" to Japan. Abrogate the mutual security pact with the Japanese. Forget the Philippines as a naval base. "If the smaller nations of East Asia, fearful of Japanese or Chinese hegemony, want a U.S. fleet presence, they can pay for it."

#4. Don't make any security commitments east of the old NATO boundary with the Warsaw Pact. Don't let Poland, the Czech Republic, and Hungary join NATO, the pleas of our "new friends" behind the old iron curtain notwithstanding. "Eisenhower would not fight in Hungary in '56 and we're not going to fight in East Europe."

#5. In fact, once Soviet troops are out of eastern Europe, the Baltic states, and Ukraine, we should abandon NATO altogether, bring the boys home, and take our theater and intermediate-range

nuclear weapons with us. "The new Germany of 80 million is rich enough and powerful enough to defend herself."

#6. Zero out all foreign aid. Close down the Agency for International Development (AID), and drastically cut back the United States Information Agency. Withdraw U.S. funds from the "African Development Bank, the Asian Development Bank, the Latin American Development Bank, etc. If Uncle Sam wants to guarantee state loans, let's set up an Arkansas Development Bank or a West Virginia Development Bank."

#7. Stop making new grants to the International Monetary Fund and the World Bank, "and demand a hard balance sheet from each, with loans written to market value. Both are global S&L's; we are going to have to pay off the lion's share of the lousy paper."

In sum:

"Powerful as she is, America cannot dictate the shape of the world to come. Nor should we try. Like surfers, we need to watch the great waves roll in, closely, to discern the elemental forces at play, and to ride those that move mankind to ends commensurate with our values: freedom, liberty, self-determination. Our war, the Cold War, is over. Time for America to come home."[6]

THE CASE AGAINST THE NEW ISOLATIONISTS

There are at least six reasons why Pat Buchanan's America Firstism is mistaken, wrongheaded, and dangerous.

1. Buchanan misrepresents the history of the Cold War world, and particularly the history of the 1980s.

American leadership was indispensable to the success of the Freedom Party in World War III, the Cold War. In 1947, the impoverishment of the British exchequer made it necessary for the United States, in the Truman Doctrine, to draw the line against the further expansion of Stalin's empire. American leadership was crucial to the formation of NATO, to the Marshall Plan, and to the repelling of Communist aggression in northeast Asia. More recently, American leadership—which meant Ronald Reagan's leadership—was essential in braking the 1970s expansion of Soviet power (in the invasion of Afghanistan, and in Africa and Central America), in checkmating the new nuclear power of the USSR and its threat to "Finlandize" western Europe, and in seizing the opportunities presented by Mikhail Gorbachev to drive the Cold War to a successful conclusion. Pat Buchanan was right in saying that a lot of people owe Uncle Sam a lot of thanks.

He was wrong, though, to suggest that Uncle Sam bore the burden of the long, twilight struggle alone. We didn't. Moreover, it was our idea—and a very wise idea—to disarm Japan and to accept post-war German rearmament only in the context of NATO. If Pat Buchanan thinks that was a dumb policy, or if he contends that there aren't reasons to be concerned about a Germany-*sans*-NATO and a remilitarized Japan, then he isn't much of a student of modern history, and he hasn't been talking to very many central Europeans or east Asians in recent years.

Could Germany and Japan have picked up more of the tab in the last decade? Absolutely. Would a militarily oversized Germany and a remilitarized Japan be safe for the world of the 1990s and the twenty-first century, or for the United States? I very much doubt it.

Then there is the question of the 1980s. Pat Buchanan frequently presented himself, during his 1992 campaign, as the true legatee of a Reagan Revolution that had been betrayed by the limp policies and board-room personalities of the Bush administration. There was an uncomfortable amount of truth in the latter part of this: the failure of President Bush and Secretary of State Baker to grasp and articulate the meaning of the end of the Cold War led to dubious policy abroad and opened the path for a new, leftist revisionism at home ("See, the Soviet Union wasn't all that much of a threat. It was going to self-destruct anyway. The anti-Communists really were hysterics").

On the other hand, for this self-professed America Firster to claim the mantle of Ronald Reagan, democratic internationalist *par excellence*, is *chutzpah* of the first chop. Ronald Reagan was no isolationist. If there were blind spots in his worldview, they had to do with the sunny optimism of his confidence in the democratic possibility, and the expansive nature of his understanding of the American role in securing a democratic future for the world.

Reagan's views of the world, and of America's role in it, were shaped during the late 1930s, in the face of the totalitarian threat of Nazism. Pat Buchanan celebrates the memory, and has tried to revive the battle cry, of the "America First" crowd of that time. Ronald Reagan was on the other side of the argument then, as he is now.

  2. *Buchananism badly misunderstands the international situation that faces us today.*

Pat Buchanan was right that America is, in the vulgate, Number One. But the conclusions he drew from that fact were deeply misconceived.

To argue that ours is a unipolar world is not an act of American hubris or self-congratulation; it is the acknowledgment of a fact. The theoreticians of international relations were, in the main, wrong: the post–Cold War world did not move quickly from bipolarity to multipolarity. It moved from bipolarity to unipolarity.

Moreover, the lesson of the Gulf War, and of the sad implosion of Yugoslavia into a charnel house, is that the alternative to an American leadership role today is not an instinctive reach by the nations of the world for "mutual security" arrangements. It is chaos. A chaotic world is not safe in itself. But neither is it safe for America, economically or in security terms. There is no hemispheric bunker into which Americans can retreat and lock the door: the microchip and the ballistic missile have seen to that.

Moreover, in the debate that took place between Desert Shield in August 1990 and Desert Storm in January 1991, Buchanan and the new/old isolationists had a chance to demonstrate their acumen in reading the signs of the international times. And they failed. The Buchananites warned that if the United States used military force against Iraq, the "Arab street" would rise in revolt, the Security Council wouldn't remain behind us (and neither would our NATO and Arab allies), and thousands of American body bags would be stacked up at Dover Air Force Base. They were wrong on all counts. Had Patrick Buchanan's advice been followed after the Iraqi invasion of Kuwait, Saddam Hussein would now have completed the annexation of his nineteenth province; the Saudis and the other Gulf states would have cut their deals with the new regional hegemon; unemployed Soviet nuclear technicians would be en route to Baghdad; and 40 per cent of the world's proven oil reserves would be effectively under the control of the man who even now is working feverishly to develop weapons of mass destruction and to expand his ballistic-missile capability.

But back to the implications of "unipolarity." To assert that American leadership is indispensable in the world today is not to deny that the Agency for International Development is in desperate need of fundamental reform. Nor is it to suggest that the United States can "dictate the shape of the world to come," as Buchanan suggested democratic internationalists believe.

In the wake of the Cold War, the choice before us is not between "interest-oriented" isolationism and gullible internationalism, but between isolationism and smart internationalism. On the isolationist telling of the story, every democratic internationalist in America is (if not dubiously patriotic, because of "double loyalties") a kind of naïve and vaguely *gauchiste* do-gooder, of the sort that one imagines chairing the United Nations Association in Evanston, Santa Monica, or Marin County. But this is silly. It was, after all, the democratic internationalists who had the more accurately realistic reading of the power politics of the Middle East in 1990–91, not the isolationists.

Then there is the continuing problem of Buchananite protectionism. Let us stipulate, as the lawyers say, that the world has a long way to go before the practice of "free trade" matches many nations' rhetorical devotion to it. Let us stipulate further that a far more aggressive American posture toward some of our friends in east Asia and western Europe is required if the new protectionism in those quarters is to be successfully resisted for the good of the international trading system, as well as in terms of more equitable treatment for our own goods. But Buchanan seemed to have in mind something other than tough-minded free trade.

Paul Johnson, whose work Pat Buchanan undoubtedly admires, had something to say in *Modern Times* about the inconsistencies of those who putatively celebrate the free economy while advocating and executing protectionist policies:

If Harding, Coolidge, and Hoover had acted on the entrepreneurial principles they proudly proclaimed, they would have resumed Wilson's . . . policy of 1913 of reducing U.S. tariffs. In fact, they did the opposite. The Fordney-MacCumber Tariff Act of 1922 and, still more, the Hawley-Smoot Act of 1930, which Hoover declined to veto, were devastating blows struck at world commerce, and so in the end at America's own. The fact is that America's presidents, and her congressional leadership, lacked the political courage to . . . pursue internationalism in the most effective way open to them and the one that conformed most closely to the economic views they claimed to hold.[7]

Protectionism isn't the answer to unfair trade practices, or to the problems of American competitiveness. It is a prescription for international economic disaster—and at a time when the argument for the free economy has won the day in Latin America and central and eastern Europe.

3. Buchananism misconstrues the cause of our domestic problems, and the relation between those problems and internationalism.

Another curious aspect of Buchanan's isolationism was that its analysis of the cost of internationalism was quite similar to that of Yale's Paul Kennedy, whose 1987 work, *The Rise and Fall of the Great Powers,* put the phrase "imperial overstretch" into the common parlance. Why should Pat Buchanan, of all people, adopt an economistic, indeed vaguely Marxist, reading of the dynamics of history?

There are also serious problems with the new-isolationist argument that an "America First" foreign policy will create the conditions for a more successful address of our domestic woes. Infrastructure—roads and bridges, airports, urban mass transit, the national rail grid—is one thing; here money is needed, and long overdue. But the problems that Buchanan rightly laments—crime, drugs, teenage pregnancy, unsafe public spaces, bad education, racial and ethnic animosities and tensions—are born of deficiencies of character, not deficiencies of infrastructure.

They are not, in other words, problems whose resolution lies in the redirection of federal megabucks out of the State and Defense Department accounts. High school SAT scores aren't shamefully low, and out-of-wedlock teenage pregnancy rates shockingly high, because the United States puts dollars into foreign aid that might otherwise go to Health and Human Services or the Department of Education. We spend far more money per child on education than any number of countries that get much better results than we do. For Pat Buchanan to have adopted the line of the National Education Association—that American educational incompetence is a funding problem—is quite simply bizarre.

Buchanan's suggestion that our foreign and military spending levels are the cause of our domestic difficulties marked yet another point at which his new/old isolationism embraced classic New Left themes. And that, in turn, is another indication of the deep confusions—and their roots in the politics of resentment—with which the new America Firstism is rife.

4. Buchanan's isolationism flirted unnecessarily with nativism and racism.

One is never quite sure whether Pat Buchanan's more volatile statements about, say, immigration policy reflect too many hours spent in "Crossfire" and "McLaughlin Group" forums—which put a premium on fervid formulations—or whether they are meant to appeal to the baser prejudices and fears in the American body politic. But there are surely better ways to address the ancient question of U.S. immigration policy than to suggest, as Buchanan did in late 1991, that the troops coming home from NATO should be redeployed "as border guards in the Southwest."

Moreover, Buchananite concerns about the new immigrants have, at times, a disturbing affinity with the no-holds-barred nativism on display in such paleoconservative publications as *Chronicles*, whose editor is given to lamenting our weakening ethnic "stock" and hymning the glories of blood-and-soil. Buchananite concerns about immigration policy might contribute to a genuine debate on the issue were they not cast in terms of worries about how the country can absorb so many of those brown, black, and yellow folks. Oddly enough, Buchanan's flirtations with nativist code language were reminiscent of the racist frettings that the "Old Republic" English raised about Buchanan's

Irish forebears. A man whose ancestors were the objects of "NINA"—"No Irish Need Apply"—signs a hundred and fifty years might have been expected to be more sympathetic to the huddled masses of today. (Buchanan once got off a crack to the effect that a million Englishmen would be self-evidently easier to "assimilate" in Virginia than "a million Zulus." As one wag put it subsequently, the case isn't clear at all. Zulus tend to be conservative, entrepreneurial, and religious. Englishmen today tend to be secularized, besotted with socialism, and the carriers of a dreadful cuisine. Virginia would quite probably be better off with the Zulus—who could, among other things, be counted on to vote Republican!)

Yes, there are circumstances in which other aspects of the common good require us to be rigorous in screening immigrants. But the general rule ought to be generosity, and for reasons of self-interest as well as common decency. In an international economic environment in which imagination, creativity, inventiveness, and entrepreneurial energy are the keys to success, the fact that the United States is the most immigrant-friendly country in human history is a great advantage, for immigrants tend to have been among the most active, energetic people in their native societies. Japan's xenophobia, on the other hand, may prove to be its greatest weakness in the long run. Immigration plus assimilation plus welfare reform and educational reform is a more likely formula for American national economic success than pulling up the drawbridge and filling the moat.

5. Buchanan's vision of "America First" is softening up the political culture for a revival of New Leftism.

Although stranger things have happened, it seems unlikely that Pat Buchanan will be the Republican nominee for president in the foreseeable future. Indeed, one suspects that he realizes this, and that what he really hoped to do, in declaring his candidacy in 1992, was to position himself as the ideological arbiter of the conservative movement for the 1990s, holding open the prospect that such a position might eventually lead to public office (for himself, or for someone else with his views) in the future.

In fact, though, what Pat Buchanan did in the 1992 campaign was to plow ground that would be sown and reaped by liberal and

leftist Democrats who saw in "America First" populism an antidote to their image as wimps. By redrawing the boundaries of the
acceptable, Buchanan changed the ideological rules of the presidential game. But was he the beneficiary of his populist evangel-
ism? The evidence in 1992 suggested that others, with very
different agendas indeed, quickly moved in on the "America First"
turf, in ways that further softened George Bush for the knock-out
blow administered in November of that year.

Thus left-liberal Democrat Tom Harkin of Iowa argued on the
stump during the early 1992 primaries that "Bush is working on a
recovery plan for Turkey, for Bangladesh, and the Soviet Union"
but "doesn't have a vision about how to get our country moving
again." Majority whip David Bonior had the following to say on
the floor of the House of Representatives: "To those who say 'No,'
we have to save our emergencies for the Kurds and the Turks this
week, the people in the Baltic states; save our emergencies for
them, I say it is time to help people right here in the United
States." Democrat Harris Wofford's Senate campaign in Pennsyl-
vania had carried the same message, even more bluntly: "At a
time when government seems to care about everyone in the world
but us, Harris Wofford says it's time for Americans to take care of
Americans again. It's time to take care of our own."

This demagogy, to which the Bush campaign made no effective
response, helped elect a left-leaning Democrat in 1992. And the
ground for that surprising outcome was softened up by the
Buchananite isolationists, whose undisputed patriotism gave a
veneer of respectability to the isolationism of others whose views
of America were very different indeed.

6. Buchananite isolationism is morally diminishing.

The first responsibility of any government is to those people in
whose name, and by whose grant of power, public authority is
exercised. But that is not government's only moral responsibility,
particularly in a democracy in which the government represents a
people who have duties beyond their borders.

Moreover, to argue that the moral responsibilities of the American people end at the water's edge is to opt for a selfish, crabbed,
and almost inevitably xenophobic construal of the American

experiment in democratic republicanism. The American people don't believe that about themselves—hence their massive giving, every year, to religious and secular charities that work abroad. We may also assume that the American people want a foreign policy that defends their legitimate interests. Americans understand that the U.S. government cannot be a charitable institution. Because of its fiduciary role, government has a moral (not simply pragmatic) responsibility to act in ways that enhance the well-being of the people who pay to make government's activities possible. But while there may be tensions at times between morally obligatory realism and morally desirable idealism, the thing to remember is that these are tensions—not fundamental contradictions.

Buchananite isolationism tends to be a zero-sum game morally, as well as in its reading of the international economic situation. To care more about "us," in this view, means we must care less about "them." But this makes as little moral sense as protectionism makes economic sense. According to classic Jewish and Christian understandings of the moral life, we are enlarged, not diminished, by transcending the temptations of solipsism and selfishness. Moreover, a rigid division between "us" and "them" in thinking about the world will, sooner or later, come home to roost domestically. The mental habit of division dies hard.

Buchananite isolationism rightly stresses that national identity is important and that patriotism is a virtue. But in the Catholic construal of these things, which ought to be of special interest to Pat Buchanan, patriotism is not an absolute virtue, and national identity is a secondary, if honorable, definition of one's self. Patriotism does not absolve us from the moral responsibility to subject the policies of our government to moral scrutiny. And our national identity is subordinate to our identity as members of the Body of Christ, the Church. That subordination does not render us suspect as citizens. Properly understood, it makes us precisely the kind of citizens necessary for a democracy, in which the virtue of the people is the ultimate guarantor of their liberties.

Twentieth-century Catholic social teaching has arguably been too optimistic in its internationalism, too ready to remand authority over from national to transnational and international institutions. And, like most of the rest of us, Catholic social teaching may have failed to measure accurately the enduring attractions and passions of ethnic and national identity in late modernity—particularly as nations and peoples emerge from under the rubble of the totalitarian state. On the other hand, the authentic mainstream of Catholic social ethics reminds us that the absolutizing of any virtue tends to lead to the corruption of the other virtues. And the history of this violent century surely ought to have taught us that patriotism best contributes to the full flourishing of the human spirit when it is inculcated against a capacious, rather than narrow and cramped, horizon.

America best models the possibilities of genuine freedom and a true pluralism when America works as well as it should. It will not work as well as it should if it hunkers down in a hemispheric bunker like an adolescent whose moral horizons are defined by the power of his or her own self-absorption.

PART THREE

The World and Us—
Five Issues

"Let us thank God that He makes us live among
the present problems. It is no longer
permitted to anyone to be mediocre."

POPE PIUS XI

9

Just War After the Gulf War

Those inclined to pessimism about the quality of public life in the republic would do well to remember that just a few years ago Americans conducted a sustained and thoughtful argument about grave issues of the national interest and the national purpose. The debate began with Iraq's invasion of Kuwait on August 2, 1990. It was loud, sometimes heated, occasionally confused, often insightful; in a word, democratic. And it was frequently couched in explicitly moral terms, drawn from the classic wisdom of the just war tradition. Was ours a just cause? What were our intentions? Who could authorize the resort to armed force? Did we have a reasonable chance of success? Was military action a last resort? Could we conduct military operations that respected the rights of innocent civilians? Questions like these were argued by Americans from all walks of life, in homes, schools, churches, offices, bars, cabs, subways, barber shops, in newspapers and magazines, and on radio and TV talk shows from coast to coast.

The "lessons of Versailles" gave us isolationism in the 1930s. The "lessons of Munich" led to U.S. military action in Korea and Vietnam. The moral "lessons of Vietnam" as defined by the Vietnam-era New Left led to the floundering that beset U.S. foreign policy during the Carter administration. The military "lessons of Vietnam" were hotly debated in the armed forces after 1975, and the results were evident in Desert Storm (a point made to great effect by Colonel Harry G. Summers, Jr., in his 1992 study *On Strategy II: A Critical Analysis of the Gulf War*[1]). Similar "lessons of the Gulf War" have already had an impact on the intellectual architecture of U.S. policy in the 1990s, in our intervention in Somalia and non-intervention in ex-Yugoslavia. And we may expect that these "lessons" will continue to be invoked for quite a while. Thus a careful reflection on "just war after the Gulf War" is very much in order.

ASSESSING THE WAR

The post-war debate on the morality of U.S. military intervention against Iraq has most often focused on two *ius in bello* (war-conduct) issues: (1) *Proportionality*: Did the United States and its allies use no more military force than was necessary to achieve morally legitimate political and military objectives? (2) *Discrimination*: Did military operations rigorously distinguish between combatants and non-combatants?

There seems to be general agreement that the allies intended to conduct a discriminate military campaign, beginning with the air war. The rules of engagement and target-recognition—two empirical tests of "intention"—were strict. And for the most part they seem to have been observed, even when doing so meant that allied pilots had to assume a greater risk, e.g., by returning from missions with unexpended ordnance because target-recognition was below minimum requirements.

Although questions have been raised about the "collateral damage" inflicted on civilians by the air war, there is considerable agreement that we did what we intended to do: namely, to distinguish in practice, and not just in theory, between combatants and non-combatants. (*The Nation*, a magazine with little interest in supporting American policy in this or any other area, sent an investigative team to Baghdad after the war, expecting to find tens of thousands of Iraqi civilian casualties. The team concluded that, at the worst, the bombing may have killed 3,000 civilians; the actual number was probably much smaller, given the official Iraqi count of some 1,600 fatalities.) This discriminate targeting was made possible by the allies' success in suppressing Iraqi air defenses, by the formidable capabilities of the stealth F-117A fighter-bomber, and by precision-guided munitions (smart bombs). Taken together, these three factors meant that highly skilled allied pilots had enough time (particularly over Baghdad) to make sure that the bombs went where they were supposed to go.

The Infrastructure Debate

Far less agreement has been reached on the damage done to the civil infrastructure of Iraq and the civilian suffering this has caused, during the war and afterwards. There has been an element of irony in this debate: many of those who argued that the damage to Iraq's infrastructure breached the moral boundaries set by the principles of proportionality and discrimination were the same people who argued in the fall and winter of 1990 for "letting sanctions work"—a strategy whose victims would have been, precisely, civilians. Nonetheless, the issue is serious and must be engaged. Did the allied air campaign, by doing grave damage to the infrastructure of Iraq—its electrical grid, its water and sewage systems, its communications and transportation networks—inflict disproportionate and indiscriminate harm on Iraqi noncombatants?

The question cannot be answered mathematically, for just war thinking is not a moral equation in which "damage assessment x" on one side automatically yields "moral assessment y" on the other, irrespective of other relevant factors. To oversimplify, we cannot arbitrarily say that destroying 40 per cent of Iraq's civil infrastructure would have satisfied the criterion of proportionality while destroying 60 per cent would have violated the moral limits.

The key is this matter of "other relevant factors." And here the chief factor to be considered is the nature of the Iraqi regime and the way it had organized Iraqi society—including that society's material and technological infrastructure.

Although its messianism was more muted than that of the Nazis and the Leninists, the Ba'ath regime of Saddam Hussein had—and, regrettably, still has—many of the characteristics of a totalitarian state. The country is ruled by a small vanguard party, opposition to which is ferociously suppressed. Within Iraq there is widespread use of state-sponsored terrorism to maintain the power of the party and its maximum leader. Both the software and hardware sides of life—the media and the education system, and the industrial and technological system—are organized to support and extend the power of the state. Public life is demonstratively militaristic, and the regime engages in a broad program of ideological indoctrination. There is no cultural life that is not regime-approved. Commercial activity is closely monitored so that it poses no threat (and in fact provides support) to the regime.

Whether one judges the Ba'ath regime of Saddam Hussein to be a kind of totalitarianism or a case of advanced authoritarianism, Iraq is indisputably a thoroughly centralized dictatorship in which the state controls as much of life as it can bring within its grasp. And this regime-analysis has to be factored into the moral assessment of both the damage done to Iraq's infrastructure (the *proportionality* issue), and the wartime and post-war civilian suffering caused by allied military operations (the *discrimination* issue). Saddam Hussein designed the modern infrastructure of Iraq so that it could be centrally controlled. Iraq was not like an American state, in which a number of independent private and/or public power companies might operate a complex of electrical grids. Everything was organized into one national system precisely so that Saddam could maintain control. Thus any attack on Saddam's control systems would inevitably have effects beyond his immediate ruling circle and his military.

Because Saddam had organized his society on a centralized-militarized model, the destruction of his communications electronics in the first phase of the air war inevitably had an impact on civilians. Because he had organized his national electric grid in the same fashion, the destruction of the electrical system that was the lifeblood of his military and political machines (and the power source for the factories in which he was working feverishly to produce weapons of mass destruction) also resulted in severe damage to the system that supplied power to Iraq's hospitals and that lit and heated its homes. And because Saddam ran the kind of regime he did, there were backup electrical, water, and sewage systems for his bunkers, command posts, and military headquarters but not for the hospitals and the neighborhoods. (The effects of infrastructure destruction on the civilian population have been magnified, to be sure, by the continuation of U.N.-sponsored sanctions—but those sanctions are in place because of Saddam's intransigent refusal to abide by the ceasefire agreement he accepted in March 1991. Moreover, a Saddam Hussein who can afford to rebuild his armored divisions is one who can surely afford infant formula.)

In a situation like this, it does not seem right to say that we cannot attack legitimate military targets because there may be, as a consequence, damage to the nation's infrastructure. For this would concede to the tyrant an unjustified (and perhaps even decisive) military advantage in prosecuting a war that on his part is already unjustifiable. The more persuasive argument is that, if the enemy's regime is structured in such a way that legitimate military actions inevitably result in damage to the infrastructure that supports civilian life, the attacking party (and, in the case of the Gulf War, the international community that authorized the military action) assumes a measure of post-war responsibility to help reconstruct what was destroyed, in order to help restore normal civilian life.

But a commitment of that sort cannot be fulfilled unless the war is prosecuted to an appropriate political end. And that, alas, did not happen in the Gulf War. Had we pressed on until Saddam was removed from the scene (which would not, in my judgment, have militarily required any more damage than had already been done to the Iraqi infrastructure), we would have been obliged to help the country back to its feet. (Such a policy would also have made eminently good political-strategic sense.) But given the current situation, the suggestion that the international community and the United States are somehow obliged to rebuild the infrastructure that is part and parcel of Saddam Hussein's system of social control is not morally compelling.

The grim situation in Iraq years after the war further illustrates how important regime-assessment is in analyzing these difficult problems of proportionality and discrimination—and in thinking through the relationship between justifiable military means and just political ends. The continued suffering of the Iraqi people should give no satisfaction to even the most enthusiastic supporters of the Gulf War. As the United States and its allies insisted from the outset, the enemy was Saddam Hussein, not the people of Iraq—who are his victims, as were the people of Kuwait. But primary responsibility for the current suffering in Iraq cannot be laid at the feet of the allied coalition.

It may help to think about this analogically. Is the situation in Iraq today comparable to the devastation that marked Germany after World War II—where there was mass destruction of urban industry and housing, wholesale displacement of populations, epidemic disease, and starvation? Certainly not. Yet within two years, Germany was on the road to economic and political recovery (at least in its Western-controlled sectors). Why? Because an evil regime had been removed, and because the people who had won understood that their responsibilities did not end with military victory. That the Ba'athist regime was not removed in Iraq is the primary reason why the suffering of the Iraqi people has been prolonged.

The debate on these questions of proportion, discrimination, and infrastructure destruction will and should continue. We should not expect that debate to produce neat answers; that is not what the moral calculus of the just war tradition gives us. But if the "regime factor" is given sufficient weight, the ongoing debate can enable us to confront future situations and options more wisely, and with a full measure of concern for all "other relevant factors" in the moral-political-military equation. Taking the regime factor into account does not mean thinking rigidly and algebraically: increments of regime awfulness do not necessarily yield increments of justifiable destruction. But an analysis of the Gulf War that focuses on infrastructure damage without considering the nature of the Iraqi regime misses something crucial; and the "lessons" thus drawn cannot be taken as wise counsel—moral or military—by the U.S. government or by international institutions.

Iraqi Military Casualties

Another ongoing argument about proportionality of means concerns the number of Iraqi military casualties, and both policy realists and activists who were dubious about the war from the start have condemned the allied coalition for inflicting disproportionate casualties on the Iraqi army. Among the critical realists was Robert W. Tucker: deeply disturbed by what seemed to him the gross disparity between allied and Iraqi casualty figures, Tucker attributed this to the politically motivated determination of U.S. leaders to avoid heavy allied casualties.[2]

Concerns about the ethics of proportionality shaped the endgame of the war. The Bush administration chose to stop military action on February 28, 1991, for a number of reasons—among them, pressures from several of our allies who fretted about the "instability" that would follow the collapse of the Saddam Hussein regime. (One of those allies, Saudi Arabia, changed its mind a year later and, if news reports are to be believed, urged the United States to take the lead in eliminating Saddam Hussein. King Fahd's sense of timing does leave something to be desired.) But both published accounts and my own conversations with some of the principals involved, at the White House and the Pentagon, suggest that senior American officials believed that the United States and its allies were bumping up against the boundary of proportionality in our attack on the Iraqi troops fleeing Kuwait on the second and third days of the ground war. General Colin Powell, for example, has been widely quoted as advising the president that further military action against the retreating Iraqis would be "unchivalrous." The theater commander, General Norman Schwarzkopf, apparently had a different view. But it seems fairly clear that at the highest level of American decision-making, concerns about potentially "disproportionate" Iraqi losses influenced the decision to halt military action.

In looking at this issue now, we are still in something of an empirical fog. Iraq never released its military casualty figures; nor did the Pentagon ever assay an official count of Iraqi combat deaths, though estimates have suggested a range from 50,000 to 150,000. Other analysts have come up with very different figures. Anthony Cordesman, a defense analyst for ABC-TV during the war, "guesstimates" that the maximum number of Iraqi soldiers killed was 25,000, and believes this figure is probably on the high side. George Kuhn, one of the analysts consulted in the fine *U.S. News & World Report* study *Triumph Without Victory*, used figures assembled by a leading expert on the Iraqi army to come up with an Iraqi military death toll of between 6,500 and 18,000 during the ground war. We just don't have reliable data, though the consensus does seem to go against those who argue for an Iraqi death toll as high as 100,000.

What we do know, however, is what happened after the ground war was stopped. Several of Saddam Hussein's prize Republican Guard divisions—the Adnan, the Nebuchadnezzar, the Al Faw, the 8th Special Forces, and part of the Hammurabi—escaped General Schwarzkopf's double-envelopment trap, remained intact, and went on, the next month, to slaughter tens of thousands of Shi'ites and Kurds. And it is not clear that closing the trap and dealing with these crack troops would have meant endless slaughter. While some allied commanders believe that fighting on would have required bloody, house-to-house combat in Basra, others think that continuing the double-envelopment would have trapped the Republican Guard divisions in the Basra pocket without sufficient supplies. They could then have been left to stew until they chose to surrender themselves and their materiel. Since the entrapment of his remaining elite troops might well have led in short order to the overthrow of Saddam Hussein, that surrender might not have been very long in coming.

It also seems, in retrospect, that the so-called Highway of Death out of Kuwait—images of which were crucial in raising the proportionality issue at the end of the war—was nowhere near as lethal as it was originally reported to be. According to *Triumph Without Victory*,

> [Anthony] Cordesman walked that highway through the Mutlah pass after the war. "It was an incredibly impressive achievement of air power," Cordesman said, "but it was not a highway of death." When the lead and rear vehicles came under attack, most of the drivers and passengers fled the scene. Cordesman said that most of the vehicles he saw were intact and abandoned. "There weren't that many bodies, and on the other vehicles, there certainly wasn't any blood."[3]

Weighing all the available evidence on Iraqi combat deaths, one can still, it seems to me, make a reasonable case that proportionality of means was observed in the Gulf War. Robert Tucker's argument, that the relevant factor is the disparity between allied and Iraqi casualties, betrays a profound misunderstanding of the *in bello* proportionality criterion. Would a slaughter like Antietam or Verdun be more likely to satisfy the criterion of proportionality because there was massive bloodshed on both sides? That is morally absurd. The disparity of casualties in the Gulf War was the result of superior allied technology, training, and leadership; it was not the result of excessive ruthlessness, deployed for ignoble political ends.

The death of tens of thousands of Iraqi soldiers was a human tragedy. But did the allies engage in indiscriminate slaughter, in a "turkey shoot"? According to all the available evidence, no.

Techno-War: Some New Moral Issues

Some analysts and activists have long argued that modern war is inherently disproportionate and indiscriminate; others have claimed that any "conventional" war in the late twentieth century would inevitably escalate to involve the use of weapons of mass destruction. The Gulf War made such claims seem even more excessive than they had previously.

Technological advances such as real-time intelligence, stealth capability, and precision-guided munitions have in fact made it more possible for the morally serious commander to observe in operations, and not just in intentions, the boundaries of proportionality and discrimination. Wars without collateral damage are inconceivable; combat is an inherently risky and uncertain business, and the innocent will never be out of harm's way in war. But modern technology, far from making the theater of operations into a gigantic free-fire zone, has made it possible to limit collateral damage in impressive ways.

The Gulf War also falsified the claim that modern war would inevitably escalate to the use of weapons of mass destruction. That risk is inherent in a world in which unstable regimes get their hands on nuclear, chemical, or biological warheads and the ballistic missiles capable of delivering them to targets far away. But "inevitability" is not the category in which the risk of escalation should be assessed. To do so would be to give crazy regimes and their weapons of mass destruction a kind of blackmail power in international politics.

The military conduct of the war has, however, come under close and deserved moral scrutiny on several other grounds. One is the use of "fuel-air explosives" against ground forces: do these munitions, which ignite the oxygen in the target area and render it an inescapable inferno, violate the ancient proscription against gross anti-personnel weaponry? Also worrisome were some of the tactics reportedly employed by U.S. armored forces in their charge across the desert. Reports of tanks equipped with bulldozer plows that buried conscript Iraqi troops alive before they had a chance to surrender put disturbing questions on the ethical agenda that must not be avoided in future tactical planning.

So the moral assessment of the means employed by U.S. and allied forces in Desert Storm will continue; and as it does, we would do well to remember a caution raised by the late Jesuit social ethicist John Courtney Murray. The weighing of ends and means in just war thinking, the "casuistry" of the tradition, is "endlessly difficult," wrote Murray. The difficulty is especially acute "when the moralist's refusal to sanction too much force clashes with the soldier's classic reluctance to use too little force"[4] —and when we recognize that this "soldier's reluctance" is often based on a moral concern for those under his command.

But to say that the weighing is difficult is not to say that it is either meaningless or avoidable. No tradition of moral reasoning can deliver prefabricated answers to the complexities faced by statesmen and soldiers. The task of refinement continues.

JUST CAUSE, REVISITED

The post–Gulf War focus on issues of proportion and discrimination reflected the tendency of the just war debate to focus, over the past forty-some years, on *ius in bello* (war-conduct) issues. This has been especially true in Christian circles influenced by the late, great Paul Ramsey, whose two books, *War and the Christian Conscience* (1961) and *The Just War* (1968), focused attention on the conduct of war in their attempt to specify a distinctively Christian form of just war thinking. As James Turner Johnson has written,

> Ramsey argued that Christian just war theory is based on the moral duty of love of neighbor. The obligation to protect the neighbor who is being unjustly attacked provides justification for Christians to resort to force; at the same time, love also

imposes limits on such force, requiring that no more be done to the unjust assailant than is necessary to prevent the evil he would do, and that no justified use of force ever can itself directly and intentionally target the innocent.[5]

It may well be, however, that the focus of the just war debate in the 1990s will be expanded to include more careful attention to the *ius ad bellum* (war-decision) rules that govern when the resort to armed force is morally justifiable. The new debate was evident during the Gulf crisis in the argument over "proper authority." Who could legitimately authorize the use of military force to reverse Iraqi aggression in Kuwait? The president? The president with the consent of Congress? The "international community," acting through the United Nations Security Council?

But the *ad bellum* issue that events are most likely to force onto the public agenda in the 1990s is just cause. During the Gulf crisis, several rationales for the justice of the allied cause were explored: reversal of an aggression already committed; rescue of the beleaguered people of Kuwait; regional stabilization; nuclear nonproliferation; defense of oil resources. The relevant Security Council resolutions under which the allied military action took place identified the *casus belli* as the violation of Kuwaiti sovereignty by Iraq's invasion and occupation. Clearly, however, the plight of Kuwait was not the only condition moving the leaders of the allied coalition to action.

Banning the Bomb, Energetically

Traditionally, three kinds of action satisfied the just cause criterion: defense against aggression, or the recovery of something wrongfully taken, or the punishment of evil. In recent years however, the first of these types of action—defense against an aggression already under way, or imminent—has been taken to be the primary, even sole, component of just cause. That definition of "just cause" informs Articles 2 and 51 of the U.N. Charter, for example.

Now, developments in both international politics and weapons technology have conspired to suggest that it may be time to reopen the debate over just cause. Take the preemptive Israeli attack that destroyed Iraq's Osirak nuclear reactor in 1981—an action sometimes described as exemplifying an "energetic nuclear non-prolif-eration policy." According to many contemporary conceptions of just cause, that action was quite probably unjustified. Yet who would deny today that the Israeli attack embodied precisely what the just war tradition is intended to facilitate: the use of propor-tionate and discriminate armed force in the service of peace and security?

Two other areas in which the question of preemptive action arises are the problem of nuclear non-proliferation and the threat of terrorism. How to respond to terrorism within the moral boundaries set by the just war tradition will be explored in chapter 12. Here I want to focus on the nuclear non-proliferation issue, which is likely to sharpen the debate on the boundaries of just cause rather quickly. For we now are faced with two situations in which despotic and aggressive regimes—in Iraq and North Korea —are working overtime to build nuclear weapons (in violation of the nuclear non-proliferation treaty that both signed). We also know that both of these regimes have, or can fairly easily acquire, ballistic-missile capability. Thus the world may well have to confront the reality of nuclear-armed states whose patterns of international behavior do not, to put it gently, inspire confidence.

Father J. Bryan Hehir, a veteran student of the just war tradition and the principal counselor on world politics to the Catholic bishops of the United States, does not want to see the world's concern for nuclear non-proliferation become the occasion for stretching the boundaries of just cause. Writing in 1992 in the Catholic journal *Commonweal*, Father Hehir had this to say:

> I am prepared to argue that only the resistance-to-aggression rationale should be accepted . . . as a *casus belli*. In a world where threats to proliferation are likely to increase . . . the moral arguments should strictly limit what constitutes cause for war. Proliferation, for example, is a deadly serious threat to international order but there are a range of methods to address the question which are short of war. Establishing a precedent that resort to force is an appropriate method to restrain prolif-eration erodes the case which should be made about other means to address proliferation, and it increases the likelihood that force will be used.[6]

Something seems to be missing in this position, and once again the "something" is the "regime factor." No sane person, no matter how devoted to the cause of non-proliferation, would suggest a preemptive attack on the British nuclear submarine force or the French nuclear *force de frappe*, either of which could wreak havoc far beyond anything that Saddam Hussein or North Korea's Kim Il-sung is likely to be able to accomplish in the near future. And yet there may be a morally compelling case for preemptive military action against the modest nuclear capabilities that Iraq and North Korea are acquiring. Why? Because of the nature of the regimes in Baghdad and Pyongyang.

The Iraqi and North Korean nuclear-weapons programs do not exist in a historical vacuum. They are the expressions of evil, real-world political intentions whose character has been made plain over many years. Precisely for the same reason that we do not think about preemptive action against Britain and France, we can, without collapsing into the moral vulgarities of Realpolitik, consider proportionate and discriminate preemptive action against Iraq and North Korea to prevent their acquisition of nuclear weapons, should other means of persuasion fail.

And we ought to be able to do so in ways that strengthen the case against the premature resort to force, rather than weaken it, as Father Hehir seems to fear will happen. Would a discrete use of preemptive force against the nuclear capabilities of a state like North Korea or Iraq weaken the argument for using all available non-military means for dealing with proliferation threats? Would it increase "the likelihood that force will be used" in the future? Perhaps. But I think the opposite is more likely.

Non-proliferation efforts of the sort that have been persistently frustrated by Iraq are going to look very much like a paper tiger to other would-be nuclear powers (Libya? Iran? Syria? Algeria?) unless it is made clear that, should non-military means fail, other forms of non-proliferation enforcement are available and will be used. They will be used, that is, in these limited circumstances, where the weapons threat is amplified dramatically by the nature of the regime involved. If such military action succeeds, it will strengthen non-military non-proliferation efforts in the future, for they will be seen to have teeth. Further, by discouraging proliferation fever among more rational states, preemptive, discrete military action in the case of genuine outlaw regimes (when other reasonable, non-military efforts have failed) could actually decrease the "likelihood that force will be used" in the future.

Preemptive military action to enforce the global ban on nuclear non-proliferation when the "regime factor" warrants it is no panacea. Military action never is. But if any contemporary circumstance bids us to reopen quickly the discussion of the boundaries of just cause, it is this.

It may even be possible to make the moral case for preemptive action, in the limited circumstances identified above, within the traditional limits of just cause. For the "regime factor," properly weighed, may allow us to consider the possession of nuclear (or chemical, or biological) weapons and the means to deliver them over long distances by certain extreme types of regimes to constitute in itself "imminent aggression," in the face of which proportionate and discriminate military action is morally justifiable. A similar calculus could apply in another nightmare scenario, one in which a terrorist organization gets hold of a nuclear weapon or other weapon of mass destruction (perhaps during a collapse of public order in what used to be the Soviet Union).

Cross-border aggression will remain the most "obvious" justification for the resort to armed force in the defense of peace and security. But it cannot be the only legitimate *casus belli*. Otherwise, we end up holding the untenable position that a just cause exists when Burkina Faso invades Mali but not when Saddam Hussein or Kim Il-sung threatens to do vast damage with weapons of mass destruction.

Resources and Rescues

The other possible components of *casus belli* debated during the Gulf crisis were protection of access to a vital resource—oil—and humanitarian assistance to the beleaguered people of Kuwait. Similar situations are likely to confront us in the future.

The debate over resources as a possible *casus belli* was foreshortened by events, but also by the silly sloganeering that passes for moral argument in some quarters ("We won't fight for Texaco," etc.). It was said during the debate before Desert Storm that the

United States wouldn't have fought Saddam Hussein if Kuwait had been a vegetable patch. Perhaps not; but neither would Saddam have invaded and subjugated Kuwait if its only products were carrots and rutabagas. Moreover, as the oil embargo of 1973–74 should have made clear (and particularly to those whose primary concern is the "North/South" divide in the world), it is the poor countries that are hit hardest by massive oil price hikes. Such increases would surely have followed in short order had Saddam successfully made Kuwait into his nineteenth province and brought the Saudis to heel.

Oil is not just any commodity: it is, for better and for worse, the chief lubricant (so to speak) of the international economy today. And the "international community" seems to have recognized, if tacitly, that reasonable access to oil at reasonable prices (as, unfortunately, those prices are manipulated by OPEC) is one of the prime components of the minimum of world order we enjoy today. Those who chanted about "Texaco" were indulging in a luxury (politically and economically) that is not enjoyed in most of the Third World.

In this case, the "regime factor" also invested the "resource factor" with a particular gravity. Had a benign party suddenly cornered the world oil market, that would surely not have constituted a *casus belli*. But it was *Saddam Hussein* who threatened to get a stranglehold on 40 per cent of the world's proven oil reserves, and so the threat was (correctly) perceived as grave enough to require action.

As we think about broadening the components of just cause, an even harder case to make is for military action to stop a gross abuse of human rights where no threat to U.S. national security or to international order is involved. Here one wishes fervently that "U.N. peacekeeping forces," or some other form of multilateral interventionary force, could be used more intelligently. The United States cannot be obliged to intervene militarily whenever there are gross abuses of human rights. But, as I argued above, a devotion to state sovereignty (on the international legal side) and the parallel inclination to justify military action only in cases of cross-border aggression (on the just-war/moral-reasoning side) are not exceptionless norms; they are not trump cards that override every other consideration. If that were the case, then we would be reduced to arguing, in a grotesque parody of the just war tradition, that there would have been no *casus belli* in the Nazi "Final Solution" had Hitler kept the Wehrmacht and his concentration camps within Germany's borders. Sorting out the meaning of "order" in the post–Cold War world is thus going to require very careful thought about how the world responds to specific cases in which genocide is a real and present danger.

JUST WAR AND THE PURSUIT OF PEACE

Following Martin Luther's counsel in his *Small Catechism* that we should put the best construction on everything, let us assume that the heart of today's agitation among some religious ethicists over the alleged "obsolescence" of the just war tradition is an intuition that the world, at the turn of the third millennium of the common era, ought to be able to devise a more morally satisfactory way to handle international conflict than war. This intuition, which is admirable and understandable, has also been influenced by the successes of non-violent resistance in the Revolution of 1989 in central and eastern Europe and in the New Russian Revolution of August 1991.

It would be a mistake to dismiss this as mere romanticism or frivolous utopianism. The hope for a better future that animates many spirits at the end of this most sanguinary of centuries should not be extinguished in the name of a realism that, below the surface, is really a tired cynicism.

This hope for peace needs to be informed, however, by the moral wisdom of the just war tradition. Neither the contemporary critics of just war thinking nor its defenders have thought very carefully about the tradition as a tradition of peace. But that is really what it is. The just war analyst tries to order the proportionate and discriminate use of force, in circumstances in which other means of redress have been tried and have failed, to the pursuit of the five great ends of politics: justice, freedom, order, the general welfare, and peace.

There is no way around this argument. If international politics were ever "domesticated"—if a genuine international political community were to evolve over time—it would have to wrestle with these questions every bit as much as we do in the age of nation-states. For, as Paul Ramsey taught us almost thirty years ago, the moral-political "logic" within the criteria of the just war tradition is also the moral "logic" that has to guide any meaningful political action. To put it another way, the just war criteria are the "moral economy" that tempers and orders the use of force, which, this side of the coming Kingdom, is an inescapable part of all political life.

Is the just war tradition obsolete? One might as well ask whether politics—the organization of human life into purposeful communities—is obsolete. What we must do is refine the moral logic of the just war tradition to take account of the new political and technological circumstances in which we find ourselves. The Gulf War and the world that has emerged from the Cold War demonstrated just how urgent a task that is.

10

"Humanitarian Intervention": History, Strategy, and Morality in the Bosnian Crisis

The Bridge on the Drina, which won its Bosnian Serb author, Ivo Andric, the 1961 Nobel Prize for Literature, should have been required reading for anyone trying to think seriously about the Balkan crisis of the early 1990s. Andric's story is full of memorable characters—some memorable chiefly for their awfulness. But the real protagonist of this epic tale is the great stone bridge itself: an expression, and finally a victim, of the ancient passions of that turbulent region—passions that by 1991 were no longer hidden but were being broadcast daily into our homes in living (and, too often, dying) color.

Early in the novel, which spans four centuries, the Islamic religious foundation that had traditionally maintained the caravan-serai (the travelers' quarters, or *han*) beside the great bridge runs out of money. One of the local Bosnian Muslims tries to secure other funding for the building but fails. No one, it seems, is interested in the local troubles. And thus, as Andric writes,

> The travelers had to look after their own needs and cleaned up the *han* as much as they found necessary for their own convenience, but as each one went his way he left behind manure and disorder for others to clean up and put right, even as he himself had tidied up whatever he had found dirty and in disorder. But after each traveler there remained just a little more dirt than he himself had found.[1]

161

It is difficult not to see in this image a portrait of the Balkans: disaster after disaster, each leaving behind its residue of resentment, each contributing to a thick memory of grievance whose perpetuation (and, no doubt, embellishment) over time becomes part of the psychic rhythm of life in the region. Andric nicely evokes this dynamic, too, in describing how the old men of Višegrad, the town near the bridge, gather in the evening to tell stories of the river floods that sometimes devastated the lands:

> They loved to recall memories of the hardest blow dealt them in their lives. Their recollections were inexhaustible and they repeated them continually, amplified by memory and repetition; they looked into one another's eyes, sclerotic and with yellowing whites, and saw there what the younger men could not even suspect. They were carried away by their own words and drowned all their present everyday troubles in the recognition of those greater ones which they had experienced so long ago.[2]

And the kinds of tales the old men told about natural disasters were also told, repetitively and with amplification, about political and religious and ethnic disasters. Even in relatively tranquil times, Andric writes, the churnings of memory were at work, like undercurrents in the Drina itself. On the surface (as in the quiet years of the Austro-Hungarian empire), things seemed placid. But "everything else was flushed away into that dark background of consciousness where live and ferment the basic feelings and indestructible beliefs of individual races, faiths, and castes: which, to all appearances dead and buried, are preparing for later, far-off times unsuspected changes and catastrophes without which, it seems, peoples cannot exist and above all the peoples of this land."[3]

Thus the Thoroughly Modern West, in which a sense of *anamnesis*, of identity-creating historical memory, has largely evaporated, was shocked and disoriented by the turmoil in its southeastern borderlands: turmoil whose origins go back at least a millennium to the migrations that roiled Europe at the end of the Dark Ages. Moreover, the flaccid Western response to the Balkan crisis was marked by an almost palpable sense of disappointment, bordering on petulance: these things were just not supposed to happen in our post–Cold War world.

The Balkan crisis also led to a curious role-reversal in the foreign-policy debate. Commentators, politicians, and clergymen who have been notably dovish ever since the 1960s were, in some instances, positively bellicose about the necessity of Western (or, if need be, unilateral American) military intervention in Bosnia. Conversely, many public figures who had urged a militarily robust anti-Communism during the 1980s and who had supported a vigorous response to the Iraqi invasion of Kuwait were much less inclined to see the United States militarily involved in Balkan affairs. (This role-reversal is not so surprising as it may at first appear. Among the new hawks, it not infrequently reflected the classic modern liberal tendencies to countenance the use of military force precisely when the "dirty" issue of "national interest" is not directly engaged, and to avoid the hard question of how military means serve real-world political ends.)

Finally, the Balkan crisis raised all over again the question of whether there is something called "Europe," even as it thrust back onto our public agenda the pressing question of America's role in a unipolar world. And if the Balkan turmoil turns out to be a dress rehearsal for the kind of chaos that could break out in the old Soviet Union at some point in the 1990s (indeed, has already broken out in the Armenian-Azeri conflict), then the West's inability to gather itself to impose order in southeastern Europe will look even more shortsighted.

THE PUSILLANIMOUS WEST

Has western Europe entered a period of political decadence such that it cannot even police its own neighborhood?

The question became unavoidable in 1991–92. For the Balkan crisis was, first and foremost, a European crisis. The people directly involved are Europeans (including the Bosnian Muslims). The people most likely to suffer the consequences of a spillover from an expanding Balkan war are Europeans. But where were the leaders of western Europe? It was said that there was no political will in western Europe to impose a settlement in ex-Yugoslavia. But isn't it one of the functions of political leadership to *forge* the necessary political will within a democratic citizenry when a moral and strategic crisis presents itself? Instead of leading on a matter in which their own strategic interests are directly at stake, western European politicians kept trying to wish the problem away.

Not that the United States has a record to be proud of in this matter. Indeed, one can date the beginning of the disaster in ex-Yugoslavia with some precision: to June 1991, when Secretary of State James A. Baker III informed the Serb-dominated leadership of a strained Yugoslav federation that America's interest in their neighborhood, then beginning to show the first telltale signs of crackup, was order and stability. Not peaceful, democratic, non-violent change; not a careful process of adjustment, within the old South Slav federation or among the micro-states that might succeed it; but order and stability. Not unreasonably, this was taken by thuggish leaders like Serbia's Slobodan Milosevic as a signal that Washington (and the West) would not object to a bit of head-knocking if that was what was required to keep the lid on in Yugoslavia.

And so the war came. U.S. policy didn't cause it. But U.S. policy under Bushbaker did nothing to make the war less likely, and a lot to make a disaster virtually certain.

Bushbaker's crude power realism and the general pusillanimity of the western Europeans led to a policy towards Yugoslavia that was, in truth, not a policy but rather a comprehensive abdication of responsibility. Michael Ignatieff of the London *Observer* caught the full measure of the fecklessness in a 1993 essay:

> . . . Western failures of policy were caused by something deeper than inattention, misinformation, or misguided good intentions. The very principles behind our policies were in contradiction. In the light-headed euphoria of 1989 our political leaders announced their support for the principle of national self-determination and for maintaining the territorial integrity of existing states, without recognizing that the first principle contradicted the second. We insisted on the inviolability of frontiers, without also making clear whether we also meant the frontiers between the republics within federal states like Yugoslavia.
>
> Most of all, we allowed guilt over our imperial past to lead us to evade our responsibilities for defining the terms of the

postimperial peace. The Western Europeans and the United States could have ended the cold war with a comprehensive territorial settlement in Eastern Europe, defining new borders, establishing guarantees to minority rights, and adjudicating between rival claims to self-determination. After Versailles, after Yalta, the collapse of the final empire in Europe gave us a third opportunity to define a durable peace for the whole continent.

Yet so concerned were we to avoid playing the imperial policeman, so self-absorbed were we in the frantic late-Eighties boom, that we let every post-communist demagogue exploit the rhetoric of self-determination and national rights to their own nefarious ends. The terrible new order of ethnically cleansed states in the former Yugoslavia is the monument to our follies as much as it is to theirs.[4]

Enter the New Kids on the Block

Candidate Bill Clinton seized on this pattern of incomprehension and irresponsibility and urged a more assertive U.S. posture toward the Yugoslav war (especially toward the vicious cruelties of "ethnic cleansing") during the 1992 U.S. presidential campaign. But in the early going, President Clinton and his administration did not show any greater leadership at the level of actual policy and performance than their conventional Realpolitik predecessors. The rhetoric was stiffer, but the performance was limp. And if the performance be taken as a preview of coming attractions, there is cause for serious worry.

The president remained in campaign mode during most of his first four months in office, seemingly unable to decide just how high a priority the Bosnian crisis should have. Then there was the Christopher mission to western Europe in early May 1993. Did the Secretary of State go to Europe to lay out a bold and imaginative plan and get the allies lined up behind it? No, he went to "seek consensus," or somesuch. Thus we were treated to the spectacle of the secretary going hat in hand from capital to capital, being politely stiffed by such proconsuls of empire as the Italian foreign minister.

Note to Foggy Bottom: When difficult decisions have to be taken, diplomacy in the post–Cold War world should not be understood on the analogy of lawyers meeting in a dark-paneled room over after-dinner Courvoisier to "work things out." There is no consensus and there will be no consensus, on the Balkans or on virtually any other serious security issue, until the United States defines a policy that others are then persuaded (or, more likely, obliged) to accept. That is what happened during the Gulf crisis of 1990; and that is what is likely to happen throughout the rest of the decade.

The Balkans are, to repeat, primarily Europe's problem. But "Europe" doesn't exist, as an effective instrument of policy. American leadership in forging a pan-European policy, and then in helping to provide the diplomatic and perhaps military muscle to back it up, was the key missing ingredient in the diplomatic mix throughout the early 1990s. Bushbaker "realism" and Clintonite "multilateralism" left the United States in the ridiculous position of supplicant before people who can't even rouse themselves to restrain the neighborhood hoodlums.

THE QUESTION OF U.S. MILITARY INTERVENTION

In the just war tradition, the use of proportionate and discriminate military force derives its moral legitimacy from its capacity to advance a just political goal. The end does not justify any means; but the means derive their justification from their linkage to a just end. (Or, as a Jesuit moral philosopher of the old school once put it, "If the end doesn't justify the means, what does?")

Thus the possibility of U.S. military intervention in the Balkan crisis was not, and could never be, an independent variable in the strategic and moral calculus. Which is to say, the question of military intervention at any of the levels proposed in early 1993— an air cap over all of ex-Yugoslavia, air raids on the artillery around Sarajevo, destruction of the logistical and transportation grids by which support for Bosnian Serbs (and Bosnian Croats?) got into the war zone, "turning out the lights" in Belgrade (and, according to some, in Zagreb), even an invasion to impose order—could not be seriously debated in the absence of answers to a cluster of prior strategic and moral issues.

Specifically: What political goal were we trying to achieve? It could not simply be to "stop the fighting." That was what we tried in Lebanon in the early 1980s and, to a lesser extent, in

Vietnam. But armies are not police forces. In a still contested situation, a modern army relegated to a stationary "peacekeeping" role and thus deprived of its capacity to maneuver is an army that has lost its most potent strategic and tactical asset. It is an army that has become a sitting duck, a target, rather than an instrument for achieving a just political end.

So "stopping the fighting" had to be linked to something else. Was it the Vance-Owen plan with its complex scheme of ethnic cantons within a weak Bosnia-Herzegovina? Was it Vance-Owen as an interim agreement creating the circumstances for a new negotiation on future relations among the states that once made up "Yugoslavia"? What would be, in the Vance-Owen argot, a "just and lasting political solution" to the crisis of ex-Yugoslavia? Who should define—and enforce—that solution?

Then: How committed were we to seeing this through? Could the Administration give guarantees to the American people, the U.S. military, our western European allies, the United Nations, and, last but hardly least, the people of ex-Yugoslavia that an America committed enough in month X to use military force in the Balkans would not be distracted from the effective pursuit of its goal in month Y by, say, a raging domestic debate over the b.t.u. tax? (Or homosexuals in the military. Or the latest outrageous statement from the Surgeon General. Or a Supreme Court nominee's baby-sitting arrangements. Or the pursuit of the First Lady's "politics of meaning." Or whatever.)

In the absence of persuasive answers to these strategic and moral questions, the use of military force would have resembled an act of desperation or petulance far more than an act of statesmanship.

Taking Out the Guns of Sarajevo

Some argued that the justification for limited military action in Bosnia was retribution, linked to deterrence: air strikes on the guns of Sarajevo would punish the Bosnian Serbs for their outrageous behavior, while deterring possible repeat performances. "Punishment for an evil already committed" is a classic component of "just cause" in the just war tradition (although it is not prominently cited by most just war theorists today); and the idea of a (well-deserved) punishment with a possible deterrent effect certainly had its attractions in Bosnia.

But there were serious military questions about the air-strike option that were never satisfactorily answered. When was the last time that "precision air strikes," without any followup by ground troops, effectively shut down hostile artillery in mountainous terrain? What evidence was there that spasmodic air strikes, seemingly unrelated to any other serious diplomatic or military initiatives, would have a deterrent effect? If the air strikes failed (and the Clinton administration publicly discussed tactics aimed at minimizing risk to U.S. pilots that seemed likely to result in failure), wouldn't the likely consequence have been to embolden, rather than deter, the aggressors? Moreover, if punitive and/or deterrent air strikes against the Serbian guns around Sarajevo were justified, what about air strikes against the Croat forces that regularly took advantage of the diplomatic chaos to launch their own brutal attacks in Bosnia on behalf of Great Croatia?

Air strikes as an escalatory "signal" to the Other Side, in the middle of a shooting war, to Stop It are a use of military force whose connection to a feasible political goal is not self-evidently clear. The early bombing campaigns of the Vietnam War were precisely such exercises in "signaling": and they did no discernible political-military good. Indeed, the whole concept of "signaling" grew out of the rationalist Shangri-La that was Robert McNamara's Pentagon in the heyday of the "systems analysts" and "whiz kids." "Signaling"—through "graduated steps" up the "escalation ladder"—assumes that politics is an algebraic exercise in which action taken on one side of the equation yields a predictable and commensurate reaction on the other side. That may make sense in seminars at Harvard's Kennedy School of Government. But it is hardly the way the politics of the Balkans have worked for the past millennium or more.

The Chiefs' Criteria

The role of the joint Chiefs of Staff and their then chairman, General Colin Powell, in the Bosnia debate should have put to rest any lingering notions of "American militarism" in those who had drunk too deeply from the wells of the sixties. Indeed, the chiefs' dovishness (better, their skepticism about the proposed military options cited above) served a useful role in forcing the Clinton administration to think more seriously about the use of U.S. military power in the Balkans. But not a completely useful role.

Today's senior American military leaders—most of whom were introduced to southeast Asia as junior officers—remain deeply affected by their own strain of Vietnam Syndrome. Doctrinally, they are committed to a concept of America's military strength in which technological superiority makes possible the application of overwhelming force at the decisive point through rapid, maneuver warfare (the "AirLand Battle," in the jargon). Politically, today's military leaders seem to doubt the staying power of both the populace and the politicians in conflicts where there is no direct threat to national survival. And so the chiefs, especially the highly respected General Powell, expressed deep skepticism about any use of military force in which the political goal is not clearly defined, the military tasks are not clearly achievable, the kinds of power the United States can bring to bear are not necessarily decisive, and the political will to victory is not conspicuously present.

These are all reasonable concerns. They are, in fact, specifications of the just war tradition's criterion of "reasonable chance of success." In the just war tradition, as in the minds of the chiefs today, you don't send in the troops (or the F-16s) and then "see what happens." No: if you're interested in serious (and morally justifiable) war-making rather than "signaling," you have a real political goal (which means you know how the war should end), and you use the proportionate and discriminate means appropriate to achieving that goal with the least threat to your own people and to innocents in the combat zone. By raising these issues, General Powell and others did a public service.

But one does wonder if the chiefs haven't redefined "reasonable chance of success" to mean "assured victory." "Reasonable" does not mean "certain." A reasonable chance of success is (to put the matter crudely but accurately) a better than 50–50 chance. General Powell and his colleagues seemed to want to raise the bar to, say, 80–20, or perhaps even 90–10. But that is an impossibly high standard.

Moreover, while the military's nervousness about the staying power of the political leadership and the people is not unwarranted, the most recent test of that staying power suggests that the generals may be overdoing the skepticism. The case in question is, of course, the decision, discussed above, to stop the ground war in Iraq short of the achievement of our real (if unstated) political goal, the removal of Saddam Hussein from power.

As we saw in the previous chapter, that decision was shaped in part by General Powell's concern that the pictures from the "Highway of Death" being broadcast by CNN and others would erode public support for the war effort. But we now know that there was no mass slaughter on the highway out of Basra; moreover, it has been plausibly argued that the closing of the Basra Pocket would not have required a "turkey shoot" of Iraqi forces. Stopping when we did had two entirely undesirable results: Saddam Hussein remained in power, and the Iraqi tyrant retained several of his Republican Guard armored divisions—which were then used to suppress, with far greater slaughter than took place on the wrongly named "Highway of Death," the rebellions of the Shi'ites and Kurds.

Hindsight is, of course, 20:20. But the public criticism of "stopping too soon" began almost immediately—which suggests that there are other-than-hindsight grounds for arguing that a misreading of both the situation on the ground outside Basra and the political situation in the United States led to an unsatisfactory conclusion to what had been, until then, a textbook case of military and political success.

The dovishness on the uniformed side of the Pentagon in early 1993 might also have reflected the military's skepticism about its commander-in-chief. President Clinton's relationship to the Selective Service System during Vietnam is not, I think, at the bottom of this dis-ease. Rather, there seems to be a deep-seated concern throughout "the force" that when it comes to military life, the military ethos, and the proper use of military force, the president and his people just don't get it.

The fact that Bill Clinton, Rhodes scholar, never served in uniform is no argument against the possible effectiveness of President Clinton, Commander-in-Chief. Franklin D. Roosevelt, whose only personal experience with a uniform was the sailor suit he wore as a little boy, ran a rather effective war effort. And Ronald Reagan, hardly a veteran warrior, was similarly no slouch as commander-in-chief. But President Clinton comes out of an intellectual and political milieu—the Sixties Left—that was not simply ignorant of the military but contemptuous toward it on what it took to be moral grounds. And, of course, early Clinton-administration attempts to use the armed forces as a laboratory for social engineering in the matter of American attitudes toward homosexuality did not enhance the confidence of "the force" in its boss.

This unhappy situation between the constitutionally designated commander-in-chief and the armed services he commands bore heavily on the question of what the United States ought to do in the Balkan crisis. For if all the means/end questions raised above could be satisfactorily answered, we would still be left with a hard question: Do we trust this president and his advisors to run this thing?

BAD, WORSE, AND WORST

During the martial-law period in Poland in the early 1980s, Poles used to say that there were two solutions to the Polish crisis: the realistic solution and the miraculous solution. The realistic solution would be if Our Lady of Częstochowa appeared in the heavens and the Russians fled. The miraculous solution would be if the Russians simply packed up and left under their own steam.

There are probably no "good solutions," miraculous or realistic, in the Balkans these days. History (and literature, like Ivo Andric's brilliant novel) suggests that turmoil is of the essence of a region in which three civilizations abut one another. The immediate strategic issue in the travail of ex-Yugoslavia was not, alas, how to achieve a "just and lasting political solution," for no such solution exists. The issue was to contain the conflict so that it did not lead to a general Balkan war, which would be likely to become a war throughout the eastern Mediterranean with Greece and Turkey arrayed on different sides and NATO in ruins. The reiteration of a "bright line" at the border of Macedonia (with NATO troops as a tripwire), coupled with the insistence that Serb "ethnic cleansing" not extend into Kosovo and its heavy Albanian population, was the beginning of a sensible policy in a situation where the choices are between bad and worse. But the maintenance of an arms embargo against the Bosnian Muslims undercut the purported seriousness of Western and U.N. concern, on the ground and in the minds of the leaders of Serbia and Croatia. In these circumstances, in which a form of liberal sentimentality worked to reinforce the power of the ruthless, diplomatic pressure on the Serbian and Croatian governments had little credibility.

Lessons for the Future

What lessons might we draw from this debacle? At least these three:

1. *The phrase "humanitarian intervention" may obscure more than it illuminates.* On the best possible construction, "humanitarian intervention" means that a justifying *casus belli*, a morally legitimate reason for going to war, may exist in situations in which more traditional forms of aggression—such as a cross-border invasion —have not occurred, but where genocide is taking place or is likely to take place. In this sense, "humanitarian intervention" is a specification of the limits of state sovereignty noted in chapter 6.

But that is not, one fears, the meaning that "humanitarian intervention" has acquired. Rather, the phrase has too often served as a rhetorical tool to avoid, in the political-military-moral calculus, any wrestling with the question of national interest for those who find that notion distasteful. Indeed, some erstwhile doves who became proponents of the use of U.S. military force in Bosnia seemed to think that it was precisely because there was no direct American national interest involved in ex-Yugoslavia that the use of U.S. air power was justified.

Any serious political *or moral* judgment about a possible U.S. military intervention anywhere *must* take sufficient account of the degree to which the American national interest is engaged in the dispute in question. For this and other reasons we sorely need a great national debate, issuing in a politically sustainable national consensus, on the content of the "national interest" in the post–Cold War world—a debate that will, as suggested in chapter 6, define our "interests" comprehensively, against a wider horizon of national purpose, even as it takes account of the basic security requirements of the United States.

2. *There is no justifiable military intervention that is not linked to an achievable political goal.* The notion of "humanitarian intervention" has also been used (or, rather, abused) to sever the crucial strategic linkage between politics and the use of military force. But there is no safe "middle ground" in these matters, and there is no apolitical use of military power. If the United States uses military force in any situation—Bosnia, Somalia, Sudan, Haiti, North Korea, Iraq—the United States inescapably becomes a political player in that situation.[5]

In the matter of Bosnia, indeed of all ex-Yugoslavia, the chance for a good, or at least tolerable, solution was probably lost when, as Michael Ignatieff argued in the passage quoted earlier, the West decided not to impose and enforce a general settlement on post-Communist central and eastern Europe after the Revolution of 1989 and the New Russian Revolution of 1991. Indifference and/or indecision, stemming from a lack of Western leadership and political will, did not buy time—it bought only misery, and it made a resolution of the crisis of ex-Yugoslavia even more difficult, indeed well-nigh impossible, downstream.

The enforcement of a general political, territorial, and human-rights settlement might have involved the use of U.S. troops, under NATO or U.N. auspices; and the deployment of those troops, as guarantors of the settlement, could have involved them in combat. But in this instance, U.S. military intervention would have taken place in the context of an agreed-upon political goal. We would have known what we wanted; we would have had a reasonably good idea of how to get it; and we would have been able to specify how and when our military involvement would end.

Without such a political framework, military intervention on "humanitarian" grounds almost never makes strategic, moral, or, indeed, military sense. The Somalia imbroglio in which we became involved in 1992 is another example of how the use of military force inevitably involves the United States in the politics of the nation where the intervention takes place—even when the original goal is simply to get food and medicine to starving victims of a brutal civil war. In situations like Somalia, where the root problem is the absence of any real civil order, it is virtually impossible just to go in, get the bandits under control, and leave. For unless civil order is restored (or, in some cases, created), the bad guys will just come back after the U.S. forces have left. (Such situations raise the possibility of a "new colonialism," explored in chapter 7.)

In sum: the urgent prior question, before we pull the trigger, is whether we are prepared to stay the course and see a crisis through to an acceptable political solution. If not, military intervention almost certainly will not "work." And that is a matter of grave concern to the ethicist as well as to the politician, the strategist, and the soldier.

3. *There are other-than-military "interventions" by which we can try to influence the outcome of tangled situations where military action seems imprudent*—and we ought to be more imaginative in using them.

Again, take the case of ex-Yugoslavia. The thugs who have been running Serbia and Croatia since the Yugoslav federation dissolved long benefited from the fact that they controlled the flow of information (which is to say, misinformation and disinformation) in their countries. Hard as it may be to imagine, a lot of people in Belgrade and Zagreb didn't know what was going on in Sarajevo and Mostar in 1993. These people and their fellow countrymen, many of whom might well have wanted to bring political pressure to bear on the warmongers among their brethren, needed the oxygen that is the truth. The immediate startup of round-the-clock Radio Free Europe news broadcasts in Serbo-Croatian would thus have made a lot of sense. (In fact, RFE officials proposed this, but then the bureaucratic "process" kicked in.)

It would also have made sense to identify and provide financial and logistical support to democratic forces in Serbia, Croatia, and Bosnia-Herzegovina in the early going, in order to help build an "opposition" that might, someday, have been able to make peace. Our experience in central and eastern Europe in the 1980s should have proved valuable here; but, once again, a lack of political imagination and leadership let a lesson go unapplied.

American "intervention" in a potential crisis is not limited to governmental actions. Non-governmental organizations can often achieve results that are difficult, if not impossible, for governments. In the ethnic/religious cauldron of an about-to-splinter Yugoslavia, for example, joint charitable activity by Catholic, Orthodox, and Muslim organizations in the West might have provided needed services and an important example, before the devastation began.

The Obligation of Politics

All this is far easier to discern in retrospect, of course. But if there is any grand lesson to be drawn from the wars of ex-Yugoslavia, and pondered in the full knowledge of the vast human suffering to which inept Western policy contributed in that crisis, it is that appeals to "humanitarian intervention" contain no absolution from politics. Military force is not a dramatic form of psychotherapy; it is not the way to "signal" our desire for drastic behavior modification on the part of aggressors. If an aggression involves the national-security interests of the United States directly, or if an aggression so threatens the fabric of international order that American national security will eventually be jeopardized, then the justifiable use of military force in response to that aggression must be ordered to the pursuit of an achievable political goal. And the political will must be summoned to see us through to the achievement of that goal, after the initial fighting has stopped.

Hit-and-run is a venerable tactic in baseball. It is neither morally nor politically defensible in world affairs.

11

Waiting for Augustine:
Islam and the West

For minds accustomed to tracking in bipolar grooves, it is tempting to substitute "Islam" for "Communism" on the list of possible threats to the West over the next decade, and indeed the next century. Media images and jargon have intensified the temptation by giving "Islamic fundamentalism" a graphic and frightening immediacy: mobs in the streets of Algiers, the torture of Beirut, the crazies in Baghdad, the prospect of an Iranian "overflow" into the Islamic lands of what was once Soviet central Asia, and now the threat of terrorism within the United States itself.

But it is not only the Terrible Simplifiers of the fourth estate who are sounding the alarm about a resurgent Islam. Senior Vatican officials speak in troubled tones (if privately) about the violence in Africa between aggressive Muslims and Christians, in a belt of confrontation running from Nigeria to Sudan. Human-rights activists deplore the dismal state of religious freedom in Islamic societies. Theorists and practitioners of democratization wonder whether Islamic societies will resist what Samuel Huntington has called the "third wave" of democratic transitions that has swept through central and eastern Europe, East Asia, and Latin America in the last decade. And no less respected an authority than Bernard Lewis argued, in his 1990 Jefferson Lecture, that in activist Islam "we are facing a mood and a movement far transcending the level of issues and policies and the governments that pursue them. This is no less than a clash of civilizations—the perhaps irrational but surely historic reaction of an ancient rival against our Judaeo-Christian heritage, our secular present, and the worldwide expansion of both."[1]

In academic redoubts like the Middle East Studies Association, from which a vigorous campaign against the "demonization" of "Islamic fundamentalism" has been mounted, Professor Lewis's stark analysis caused considerable heartburn. Here, it was argued, was another "outsider" misreading the Islamic world by exaggerating its pathologies while ignoring its capacities for self-renewal. But there are interesting parallels between Lewis's portrait of the contemporary Islamic scene and that of a scholar at the Johns Hopkins University who is rather more of an insider, Fouad Ajami.

Wounds Front and Back

Fouad Ajami is from a Lebanese Shi'ite family. In the 1992 revised edition of his study *The Arab Predicament*, Professor Ajami argues that the Islamic world of the Levant (Middle East) and the Maghreb (North Africa) has to be understood as a wounded civilization.[2] The wounds have been inflicted both from within and from without.

Internally, according to Ajami, the Arab Muslim world suffers from the absence of a tradition of self-criticism. In a world that does not take responsibility for its own deeds, he writes, the gradual decline in the historical fortunes of the Arabs, from the days when Muslim armies marched on Vienna to the present, has typically been blamed on "others": the Ottomans, the British and French colonialists, Israel, "the West."

This cultural deficiency, Ajami argues, has been exacerbated by the calamitous failures of leadership and ideology that have beset the Arab Islamic world in recent decades. Nasserism was shattered by the 1967 Six-Day War. Ba'athism has been discredited by the brutalities of Hafez Assad's Syria and the military defeat of Saddam Hussein's Iraq. The new oil wealth showered on the Arab world has done little to improve the lot of the common man, for the oil sheikhs have looked first to their own pleasures, and only secondarily to the flourishing of their societies.

Then there were the externally inflicted wounds. The legacy of colonialism was often bitter, and the result was what a psychologist would call an "approach-avoidance" syndrome in Muslim attitudes toward the hegemonic West. The West was the model to be emulated, insofar as one wanted to be successful and "modern"; and yet the West was run by people who still regarded their former colonials as, well, wogs. Thus the Six-Day War (a traumatic disaster for the entire Arab world) was experienced, not as a regional military defeat, but as yet another colonial incursion, a war of "the West" against the Muslims—for Israel is usually perceived as a new Western colonial salient into historically Islamic territory.

The result of this woundedness, says Professor Ajami, is a schizoid way of life in which romanticism about the glories of the past (often expressed in terms of a quest for Islamic "authenticity") lives in profound tension with a craving for the material artifacts and gratifications of the modern West. On this analysis, and according to a Syrian writer, the Islamic world of the Middle East and the Maghreb is "stalled between seasons." Or, as Ajami describes it,

> The attraction to lifestyles freer than their own draws people into the network of the world economy, into currents of world thought and culture. Then guilt asserts itself as they begin to think that the imports are not really theirs; or they experience a change of heart when their efforts to plug into the world fail, when their skills prove no match for the more polished skills of others. And it is this ambivalence, this anguish and hesitation, that is missing from much of what has lately been offered us by way of insight into the agony of the Muslim world.[3]

Serious Business

One need not succumb to the analytic sloth of simplistically replacing "Communism" with "fundamentalist Islam" to understand that the history of the twenty-first century is going to be shaped in no small way by the interaction of a religiously and demographically resurgent Islam and "the West." A map of the world that takes account of population densities and religious affiliations should suffice to drive that point home. Two civilizations are abutting each other, from the Rock of Gibraltar to East

Timor, and the results can sometimes resemble the clash of tectonic plates beneath the earth's surface. The question is whether that encounter between civilizations will inevitably lead to mass violence, or whether the energy it creates can be channeled to more peaceful purposes.

The meeting of a revived Islam with the West is going to be (as it has already been) exceedingly complex: for the worlds of Islam are not univocal, and neither are the worlds within worlds of "the West." There are people in North America and western Europe who are not unsympathetic to Islamic critiques of the moral vulgarity of Western consumerism. And there are Muslims—many tens of millions of Muslims—who do not fit the standard TV profile of the rioting mob chanting "Death to the Great Satan!" Still, it does little good to suggest, as some Western Islamicists and "Middle East experts" are wont to do, that the confrontational aspects of the interaction between the Islamic world and the West derive almost exclusively from Western incomprehension, bias, or sheer muddleheadedness. All of that exists, in spades. But there is an aggressive element to resurgent Islam at the end of the twentieth century, and that aggressiveness is not simply "evangelical" (to borrow a Christian term).

Here, as in perhaps no other area of foreign affairs, sound-bite crudities must be vigorously avoided. Too much is at stake.

CONFRONTING OUR OWN INCAPACITIES

Thinking seriously about "Islam and the West" requires an examination of conscience—intellectual conscience and moral conscience. For unless we understand why the West has such difficulties in seeing the Islamic world of the Middle East and the Maghreb accurately, we are unlikely to resist the temptations of vulgarization.[4]

There are at least six reasons why the West has frequently misconstrued (or just plain missed) the contemporary Islamic revival:

1. *Secularism.* Western academic, journalistic, diplomatic, and political elites tend to assume that modernization inevitably involves thoroughgoing secularization.[5] A book once influential in

these circles, Daniel Lerner's 1958 study *The Passing of Traditional Society*, "took for granted the supremacy of modernity over tradition," according to Fouad Ajami. "Lerner was sure that modern man was a superior species and that tradition was doomed to extinction."[6] "Tradition" connoted several things, of course: cultural, economic, and political institutions, patterns of familial and social interaction, habits of moral and intellectual life. But the "tradition" that, like the dinosaurs, was doomed to extinction most especially included religion. Indeed, the very term "Islamic fundamentalism"—a polarizing anachronism—betokens the incomprehension of the cultured despisers of religion in the West about their own society, as well as Islamic ones. People who thought that Jerry Falwell was the greatest threat to American democracy since Hitler are not likely to understand the dynamics of a religiously energetic and assertive Islam.

Reflecting on the radical secularization of the American intellectual and cultural elite over against the maddeningly diverse and yet vibrant religiosity of the American people, Peter Berger has described the United States as "a nation of Indians [Asian, that is] ruled by an elite of Swedes." That aspect of the American culture has been a major obstacle to our understanding of the Islamic revival.

2. *Colonialism*. The legacies of colonialism are a second reason why the West, and particularly Britain and France, has persistently misread the realities of the Arab Islamic world. Guilt over previous exploitation is one dimension of the problem; continuing (if discreetly subtle) deprecation of "the wogs" is another. Of even greater consequence has been the falsification of history that accompanied the colonial experience. Atavistic French fantasies about Louis IX, the Crusades, and the French *mission civilizatrice* have posed one set of problems. But even more damage was done by "Lawrence of Arabia."

For all their literary elegance, the fictions of T. E. Lawrence about the "Arab revolt" against the Ottoman Turks during World War I have left a long, bloody trail of diplomatic and political errors in their wake. Lawrence, a great romantic, fundamentally misjudged the difficulty of erecting a modern state system on the shaky foundations of Bedouin political culture, in a region where tribal and sectarian loyalties remained (and in some instance still remain) primary. But the romance of the Arabs and the desert— not infrequently accompanied by old-fashioned, upper-crust English anti-Semitism—proved remarkably resistant to the contradictory evidence regularly thrown up by the real world of the Middle East.[7] And so the follies of British policy during the inter-war mandate period eventually yielded the British scuttle from the region in 1948, which in short order led to the first of five (or nine, depending on how you count them) Arab-Israeli wars.

3. *Theological Liberalism.* A third factor shaping Western incomprehension about the Islamic world is theological: Western liberal Christians cannot grasp the radical nature of Islamic supersessionism, the core Islamic belief that the revelation to Muhammad completes—and thus dramatically supersedes—the divine revelations to Abraham, Moses, the Hebrew prophets, and Jesus. Having adopted a soft universalism in their own conception of the relation between God's revelation and the salvation of the world, Western liberal Christians find it almost impossible to understand a religious conception of reality in which the superiority (indeed, finality) of one religious tradition is proclaimed without any hint of embarrassment.

4. *Socialism.* The obverse of this last problem is the peculiar distortion caused by the secular Western Left's faith in a mundane utopia, and the projection of that creed onto the phenomenon of "Arab socialism." Once identified with Egypt's Nasser and his leadership in the "Non-Aligned Movement," this statist approach to modernization and development proved disastrous for the poor of the Middle East and the Maghreb; nonetheless, it bewitched Western secular liberals and radicals, who saw in it a possible fulfillment of their own political-economic aspirations. (A similar process of projection also befogged Western understandings of the "African socialism" of Ghana's Kwame Nkrumah and Tanzania's Julius Nyerere, the results again being the suffering of millions of human beings and the wasting of billions of dollars of aid money.) Moreover, the ideology of "Arab socialism," with its barely masked disdain for such "pre-modern" artifacts as religion, compounded the Western secularist myopia noted above, even as it resonated with the Western Left's own sense of cultural alienation.

5. *Pragmatism*. The Western (and particularly Anglo-American) instinct for the politics of pragmatism has made it difficult to comprehend a region whose history has been shaped by the Arab cultural predisposition to the politics of ideology and drama. In the modern West, "politics" has had less and less to do with great moral commitments and more and more to do with the accommodation and adjustment of competing material interests. Thus Westerners find it difficult, bordering on impossible, to comprehend a political culture in which, as Ajami puts it, the service of "interests" is often considered "craven and unprincipled." This tendency of modern Arab politics toward "the lofty world of metaphysics" may, in fact, be drawing to an end among the contemporary political and business elites (one result of the impact of nationalism, as exhibited during the Gulf War). But it has proven to be another hindrance to a clear-eyed Western view of the realities of power in the Levant and the Maghreb.[8]

6. *Clientitis*. Finally, clientitis among Western diplomats and scholars—the tendency to make excuses *ad infinitum* for the brutal politics of the Arab Islamic world—has impeded Western understanding. Recall, for example, the doomsday forecasts of the probable results of Western military action in the Gulf that were routinely issued by sundry Middle East specialists and Islamicists during the months between Saddam Hussein's invasion of Kuwait and the launching of Desert Storm: the "Arab street" would rise in revolt; the coalition would never hold together; the West would be ruined in the eyes of the Arab world; etc., etc. None of it happened.

Some of this clientitis is an understandable reaction to the crudities of the Terrible Simplifiers. Some of it comes from a concern (sometimes sensible, sometimes pusillanimous) for continued access to Arab and Islamic leaders who are not known to take criticism kindly. Some of it is standard academic secularism, positivism, and "multiculturalism" (i.e., anti-Westernism). Some of it is simply the result of being too close to the mirror—a position that is sure to distort the image one sees. But whatever the components, the pattern remains: just as the Sovietologists were among the last people to grasp the collapse of the old USSR, so the Middle East studies guild has too often been behind the historical curve in its assessments of the Middle East. Western foreign offices have followed suit.

TOWARD A MORE COMPLEX COMPLEXITY

A book published in 1992 by the Oxford University Press, *The Islamic Threat: Myth or Reality?*, tries to set Western appraisals of the worlds of Islam and their relationship to the worlds of politics on a firmer foundation. The author, John L. Esposito of Georgetown University, is one of America's most prominent Islamicists and a former president of the aforementioned Middle East Studies Association.[9]

Professor Esposito exhibits, alas, some of the traditional analytic and literary deficiencies of his tribe: a tendency toward euphemism when unpleasant subjects arise (". . . one can expect that where Islamic movements come to power . . . issues of political pluralism and human rights will remain sources of tension . . ."[10]); a touch of ideological insouciance ("the Third World socialist outlook of Frantz Fanon and Che Guevara"[11]); a peculiar reading of recent Western history ("The exaggerated fears and static vision which drove us to take herculean steps against a monolithic enemy blinded us to the diversity within the Soviet Union and the profound changes that were taking place . . ."[12]); and a certain petulance in making comparisons and drawing analogies ("How often do we see articles that speak of Christian rage or Jewish rage?"[13]). But if one reads *The Islamic Threat* carefully, making allowances for Professor Esposito's lapses into guild-speak, there are things to be learned about what the media insist on describing as "Islamic fundamentalism."

The Roots of Revival

The first thing to be learned, according to Esposito, is that the phrase "Islamic fundamentalism" is a projection of certain secularist and academic biases onto a complex reality that is bent and distorted by the projection. In this, Professor Esposito is surely right. Indeed, the drastic overuse and misuse of "fundamentalist" to describe American Christian sects and movements should be a caution against the temptation to apply the term to Islam. (Martin Marty, please call Georgetown.)

Esposito proposes, as an alternative, either "Islamic activism" or "Islamic revivalism," both of which strike me as superior. Moreover, and like Fouad Ajami, John Esposito sees in the very fact of the contemporary Islamic revival a profound challenge to Western theories of modernization and its alleged handmaiden, secularization. The Islamic revival doesn't fit the historical template cut by secularist theorists of development; and their response has been, typically, to dismiss Islamic revivalism as a kind of weird atavism into which primitive peoples, alas, sometimes fall. Esposito suggests that a more intelligent response to this new phenomenon would be to change the template.

Most importantly, Esposito argues that the roots of the Islamic revival have to be understood spiritually or they will not be understood at all. Islamic revivalism is, first and foremost, one potent expression of a widespread desire in the Muslim world "to lead a more Islamically-informed life."[14] That desire is not confined to the margins of society: it can be found among middle-class and upper-class people, professionals as well as peasants, those with Western educations as well as those with virtually no education. Moreover, the wish to live a more Islamically centered life takes many forms throughout the Muslim world, even when it touches questions of the ordering of society, and not all those forms are violent. But to miss the religious core of contemporary Islamic activism—to reduce the phenomenon to one with an essentially political motivation—is to miss the mark badly.

Clio's Revenge

Professor Esposito concedes that the contemporary Islamic revival is also a reaction to certain historical developments: "a sense that existing political, economic, and social systems have failed; a disenchantment with, and at times a rejection of, the West; a quest for identity and greater authenticity."[15] The "heart of the revivalist worldview," Esposito writes, "is the belief that the Muslim world is in a state of decline," and the conviction that the cause of that decline is a "departure from the straight path of Islam."[16] Thus the "cure," so to speak, is "a return to Islam in personal and public life" that will, in turn, "ensure the restoration of Islamic identity, values, and power."[17]

This reading of history is not without its sourness, and here the colonial legacy—and indeed the general pattern of interaction between Islam and the West since Jan Sobieski and his winged hussars stopped the Muslim assault on Vienna in 1683—rears its head yet again. As the distinguished Harvard scholar Wilfred Cantwell Smith put it over a generation ago, "the fundamental spiritual crisis in Islam in the twentieth century stems from an awareness that something is awry between the religion which God has appointed and the historical development of the world which He controls."[18] We may have—we do have—a rather different reading of that history than a devout Muslim, especially a devout Muslim from the Middle East or the Maghreb, would have. But the point to be grasped is that the Muslim's reading is shaped by a spiritual vision of history that has been largely absent from the West since the end of the European wars of religion in 1648.

Thus the various movements of "Islamic activism" share an assumption: as Professor Esposito puts it, "that Islam is not simply an ideological alternative for Muslim societies but a theological and political imperative."[19] And that assumption has revivified the traditional conviction that "Islam provides a self-sufficient ideology for state and society, a valid alternative to secular nationalism, socialism, and capitalism."[20] (On this analysis, the Islamic revival has striking affinities to certain Christian—and especially Catholic—quests for a "third way" that is neither "socialist" nor "capitalist." It is also worth noting that, with Pope John Paul II, the leadership of world Catholicism has explicitly rejected the quest for a "third way," in favor of an analysis that proposes a vibrant moral-cultural system as the essential third leg of a pluralistic social triad whose other parts are a democratic polity and a free economy.)

A Dyad of Goals

The aim of Islamic activism is not, according to Professor Esposito, some sort of repristination, a return to the glories of a mythic past. Rather, Islamic activists today envision a complex amalgam of religious revival and economic-social-political modernization. Some groups emphasize modernization, in some cases to the point where the religious revival gets lost in the shuffle. Others stress the religious revival and give modernization a decided back seat. The tensions between "revival" and "modernization" have never been satisfactorily resolved. The cassette tape players that make possible the widespread diffusion of revivalist religious instruction (as in the Iranian revolution) can also play Madonna's "Material Girl." The cheap transistor radios that pick up Islamic religious broadcasting and the reporting done by state-controlled news agencies can also pick up the Voice of America, BBC, and Deutsche Welle. But, in the main, the Islamic revival has remained committed to its double goal—interestingly enough, in part because of the example of Israel, which is often perceived (if rather simplistically) as an example of the successful blend of religious conviction and a modern state.

Professor Esposito also makes some useful distinctions among the political movements that have arisen out of the various forms of the Islamic revival. Qaddafi's Libya is not the Egypt of Sadat and Mubarak, and neither of those states is the Iran of Khomeini and his successors. Put that way the point seems obvious enough; but it has often been ignored or drastically minimized by Western commentators. The complex phenomenon of Islamic revival, mediated through the further tanglements of national histories, tribal loyalties, and geopolitical realities, can inform quite distinct political, economic, legal, and social experiments.

So the Islamic revival is a multifaceted mix of thought and aspiration that can have many different outcomes. But because it is an *Islamic* revival, a revival rooted in a commitment to Islam as the definitive revelation of God's will and purposes for humanity, the many variations of the new Muslim activism display an important common dynamic: an impulse toward the revitalization of a holistic Islam in which society, as well as the individual Muslim believer, is decisively "liberated."

Some Simplicities Amidst the Complexity

The Islamic Threat is a lengthy plea on behalf of a worthy cause: breaking down the stereotypical dichotomies (secularism/religious-primitivism, modernization/tradition, social-dynamism/

faith) that have too often distorted Western understandings of the third great monotheistic religion and its public consequences. But then what? For surely the issue, once we have cleared our heads of falsehoods, biases, and myths, is whether or not there are truths lurking within those stereotypes. If we are to accept (as I think we should) Esposito's call to see the more complex truth within the media stereotype of "militant Islam," then we must see that truth in *all* its complexity. We can, for example, sympathize with the Islamic rejection of Western secularism. But that acknowledgment need not blind us to another piece of the puzzle, namely, the sorry state of religious freedom in Muslim societies.

This quest for the truth in all its complexity—and simplicity— leads us to the question of Islam and democracy. Professor Esposito argues for a sympathetic understanding of the difficulties inherent in the current situation:

> The political realities of the Muslim world have not been conducive to the development of democratic traditions and institutions. European colonial rule and postindependence national governments headed by military officers, monarchs, and ex-military rulers have contributed to a legacy which has had little concern for political participation and the building of strong democratic institutions. National unity and stability as well as political legitimacy have been undermined by the artificial nature of modern states whose national boundaries were often determined by colonial powers and whose rulers were either placed on their thrones by Europe or seized power for themselves. Weak economies, illiteracy, and high unemployment, especially among the younger generation, exacerbate the situation. . . .[21]

Moreover, Esposito contends, there are Islamic activists who do not share the radicals' root-and-branch rejection of "democracy" as inherently "Western," i.e., colonial, and therefore inappropriate for Muslim societies. These activists argue, instead, for an "Islamicization" of democracy, a reinterpreting of traditional Islamic concepts of consultation, consensus, and Qu'ranic interpretation to support projects of political reform. Still, Esposito concedes, "there are differences between western notions of democracy and Islamic traditions." Indeed there are. And even among the Islamic liberals, the claim is that "Islam possesses or can generate its own distinctive forms of democracy in which popular sovereignty is restricted or directed by God's law."[22]

Although it would doubtless cause howls of protest in the faculty lounge at the Harvard Law School, such an assertion about religious conviction and democratic practice is not, in fact, preposterous. The American democracy, for example, was founded on the assertion of self-evident truths about divinely warranted, inalienable rights: which is to say, American democracy was founded on the notion that there is a transcendent and normative order of truth that stands in judgment on the American state, to which the state is accountable, and whose authority the state must acknowledge if it is to retain moral legitimacy. So the question of the relation between religious truth and democracy—between God and the liberal democratic *polis*—is not easily resolved by the incantation "thewallofseparationbetweenchurchandstate."

On the other hand, Professor Esposito does not, to my mind, get to the heart of the matter by suggesting that "a process of change . . . requires time" and that more "experience" will lead to the development of new Islamic "political traditions and institutions."[23] The heart of the issue of Islam and democracy, indeed of Islam and the West, is not the development of new political traditions but the possible evolution of a new (or reformed) Islamic *theological* tradition.

A Call to the Bishop of Hippo

John Esposito is right to remind us that the worlds of Islamic religiosity, piety, law, and theology are exceedingly complex, and that there are sundry variants, sects, and tendencies within the fundamental division between Sunnis and Shi'ites. But there are also striking consistencies in Islamic law and theology across the board, and it is these that are most problematic in terms of Islam and the West, or Islam and democracy.

The first is Islamic supersessionism: the core Islamic belief that the revelation to Muhammad supersedes, in a final and definitive way, the revelations to Abraham, Moses, and Jesus (all of whom are honored among Muslims, but precisely as precursors of the Prophet). Esposito stresses the "common theological roots" of

Judaism, Christianity, and Islam (a problematic formulation, but let it stand). And no doubt the three monotheistic faiths are related to one another in a different way than any one of them is related to, say, Buddhism, Hinduism, Shinto, Confucianism, or the New Age. But the deep cleavage here is not resolved by appeals to the common ancestor, Abraham.

The history of Christian supersessionism *vis-à-vis* Judaism is a familiar and painful one. Christians do believe, indeed must believe, that God's revelation in Christ is in continuity with, and from the Christian point of view fulfills, the revelation to Abraham, Moses, and the Hebrew prophets. But no orthodox Christian can claim, in the light of Romans 9–11, a relationship to Jews and Judaism similar to that radical supersessionism with which Islam regards Christianity and Judaism. Whatever else Christians say about God and his purposes in history, they cannot claim that God breaks his covenantal promises. The covenants with Abraham and with Moses are, in the mysterious ways of God, abiding covenants. Living Judaism is part of the economy of salvation, as Christians understand it—and no orthodox Christian today would argue that the role of Judaism in post-Easter salvation history is simply to illustrate God's judgment on those who rejected Jesus as Messiah. Nor is this understanding of the divinely ordered entanglement of Christians and Jews a monopoly of Christians. Eminent twentieth-century Jewish theologians and philosophers—perhaps most prominently Franz Rosenzweig—have worked to "fit" Christianity into salvation history from a Jewish perspective.

There is no parallel to this multi-faceted image of "entanglement" in Islam's conception of itself *vis-à-vis* Judaism and Christianity. For the Islamic believer, and on the basis of the Qu'ran itself, both the Torah and the New Testament are corrupted revelations: "a composite of human fabrications mixed with divine revelation," as John Esposito described it in an earlier book.[24] The revelation to Muhammad purified Christianity and Judaism of the pagan accretions that had corrupted them; and thus Islam is the only true "straight path" to God and a knowledge of his will and purposes. (The New Testament "corruptions" include what the Qu'ran regards as the fictions of Jesus' death on the cross and his resurrection. Moreover, Islam considers the bedrock Christian doctrines of the incarnation and the trinitarian nature of God as relapses into polytheism.)

This conviction of its finality has given Islam a dynamic "evangelizing" thrust; but that dynamism is often understood rather more militantly than Christians would understand their missionary endeavors today. In his 1990 encyclical on the missionary obligation of the Church, for example, Pope John Paul II says flatly: "The Church proposes; she imposes nothing." That concept finds little resonance among leading Muslim activists today.

This brings us to another of the striking consistencies within the worlds of Islam: what we might call "Islamic monism." By this I mean the claim, found in virtually all strands of Islam, that the rightly ordered society is an Islamic society. There is no Qu'ranic text that parallels the famous injunction in Matthew 22:21 to "render unto Caesar what is Caesar's, and to God what is God's." Rather, according to Esposito, and beginning from the originating experience of the Prophet himself, "to be a Muslim was to live in a state which at least nominally was a Muslim community guided by the laws and institutions of Islam."[25]

Christians have succumbed to the monistic temptation on more than one occasion: but, save among certain extreme radical millenarians, the one-to-one identification of the *potestas* (power) of the state and the *auctoritas* (authority) of the Church has been rejected by Christians as unorthodox—even if some of those Christians willingly used the *potestas* of the state to enforce their understandings of orthodoxy. And while it is true that, in many circumstances, Christians and Jews lived less-threatened lives in Islamic societies than non-Christians did in Christian states, it is also true that Islam, in its *dhimmi* system (of "head-taxes" for "people of the book," i.e., resident Jews and Christians), has built into it a two-tiered system of citizenship that would not be congruent with Christian understandings, and with most Jewish understandings, of the relation between religious conviction and legal status before the secular law. In any "Islamic society" today, Jews and Christians cannot be other than decidedly second-class citizens. That is not true of Muslims in the societies of the West.

Before Wittenberg, "De Civitate Dei"

Pondering the possible futures of Islam, and with an eye on the relation between Islam and "the West," John Esposito suggests (along with a few Muslim scholars) that Islam, like Christianity before it, needs a Martin Luther and a Reformation.[26] But that formulation, intriguing as it is, may not cut deeply enough. For while Luther was a "religious genius" (the phrase is John Paul II's), the Reformation did not happen *de novo*. Luther appealed to an ancient Christian theological tradition that he believed had been forgotten (or, perhaps better, misplaced) by the late medieval papacy.

That was the tradition of St. Augustine, who in *The City of God* offered a theologically powerful argument for distinguishing between the earthly city and the City that was to come in its fullness only in the Kingdom of God. Augustine's distinction had many implications, but as it worked itself out in history, that idea of the "two kingdoms" or "two authorities" led to the belief that the "secular world" had a legitimate autonomy and integrity of its own, despite its corrupt condition. To put it another way, Augustine's theological explication of Jesus' command to "render unto Caesar . . ." had the effect of desacralizing politics—which, over time, opened the social space in which a politics of consent, rather than a politics of divinely sanctioned coercion, could be built. And the result, after hundreds of years of historical travail, was democracy as we know it today.

So, yes, let us shed the stereotypes about Islamic activists. However, it was not a sound-bite quotemeister but a sympathetic scholar (Professor Esposito) who neatly identified the problem of Islamic monism when he wrote that "each" of the major Islamic activist movements today "speaks of a comprehensive reformation or revolution, the creation of an Islamic order and state, since they regard Islam as comprehensive in scope, a faith-informed way of life."[27] Christians, too, regard theirs as a "faith-informed way of life." But, thanks be to God, mainstream Christians have divested themselves of the monism that once resulted in a torrent of blood throughout Europe. That happened through a Christian reappropriation and development of the Augustinian heritage.

The interaction between Islam and the West—between Islam and modernization, the market, and democracy—will be shaped in the next decades by many factors. The very experience of a modern economic/managerial/communications system is certain to have an impact on Muslim thinking about the relation between Islam and the right-ordering of social life. Still, it is not the special pleading of a theologian, but simply an adequate conception of the full complexity of the case, that leads us back from economics, sociology, and politics to theology.

For the question of Islam and "the West" is, at bottom, a theological question. Islam, in its encounter with modernity and modernization, may well need a Reformation. But right now, from a Christian social-ethical point of view, Islam is still waiting for Augustine. A lot of history depends on just how long that vigil lasts.

12

After the Twin Towers Attack: Terrorism and America

Those who think that Americans are permitted a certain insouciance about passions and politics beyond the water's edge might have been shaken out of their complacency had they been driving up the New Jersey Turnpike on the night of February 26, 1993. Looking across the river at the familiar illuminated skyline of lower Manhattan, they would have seen an eerie, Olympian darkness where the twin towers of the World Trade Center should have been. But this particular blackout was not the result of natural disaster or mechanical malfunction. No, this looked very much like the deliberate act of an enemy. Something like war—proxy war, perhaps—seemed to have been declared.

The point was driven home by a single page in the March 17, 1993, *New York Times*. Page A12 began with the continuation of a front-page story on the "tidal wave of Palestinian attacks" that had left eight Israelis dead in the previous month; a sidebar reported that things had gotten sufficiently grim that Israeli prime minister Yitzhak Rabin had canceled engagements in Washington in order to return home. A12 also carried an article on the assassination of an Iranian opposition leader, shot in the face by two gunmen riding a motor scooter in downtown Rome. And just below those gruesome tidings was the story of another attack on tourist buses at the Egyptian Museum in Cairo, where a bomb had killed three people and wounded twenty others in February. The reporter speculated that in the wake of these bombings the tourist industry, a major source of income for the hard-pressed Egyptian economy, was on the verge of collapse.

195

Meanwhile, investigators continued to explore the connections between the attack on the World Trade Center and members of an extremist group affiliated with the Al-Salaam Mosque in Jersey City. There, Sheikh Omar Abd al-Rahman had been preaching fire-breathing sermons that were subsequently circulated in the slums of Cairo on cassette tapes. The sheikh's message—that true believers must kill "the enemies of Allah . . . in order to liberate themselves from the grandchildren of the pigs and apes who are educated at the tables of the Zionists, the Communists, and the imperialists"—was thought to have been at least partially responsible for motivating the anti-tourist (i.e., anti-foreigner and anti-Western) violence plaguing Egypt.

In interviews with CNN and ABC in the month after the Twin Towers bombing, the sheikh denied any involvement in the attack on the World Trade Center but said he believed that Egyptian president Mubarak "deserves the same thing" as Anwar al-Sadat —namely, assassination. In an interview with *Al-Hayat*, a London-based Arabic daily owned by a Saudi prince, Sheikh Omar was even less circumspect, supporting terrorist attacks on tourists and foreign investment in Egypt, and indeed on any Muslim or Christian who opposes the sheikh's own interpretation of "Islamic principles." Abd al-Rahman also justified terrorist attacks on the Egyptian police: "The argument that the police are people following orders and do not deserve to be killed is unacceptable. . . . The police are one integrated unit, which justifies attacks on any part of that unit." The sheikh told the Arabic daily that while he "did not accept American laws," he abided by them in order to have a platform from which he could "confront the regime," meaning Mubarak's government. Intelligence specialists suggested that the sheikh's activities may have been funded in part by Iran.

According to the strict rules of evidence, the links among these stories—the Twin Towers bombing, the activities of Sheikh Abd al-Rahman, the travail of Egypt, and the assassination in Rome— were speculative at best; they may not even amount to a Scots verdict of "not proven," although the evidence of an alleged linkage between the sheikh and the Twin Towers attack was sufficient to convince the U.S. attorney for Manhattan, a federal grand jury, and, ultimately, Attorney General Janet Reno and

President Clinton. But however the sheikh's trial plays out, terrorism is surely back on the agenda, and demanding our serious attention.

What is "terrorism"? Defining it may seem a straightforward matter, not unlike Justice Potter Stewart's effort to define "pornography" ("I know it when I see it"). But terrorism in fact eludes precise definition: in part because of the many forms terrorism takes, and in part because apologists for terrorism confuse matters by arguing that the terrorist is really just a different kind of warrior. In *Just and Unjust Wars*, Michael Walzer formulated a description of terrorism that challenged such crudities and usefully distinguished terrorism from war:

> [Terrorism's] purpose is to destroy the morale of a nation or a class, to undercut its solidarity; its method is the random murder of innocent people. Randomness is the crucial feature of terrorist activity. If one wishes fear to spread and intensify over time, it is not desirable to kill specific people identified in some particular way with a regime, a party, or a policy. Death must come by chance to individual Frenchmen, or Germans, or Irish Protestants, or Jews, simply because they are Frenchmen or Germans, Protestants or Jews, until they feel themselves fatally exposed and demand that their governments negotiate for their safety.[1]

But even Walzer's sophisticated definition does not account for some crucial recent data. Were the attacks on Pope John Paul II, Aldo Moro, Anwar al-Sadat, and Indira Gandhi actions against people whom the terrorists considered "innocent"? No, they were attacks on people whom the assassins (or their sponsors) considered guilty. So was the murder of Nissim Toledano, an Israeli policeman, which led to the expulsion of Hamas activists from Israel in late 1992.

As the post–Cold War fractionation of the world continues apace and as new openings in the international system permit the noxious gases of political violence (as well as the clear winds of freedom) to circulate more freely, further analytic rigor is required. For mistaken understandings can lead to mistaken policies, and as the Twin Towers bombing made clear, our margin for error—yes, even in these United States—is getting slimmer all the time.

UNDERSTANDING TERRORISM: ELEVEN MISTAKES

In his revised 1987 study *The Age of Terrorism*, Walter Laqueur of the Center for Strategic and International Studies identified eleven misconceptions about terrorism whose ubiquity in the press and among government officials helps explain some of our present confusion on the subject. Pondering Laqueur's Dirty Almost-Dozen is a good way to start thinking about the problem of terrorism today.

Mistake #1. Terrorism is a new phenomenon with few historical precedents, and there is little to be learned from what meager antecedents may be found.

Not true. Modern technology, writes Laqueur, has "made a great difference as far as the character of terrorist operations is concerned." But the basic moral, political, and legal issues involved in terrorism are "anything but new," and the use of assassination and political murder as an instrument for achieving political aims has a long, bloody pedigree. Moreover, there is little in contemporary terrorist rhetoric and "logic" that was not presaged in the previous century.[2]

The metaphysics of modern terrorism—what Laqueur dubs the "philosophy of the bomb"—was first embodied by the Narodnaya Volya, a nineteenth-century Russian revolutionary clique whose three years of terror culminated in the assassination of the reformist czar Alexander II in 1881; a second Russian group, the Social Revolutionary Party, conducted a campaign of bombing and assassination from 1902 until 1911. The doctrine that shaped these movements was first propounded by the German radical Karl Heinzen (1809–1880), whose moral theology was desperately deficient: according to Laqueur, Heinzen "argued that while murder was forbidden in principle this prohibition did not apply to politics." Heinzen began his career by trying to justify tyrannicide. But it proved impossible to stop there, and as he later wrote, "If you have to blow up half a continent and pour out a sea of blood in order to destroy the party of the barbarians, have no scruples of conscience."[3]

To Heinzen's way of thinking, the revolutions of 1848 had failed because the revolutionaries had been insufficiently ruthless. And like Johann Most—another German radical who emigrated to the more hospitable United States—Heinzen hoped that technology, and specifically new explosives like dynamite, would compensate for what was lacking in the willpower of the laggardly masses. Most, inventor of the letter bomb and other terrorist refinements, was a quondam laborer in a Jersey City Heights explosives factory who extolled "propaganda by deed" in his newspaper, *Freiheit*; he anticipated twentieth-century revolutionary rhetoric by describing the enemies of the working class as "pigs, dogs, bestial monsters, devils in human shape, reptiles, parasites, scum," and so forth.[4]

Then there were the extremists who used terrorist methods in the nineteenth- and twentieth-century Irish, Macedonian, Serbian, and Armenian national-liberation movements. Anarchist and anarcho-syndicalist terrorism was also part of the early history of the labor movement in the United States, as it was in Spain, Portugal, and Italy (Spanish workers seeking higher wages were given to blowing up their factories during World War I). Thus terrorism is not exactly a *novum*, however much the motivations and the technological capabilities of terrorists have changed. Too narrow a focus on the distinctiveness of terrorism today can obscure some useful lessons from the past.

Mistake #2. Terrorism is the single most pressing issue on the international agenda, a "cancer of the modern world."

Perhaps, depending on how one defines "terrorism." (Is an Iraq or a North Korea threatening the use of nuclear weapons a "terrorist state" or an old-fashioned aggressor?) But Laqueur reminds us that the incidence of terrorism actually dropped from the mid-1970s to the mid-1980s, and while the trendline may have turned upward in the post-Soviet period, there is no compelling longitudinal evidence to sustain the cancer metaphor. Moreover, Laqueur argues, "there has not been so far a single case of a society dragged down to destruction as a result of terrorism."[5] Terrorism is a very serious problem: innocents are killed, societies are disrupted, democratization is impeded, property is destroyed. But exaggerating its extent and its impact plays into the hands of terrorists, whose power is the conviction in others' minds that terrorism is omnipresent and invincible.

Mistake #3. Repression breeds terrorism: the greater the repression, the greater the likelihood of terrorism.

Not true, at least today. Terrorism as a "response to repression" was more characteristic of nineteenth-century Russia than it is of twentieth-century societies, including the Middle East. Indeed, the hard fact seems to be that the greater the repression, the less the likelihood of terrorism. There was no terrorism in the old Soviet Union, and there is none that we know of in China, Vietnam, Cuba, North Korea, or Myanmar (Burma) today. Syria (a major supporter of terrorism outside its borders) dealt with a potential outbreak of domestic Islamic extremism in 1982 by leveling the city of Hama, killing 20,000 of its own citizens; and Syria hasn't had a terrorist problem since. Conversely, more open societies in the neighborhood, like Israel and Egypt, have had continuing problems (to put it mildly) with terrorists. Basque nationalist terrorism in Spain got going in earnest after Franco's death, and terrorism increased in the former West Germany, in Turkey, in Peru, and in Colombia under left-of-center governments.[6]

Mistake #4. The only way to reduce terrorism is to redress the grievances that cause it.

This is the false corollary to Mistake #3. No doubt grievances exist, and no doubt some of them involve real injustices. But not every grievance or perceived injustice can be resolved in this world. One group's extremist conception of the "will of God" cannot be accepted by others whose religious convictions, lives, or national existence are thereby imperiled. Nor, as we have seen, can every group claiming the "right of self-determination" exercise that right by forming an independent state; others may have legitimate claims to the territory in question, history having established facts on the ground that confound ethnic ideology and/or theological doctrine. Nor does independent statehood automatically resolve the problem of terrorism, for a newly independent state can dissolve into a bedlam of competing terrorist factions, each seeking to secure power for the future. Thus the "answer" to the problem of terrorism cannot lie primarily in the assuaging of grievances—particularly when the grievances in question are derived from violent interpretations (or misinterpretations) of a religious tradition.[7]

Mistake #5. One man's "terrorist" is another man's "freedom fighter."

This relativist cliché is both morally odious and politically repugnant. As Laqueur puts it, "there is no unanimity on any subject under the sun, and it is perfectly true that terrorists do have well-wishers. But such support does not tell us anything about the justice of their cause; in 1941 Hitler and Mussolini had many fanatical followers. Does it follow that they fought for a just cause?"[8] Moreover, the inability to distinguish between "terrorist" and "freedom fighter" debases the coinage of politics, for it brings under the honorable rubric of "political action" the indiscriminate killing of innocents. Terrorism, properly understood, is the antithesis of politics, at least as politics has evolved in the great tradition of the West. "Politics" is about persuasion; terrorism is an especially savage form of coercion.

Mistake #6. Terrorists are fanatics who cannot be brought under control until the conditions that gave rise to their fanaticism change in their favor.

This is a variant of Mistake #4. Some terrorists are fanatics; but concessions to their fanaticism will be pointless short of the terrorists' total victory, which is what fanatics require. Moreover, the historical evidence, brutal as it may be, suggests that, while the wellsprings of fanaticism may be replenished on a regular basis, "the terrorist reservoir is not unlimited." Khomeini's Iran got rid of its internal terrorist problem by killing a lot of terrorists; Turkey and Italy broke the back of the terrorism that plagued them in the 1970s by effective police work and widespread arrests and detentions. Fanaticism may indeed be an enduring fact of international public life, but terrorism need not be an omnipresent (much less an effective) expression of it.[9]

Mistake #7. Terrorists are poor, and terrorist attacks are a manifestation of the misery of the "wretched of the earth."

This is the Officer Krupke Fallacy: "We're depraved on accounta we're deprived!" And while poverty may have been the lot of nineteenth-century anarchist terrorists, that is rarely the case in the late twentieth century. Most of today's terrorists cannot afford to be poor, given the costly technology, infrastructure, and communications required in a modern international terrorist organization. Moreover, master terrorists demand, and get, handsome emoluments. One of the things that keeps terrorism going today is its ability to command serious money: thus the ugly linkages among fanatical ethnic or religious groups, outlaw states, and the oil and narcotics trades.[10]

Mistake #8. Terrorism is the result of the Arab-Israeli conflict.

The suggestion here is that a Palestinian state is the cure-all for contemporary terrorism. Given the profound divisions within the Palestinian movement today (which were evident even before the radical Islamic organization Hamas emerged as a challenger to the PLO), that is a dubious proposition at best. "Palestine" would not only be a likely launching pad for further terrorism within Israel; it would itself almost certainly be riven by terrorism as different factions struggled for power in the new state. The rapid growth of intra-Palestinian terrorism in recent years has not been sufficiently marked by the West; it is an ugly feature of the current landscape to which attention must be paid.[11]

Mistake #9. "State-sponsored terrorism" has drastically exacerbated the problem.

Yes and no. The operational and financial involvement of states in international terrorism certainly hasn't helped matters. Indeed, there would be little Middle East–based terrorism in the world today absent the willingness of Iran, Iraq, Syria, and Libya to provide terrorists with weapons, training facilities, and logistical support, and absent the willingness of Saudi Arabia and some of the Gulf states to finance these operations (protection money, they called it in Al Capone's Chicago). As noted above, terrorism today is a cost-intensive, high-tech business; the indigent anarchist with his homemade bomb is largely a figure of the past. State involvement in terrorism also complicates counterterrorist intelligence operations and raises the stakes of both preemptive and retaliatory military action against terrorists.

But there seems to be a built-in limit here: state-sponsored terrorism, says Laqueur, "will be tolerated only as long as it is not used too frequently and if it does not cause too much damage. If it becomes more than a nuisance, the political calculus changes and the inhibitions against retaliation no longer function as the public clamor for massive retaliation grows."[12] Thus far, even states like Libya have grasped the point and have declined to go beyond the point of no return in confronting the West; it remains to be seen whether Iran, to take but one example, will follow suit.

Mistake #10. Terrorism can happen at any place, at any time.

Perhaps in theory, but in practice a caveat applies: "except in effective dictatorial regimes." The more open the society, the more vulnerable it is to terrorism. The more a society is committed to a broad range of judicially enforced civil liberties and judicially monitored restrictions on its police, internal security, and intelligence forces, the more difficult it will be to mount effective counterterrorism. Surmounting those difficulties is not impossible for a democracy, but it requires facing a host of complex legal and moral issues.[13]

Many other democracies—including those that have conducted successful counterterrorist operations, such as the Federal Republic of Germany—have a less tender view of civil liberties than that which has obtained in the United States since the heyday of the Warren Court. The German legal theory (a product of reflection on the Weimar disaster and the entirely constitutional rise of the Nazis) is that those who directly threaten the constitutional order have forfeited its more expansive protections. It's not a notion that would satisfy John Stuart Mill or the ACLU, but it helped put an end to the Baader-Meinhof Gang while preserving West German democracy.

Mistake #11. Economic conditions determine the ebb and flow of terrorism.

"Terrorism is about political, not economic power, " Laqueur insists.[14] Terrorism is less likely at times of economic crisis, and more likely when economic conditions are "relatively good." In fact, terrorism has frequently flourished, not when things are getting worse in a society (or in an international situation), but when they are improving—a pattern that in modern times dates from the French Revolution. Before the rise of Hamas, for example, there seemed to be a direct relationship between progress in Arab-Israeli negotiations and the rate of terrorist incidents: the greater the progress, the more terrorism there was likely to be.

That pattern may now be changing, but the principle will remain intact: for Hamas terrorism is, in the main, driven by passions that far transcend economic grievances.

COUNTERTERRORISM: FOUR LEVANTINE STRATEGIES

While terrorism has been a major problem in Latin America and a serious problem in western Europe, analysts of terrorism and counterterrorism strategists have tended to focus their attention on the Middle East. This is a somewhat distorting prism through which to view our own problems. For, since the collapse of radical fringe groups like the Black Panthers, the Weather Underground, and the Symbionese Liberation Army, there has been virtually no domestic terrorism in the United States. Nor is this country in a protracted struggle for national survival, in which aggressive neighbors use terrorism as one component in an overall strategy of annihilation.

And yet while Latin American narco-terrorism will remain a problem, the chief terrorist threat to the United States in the foreseeable future will indeed come from the Levant, as an expression of certain passions in those sectors of the Arab Islamic world usually labeled "fundamentalist" but more accurately styled "radical" or "extremist." Not every activist or even radical Muslim is given to terrorism; the vast majority are not. But many of those who do engage in terrorism justify their activities in explicitly (if perversely) Islamic terms. Thus it is instructive to note the ways in which Islamic activism or extremism and the ensuing threat (or fact) of terrorism have been handled in their own neighborhood.

Option #1: Annihilate the Extremists.
The Syrian artillery and infantry assault on Hama in 1982 has already been mentioned; once the Sunni areas of Hama were destroyed they were paved over, creating a necropolis masquerading as a parking lot. But Hafez al-Assad was not satisfied with that Carthaginian "solution"; his agents fanned out to France, Spain, and Germany, as well as throughout the Middle East, assassinating exiled or émigré members of radical Sunni groups.

Saddam Hussein adopted a similar strategy in Iraq, executing scores of activists in the Shiite movement "Al Da'wa," including its leader, Sheikh Muhammad Bakr al-Sadr.

The Ayatollah Khomeini slaughtered his foes (some of whom had resorted to terrorism) after coming to power in Iran, and in a fashion that made the Shah's once-dreaded SAVAK look rather restrained in comparison. As Walter Laqueur puts it,

The [new] Shiite [leaders] could safely ignore Western public opinion. They had no compunction whatsoever about the number of people executed nor the choice of the victims, nor the bestiality of the torturers. Bodies were mutilated, teachers were shot in front of their pupils, some of those executed were thirteen-year-old girls, and the standing order was to deny medical help to the terrorists who had been wounded.[15]

Amnesty International estimated the death toll at almost 3,000 in one year (1981–82); the victims' allies counted over 7,500 deaths in two years (1981–83). Khomeini's draconian style of counter-terrorism drove tens of thousands of his political opponents into exile, and Iranian agents could be found "executing" these "enemies of God" as far away as France.

Annihilation works. There is no terrorism in Iran or Syria today, and there was virtually none in Iraq before Saddam Hussein's power was diminished in Desert Storm. But annihilation is no option for a civilized society.

Option #2: Coopt the Extremists.

Jordan and Algeria tried what might be called "full cooptation," encouraging Muslim activists and revivalists to organize political parties and engage non-violently in the political process. Jordan's experience with this approach had mixed results. Eleven Muslim parties ran in the 1989 elections, and activist candidates won thirty of eighty parliamentary seats, including the office of Speaker. Then it became known that two of the parties involved had also been engaged in clandestine armed insurrection, assisted by Iran. Their leaders, sentenced to life imprisonment, were subsequently pardoned by King Hussein. In November 1993, the radical Islamic Activist Front won only sixteen seats. Algeria had a more difficult time: when the radical Front of Islamic Salvation (FIS) won 180 of 231 seats in the first round of elections in December 1991, the army called off the second round and took over the government.

A struggle between FIS terrorists and the government continues to this day.

Tunisia and Egypt—countries that proscribe political activity by religious parties—tried a form of "partial cooptation," "dialoguing" with opposition Islamic radicals while encouraging their participation in politics through other parties or as independents. In 1987, with the approval of the Tunisian government, activist Muslim candidates ran as independents; but then it was discovered that some of these same activists were plotting an armed takeover of the government. End of dialogue. Egypt's travail has been noted previously, and the Mubarak government is now in an open struggle against its extremist Islamic opposition, as well as confronting the opponents' patrons, Iran and Sudan. As of late 1993, Egypt's diplomatic efforts to secure pan-Arab cooperation against Islamic activist terrorism have failed.

The strategy of cooptation has no direct bearing on U.S. policy options regarding Islamic extremism and its terrorist expressions, since whatever threat exists here is largely an external one; where an internal support system for the external threat has taken root (as it may have in Jersey City), the antidote is effective policing and much more rigorously enforced immigration laws. But the failures of cooptation are worth noting for what they illustrate about the cast of mind of those Islamic radicals who are drawn to the use of terrorism as an instrument of their politics.

Option #3: Buy Them Off and Buy Time.
This is what the Saudis have done, and it seems to have worked —so far. To be sure, professing a mutuality of religious interests and otherwise catering to the extremists involves the Saudi regime in a variety of unsavory activities, including massive funding of terrorism by groups (like Hamas) whose long-term designs the House of Saud may not find altogether agreeable. Formal adherence to the notion of an "Islamic society" also involves the extensive Saudi ruling family and ruling class in a rich menu of lifestyle hypocrisies, which further irritates the extremists. But Saudi Arabia is a distinctive case, and while the Saudi strategy did survive the supreme test of collaboration with "the infidels" in the Gulf War, it is very doubtful indeed whether the model is exportable—or even whether it is sustainable over the long haul.

Option #4: Play One Extremist Group Off Against Another.

According to Egyptian military historian Abd al-Azim Ramadan and other specialists, this modern Machiavellianism was Anwar al-Sadat's strategy of choice in Egypt after he succeeded Nasser, who had jailed Islamic activists in the 1960s. Sadat freed them, hoping they would then fight his battle against the religious and secular left for him while drastically weakening themselves in the process. But it didn't work. Like his predecessor, Sadat finally turned against the activists; they, in turn, murdered him.

COUNTERTERRORISM: A POLICY OUTLINE

International law and international conventions are of little use in confronting and confounding terrorism today. As Walter Laqueur acidly but accurately observed, international law is primarily of interest to lawyers and insurance companies. And international anti-terrorist conventions provide little leverage in a situation in which an Egypt cannot even get counterterrorist cooperation from its Islamic brethren in other countries. No, what counts is national policy and its effective implementation—sometimes, to be sure, in active collaboration with friends and allies.

U.S. counterterrorist policy will have a much better chance of success if it is based on an understanding of terrorism as a "strategic crime" that combines aspects of both warfare and criminality: which means that the problem of terrorism has to be addressed strategically and comprehensively. Moreover, counterterrorist policy has to be implemented through a clear chain of command in which military and civilian agencies are integrated. Interagency cooperation must be absolutely required and strictly enforced, and the coordinator of counterterrorism for the U.S. government should have direct access to the president.

Crimestoppers' Textbook

Deterrence is the crucial first goal of a successful counterterrorist strategy. A terrorist attack thwarted is not a draw: it is a victory for the forces of order, for it saves lives and property while demonstrating (and strengthening) society's resistance capabilities. Moreover, successful deterrence builds on itself—terrorists are rarely suicidal (mythology notwithstanding), and the success of counterterrorist deterrence in the present lowers the probability of assault in the future.

An *enhanced intelligence capability* is indispensable to counterterrorist deterrence. It is essential that the U.S. government understand the motivations, ideology, capabilities, and vulnerabilities of those groups and individuals that are the likely sources of terrorist action against the United States. Just as a clear understanding of Communism was crucial to the success of containment and deterrence in the Cold War, a sophisticated understanding of the philosophical and theological foundations of contemporary terrorism is essential to effective counterterrorism today. What is going on in the mosques of Cairo and the theological academies of Qum may have as much to do with the future security of the United States as the machinations that used to take place in the Soviet Politburo. Moreover, good intelligence will help us distinguish between those forms of Islamic extremism that pose a genuine threat to us and to our friends, and those activist Islamic movements whose passion is for religious reform and who eschew the violent politics of their brethren.

Strengthening our intelligence capabilities will require *publicly acknowledged cooperation with friendly intelligence services* in countries facing similar threats. Terrorists today rely on disagreements about the future of the Palestinians to drive wedges between the governments of friendly Arab states and the United States, or between the United States and Israel. We must make clear that we will not permit this to happen; that we will cooperate fully with cooperative allies in both the Arab world and Israel; and that differences over this or that aspect of the "peace process" will not be used as reasons to limit the sharing of crucial counterterrorist intelligence. (One of the sillier tantrums of the Bush administration was to snub the Israeli counterterrorism coordinator when in 1991 he brought to Washington some unpleasant news that the seventh floor of the State Department didn't want to hear—or have others hear.)

Counterterrorist technology may not be so well advanced as terrorist technology, but there are things we could be doing now, with off-the-shelf equipment, to provide a measure of insurance against real trouble. One nightmare scenario, of course, is that a terrorist agent or organization working at the behest of, say, Iran gets its hands on a nuclear weapon or on weapons-grade fissile material in the former Soviet Union. The problem of a rogue weapon being stolen would be minimized if electronic shackles—permissive action locks (PALs), in the jargon—were installed on all post-Soviet nuclear weapons. Providing the wherewithal to do that would be a modest investment that could pay large deterrence dividends.

Deterrence of terrorism also requires *a far more assertive non-proliferation effort* against the spread of ballistic missiles and the technology needed to use them. Severe sanctions should be imposed on any Western company that provides missile technology or the computer equipment needed to support a missile capability to any state known or suspected to be involved in terrorism. And it should be made plain to the People's Republic of China that one determinant of our future relations will be whether it stops trafficking in cruise and ballistic missiles in the Middle East. Then there is *ballistic-missile defense*: in a decade in which it seems probable, not just likely, that an outlaw state will acquire weapons of mass destruction and the capability to deliver them over long distances, ballistic-missile defense—not the Astrodome, but the kind of effective defense we could mount in the next few years against smaller attacks—is a moral and strategic imperative. We should, of course, share that capability with our friends and allies.

"Hardening" possible terrorist targets in the United States, a more rigorously *self-disciplined press*, and a more *security-conscious citizenry* are three other elements of counterterrorist deterrence. In light of the Twin Towers bombing, effective deterrence would also seem to require a *review of immigration laws and their enforcement*. Discussion of these points has raised legitimate concerns among American Muslims. Non-Muslims, as William Safire has written, can help assuage those concerns "by recognizing the great trial that millions of their fellow Americans are going through and by not thoughtlessly lumping together the orthodox, the secular and the extremist." Conversely, "Muslims can help by refusing to be intimidated by their violent minority, which is now an act of

considerable personal courage, and by recognizing that the law's worldwide counterattack against fanaticism can only strengthen Islam.''[16]

Finally, deterrence of a terrorist atrocity may, in special circumstances, require *preemptive military action*. Effective counterterrorism will thus mean a creative extension of the just war tradition. The tendency in recent decades, noted above, has been to narrow the "just cause" criterion to the point where many specialists argue that force is justifiable only in "response to an aggression already under way." But even within that (excessively constrained) definition of "just cause," the urgent question is, When is a terrorist aggression "under way"? Terrorists, for whom surprise is an essential weapon, are not given to providing advance notice of their activities. Thus it makes little moral sense to argue that, in situations where we have reasonably sure knowledge of an impending terrorist action, our ethical commitments prevent us from using proportionate and discriminate military force—if no other means of deterrence are available—to prevent that action from taking place. In the case of terrorists, the "aggression" is clearly "under way" before the action actually occurs.

Coping With Deterrence Failure

If counterterrorist deterrence fails, it goes without saying that effective police work to bring terrorists to justice is essential. But what about retaliation, particularly in the case of state-sponsored or state-abetted terrorism? Thomas Jefferson, who was not exactly a war hawk, nevertheless warned Congress not to appease the Barbary pirates after they had captured American ships, because "an insult unpunished is the parent of others." Then as now, the problem is not the principle but its implementation: What kind of retaliation? Against whom? At what level?

Neither the history of diplomacy nor the just war tradition offers formulas that provide ready-made answers to these questions. Economic sanctions take a long time to work (if they ever do), and in the case of tyrannical regimes (which are precisely the kind likely to sponsor or abet terrorism), the culprits are the least likely to feel the pinch of austerity. We do know that some retaliatory military action has been successful, while other retaliatory actions have not had the desired deterrent effect. Serious retaliation seems to have a greater effect than modest retaliation; here, an important new just war argument about proportionality has to be engaged. And here, too, what was referred to in chapter 9 as the "regime factor" is a crucial part of the moral-political-military calculus.

On Not Losing Ourselves in the Struggle

The moral values expressed in democratic governance put democracies at something of a disadvantage in facing terrorists, whose very *modus operandi* is a rejection of civilized norms of political behavior. Yet we have to cope with barbarians in such a way that we do not become barbaric in the process. According to a famous film, *The Battle of Algiers* (which celebrated the "existential authenticity" of anti-colonial terrorism in the 1950s), counter-terrorism inevitably turns the "authorities" into terrorists. This is another bit of Sartrean nonsense that has been falsified by history. The successful campaigns mounted against terrorism in democratic western Europe in the 1970s and early 1980s proved that it need not happen that way.

No one has a right to use the instruments and processes of democracy as a means to destroy democracy. Abusing civil liberties in order to deny others their most fundamental civil liberty— their right to life—is the act of an enemy of freedom, and an enemy of the United States. There is no reason why we cannot hold fast to those propositions and to our fundamental moral and political values at the same time—even in the face of terrorism.

13

The New Human-Rights Debate

In spite of, or perhaps because of, the horrors of the twentieth century, the cause of "human rights" has become one of the most powerful forces in contemporary world politics. Evidence for this is not only to be found in decent societies with a long record of protecting civil rights and political freedoms, or in the recent triumphs of human-rights activists in Solidarity and Charter 77. Compelling proof also lies in the tribute that vice pays to virtue: in the fact that virtually every tyranny in the world today tries to justify its repressions in the name of an "alternative" understanding of "human rights."

The modern human-rights movement has various roots, some of them reaching deep into the cultural subsoil of Western civilization. As Peter L. Berger once put it, a long view of human-rights advocacy today would find evidence of the movement's origins in some of the defining locales and experiences in the history of the West: "in the Temple in Jerusalem, in the *agora* of Athens, in the schools of Jewish rabbis, among Roman jurists and medieval moral philosophers."[1] The deepest of these roots is, I believe, the biblical vision of man as created in the image and likeness of God, as a moral agent with intelligence and free will, and thus endowed (to adopt Mr. Jefferson's language) with a certain "inalienable" dignity. This moral claim—that the individual has an irreducible value and dignity *prior* to his or her "public" status (as citizen, or slave, or indentured servant, or freedman, or member of the aristocracy)—is the sturdiest possible foundation for any scheme of "human rights" that seeks to protect human beings from arbitrary (and often brutal) state power.

213

Mediated through the reflections of political philosophers during the English and Scottish Enlightenments, this great Western moral understanding shaped the revolution of 1776 and 1787–89 in the United States; its influence is palpable in the most important political self-expressions of the American founders and framers, the Declaration of Independence, the Constitution, and the Bill of Rights. And in this historical tradition, "human rights" meant two things: *civil liberties*, understood as personal liberties that state power may not abrogate (thus the "right" to freedom of religion, of speech, of association, and of assembly); and *political freedoms*, such as the right to vote, to organize a political opposition, to petition for redress of grievances, and to be judged by a jury of one's peers. "Human rights," on the Anglo-Scottish-American model, meant a societal (and constitutional) recognition that certain spheres of personal and communal activity are to be protected from the tendency of all states (but especially modern states) to expand the reach of their power.

On the other side of the Atlantic, the European discussion of "human rights" was confused by two historical phenomena, not unrelated. The first was the proto-totalitarianism of the Jacobin wing of the French Revolution, which interpreted Rousseau's doctrine of the "general will" to mean that the state had the power (and even the obligation) to trump individual claims to civil rights and political freedoms. The second was the use of the language of "rights" by various Marxist theoreticians to ascribe a thick moral content to their social and economic goals. (An interesting European attempt to embody elements of the human-rights tradition that shaped the American Revolution was the Polish Constitution of May 3, 1791—a tragically short-lived experiment that came to grief just months later.)

In Europe, the older human-rights tradition—the tradition of civil liberties and political freedoms—was revivified by the French philosopher Jacques Maritain in response to the threat of Fascism in the 1930s and 1940s (a development that would have a profound effect on the human-rights thinking of the Roman Catholic Church, and that helped give birth to post-war Christian Democracy in western Europe and Latin America). But the newer Marxist notion of "social and economic rights" would prove to have considerable staying power in the post–World War II period: among intellectuals and politicians of the Left, and later among various post-colonial Third World rulers.

A Troublesome Declaration

That staying power derived in part from the follies committed by Eleanor Roosevelt when she led the drafting of the United Nations' 1948 Universal Declaration of Human Rights, the basic international legal text on the subject. While the Universal Declaration does give priority to civil liberties or civil rights and political freedoms, it also uses the language of "rights" to describe a vast array of social and economic *desiderata*, such as jobs, health care, and education. The historian Arthur M. Schlesinger, Jr., once described the politics of the Declaration in these terms: "The Universal Declaration of Human Rights included both 'civil and political' rights and 'economic, social, and cultural rights,' the second category designed to please states that denied their subjects the first"—which is, perhaps, too charitable an interpretation of the role of Mrs. Roosevelt, who was not unsympathetic to the notion that social and economic goods ought to be described as "rights."[2]

But however responsibility is assigned, the fact remains that the Universal Declaration, for all the good its norms have helped accomplish, has also fostered the confusion, and in some respects the debasement, of the human-rights debate. By using the same language to describe both the immunities an individual holds *against* the state (civil rights) and the claims that an individual is putatively justified in making *on* the state (economic "rights"), the Universal Declaration created an image of moral equivalence that dozens of tyrants turned to their advantage. How many times, during the Cold War, did we hear it said, "Well, *they* just have a different concept of human rights—they think it's more important to provide free health care and to guarantee everybody a job than to have regular elections and a free press"? Too many times, and not by cranks but by presumably serious people. The human-rights curriculum approved by the National Council for the Social Studies in the early 1980s, for example, used precisely this tactic to suggest that the citizens of the oxymoronic People's Republic of China enjoyed a large, if different, range of "human rights."

An American Argument, a European Revolution

These definitional arguments—and the ways in which they were manipulated by dictators of all stripes, but pre-eminently by Communists and their Western apologists—shaped the foreign-policy debate in the United States for a generation. In the 1976 presidential primaries, Senator Henry M. Jackson of Washington, in a challenge to the détente policies of Henry Kissinger, argued that the classic American conception of civil rights and political freedoms had universal applicability and ought to be a central concern of U.S. foreign policy. Jimmy Carter picked up the theme, but once in office his administration distorted it badly: the human-rights bureau in the Carter State Department not only argued for "economic, social, and cultural rights" but seemed to give them priority over civil rights and political freedoms. Moreover, the Carter team showed too little interest in how human rights are institutionalized in societies: which is to say, the Carter-ites paid very little attention to the linkage between human rights and democracy.

The Reagan administration is typically portrayed as having ignored human rights in its conduct of foreign affairs. But in fact it saved U.S. human-rights policy from terminal silliness—largely through the efforts of two superb appointees to the post of assistant secretary of state for human rights, Elliott Abrams and Richard Schifter. Under Abrams and Schifter, and with strong support from the president and from Secretary of State George Shultz, the priority of civil rights and political freedoms was vigorously asserted; Communist doubletalk about "alternative" human-rights "traditions" was dismissed, correctly, as self-serving propaganda; and the linkage between effective protection of human rights and transitions to democracy became a driving force in policymaking. Though this approach was all too often savaged by the prestige press and by many Democrats, its efficacy is now on display throughout Latin America and in central and eastern Europe.

The latter, of course, was the scene of the contemporary

human-rights revolution *par excellence*. Ideologically, strategically, and tactically, the Revolution of 1989 was a direct result of human-rights activism, in many cases inspired by the "Basket Three" provisions of the 1975 Helsinki Final Act. Moreover, in the Revolution of 1989 the prerogatives of genuine democracy were boldly asserted against the hoary Marxist fiction of "people's democracies" and their emphasis on "economic, social, and cultural rights." The transnational and ecumenical resistance community composed of central and eastern European human-rights activists plus kindred spirits and friendly governments in the West was also evidence that "human rights" were not a concern within one political-cultural tradition alone. And during the decade-long run-up to the Revolution of 1989, another institutional actor of great power came onto the scene: led by Pope John Paul II, and drawing on the teachings of the Second Vatican Council, the Roman Catholic Church became perhaps the world's foremost institutional defender of basic human rights, with important results in venues as various as Chile, the Philippines, South Korea, Poland, and what was then Czechoslovakia.

Back to Square One

The Revolution of 1989 and the New Russian Revolution of 1991 might have been thought to have settled the debate about "human rights." These non-violent revolutions embodied the priority of civil rights and political freedoms: they were revolutions *against* regimes that located no small part of their legitimacy in their putative provision of "economic, social, and cultural rights." The truth, of course, was that there were no "rights," economic, cultural, civil, or otherwise, in Communist societies. Jobs, educational opportunities, and health care were linked to political conformity; literature and art were rigorously policed; and the ubiquity of the secret police gave the lie to any notion of enforceable "civil rights." After the 1989 and 1991 upheavals, it should have been perfectly clear that regimes defending their records on the basis of "alternative" conceptions of human rights are to be viewed with the greatest skepticism.

Alas, it was not to be. The World Conference on Human Rights, held in Vienna under U.N. auspices in June 1993, demonstrated in painful detail just how the old rationalizations for tyranny are being recycled: now in the guise of "multiculturalism," but with the same result—people treated as chattels (and worse) by their governments. And, regrettably, the United States did far less than it should have done to reverse this backsliding trend.

THE BANGKOK CONSPIRATORS

The bad guys at Vienna were not exactly shy about what they were up to. Two months before the Vienna conference got under way, they blatantly telegraphed their punch.

At an Asian regional meeting held in Bangkok in April, an unholy alliance of Communists (China and Vietnam), anti-Communists (Indonesia), Middle Eastern despots (Iran and Syria), old-fashioned military thugs (Burma), and the gung-ho capitalist micro-state of Singapore decided that they all had something in common, after all: contempt for the classic notion of "human rights" as civil rights and political freedoms. The "Bangkok Declaration" denied the universality of human rights; such rights, it said, "must be considered in the context of . . . national and regional particularities and various historical, cultural, and religious backgrounds."

On its face, and to those unschooled in the arcana of U.N.-speak, this assertion might not seem unreasonable. The cause of human rights surely requires a careful consideration of how different religious and philosophical systems provide moral ground for human-rights claims. And effective protection of such rights over the long haul requires the exercise of common sense when the fragile institutions of a nascent civil society are threatened by fanaticism of one kind or another.

But the bad guys gave the real game away when the Bangkok Declaration went on to "[reaffirm] the interdependence and indivisibility of economic, social, cultural and civil and political rights and the need to give equal emphasis to all categories of human rights," while concurrently insisting that, as the Chinese representative baldly put it, "only when state sovereignty is fully respected can the implementation of human rights really be assured."

Decorous translation: We'll define what we mean by "human

rights"; we'll implement that definition however we see fit; and nobody else has any standing to object.

Street translation: Get outta my face.

But not so far out that they can't reach our wallets, for the Bangkok Declaration also made a great to-do about the "right to development," another bit of U.N. argot. Here is the "economic rights" notion turned into an international shakedown: by "right to development," Third World despots have meant the putative "right" to draw Western foreign aid from a virtually unlimited account. The claimants place all the blame for the widespread poverty and suffering of Third World peoples on the greedy hegemons of "the North," blithely ignoring the political, social, economic, and cultural depredations wrought by the post-colonial kleptocracies that have run these societies into the ground.

The "right to development" is the international equivalent of welfare pimping, and the Bangkok Declaration not only endorsed it but gave it another twist by condemning "any attempt to use human rights as a conditionality for extending development assistance." Translation: The fact that Sudan is committing genocide against its Christian population in no way affects its claims to vast sums of development aid money. Ditto for Burma and political dissidents, China and its colonized Tibetans, and so on.

Getting It Less-Than-Half Right

The Bangkok Declaration was, among other things, a gauntlet thrown down before the Clinton administration. The Vienna Conference would be the first major international human-rights meeting in which the new administration participated; how would the new kids on the block react?

The policy process leading up to Vienna left much to be desired. Conflicting ideological claims to the mind and soul of the State Department's human-rights bureau had buffeted the administration from the start, and the new assistant secretary of state for human rights, John Shattuck, was confirmed only a week before the conference began. More than a few Democrats wanted to revive the Carter approach to human-rights issues; this would have led to a policy in which the United States looked benignly on the "right to development," and might even have resulted in a tacit acceptance of the Bangkok Declaration's denial of the universality of human rights. Others, notably Joshua Muravchik of the American Enterprise Institute (author of *The Uncertain Crusade*, the most telling critique of Carter-administration human-rights policy), argued that the Clintonistas should build on the success of the Abrams/Schifter approach and stress the linkage between human rights and democratization, on the one hand, and successful economic and social development, on the other, while avoiding Bushbaker pusillanimity toward such Olympic-class human-rights violators as China.

Because the new administration took so long to staff the State Department (and because State itself has little institutional interest in human-rights matters—leadership on this front comes almost exclusively from political appointees), the United States went to the World Conference on Human Rights in damage-control mode. There were some things we wanted to stop (like a retreat from universality); there were some bones we were willing to throw to our adversaries to get what we wanted; there was some interest in distancing the new administration from its predecessors' policies; but there were no long-term policy goals to guide U.S. participation at Vienna.

The result was an American performance that, viewed from one angle, hit .500 (no mean average in any league), but viewed from another, barely made it over the Mendoza Line (.200).

Secretary of State Warren Christopher's speech to the conference—the defining moment for U.S. policy at Vienna—included a strong defense of the universality of basic human rights. Americans, Christopher noted, "respect the religious, social, and cultural characteristics that make each country unique." But, he immediately continued, "we cannot let cultural relativism become the last refuge of repression." Thus the United States "reject[s] any attempt by any state to relegate its citizens to a lesser standard of human dignity."

Christopher also nailed the hypocrisy of the Bangkok Declaration in sharp and uncompromising terms: "There is no contradiction between the universal principles of the [Universal] Declaration and the cultures that enrich our international community. The real chasm lies between the cynical excuses of oppressive regimes and the sincere aspirations of their people." Not bad, that.

Moreover, the Administration backed off from its previous commitment to seek Senate ratification of the "International Covenant on Economic, Social, and Cultural Rights"—a step that would have further damaged the idea of "human rights" by dulling the edge of the claims embedded in civil rights and political freedoms. Christopher also emphasized the linkage between human-rights protections and democracy, and if his rhetoric was less compelling than Ronald Reagan's, the point was nevertheless made.

So why not award Christopher and the U.S. delegation full marks?

Because what the United States asserted in Christopher's speech it then significantly undercut by accepting a conference Final Document that contradicts the secretary's key points in several crucial respects.

THE VIENNA DECLARATION

The Vienna Declaration of the World Conference on Human Rights is not reading material for the faint of heart or the stylistically squeamish. Thirty-three densely packed pages of rhetoric—divided into the standard "preambular" ("Considering . . . recognizing . . . re-affirming . . . emphasizing . . ." etc., etc.), a thirteen-page statement of principles, and a sixteen-page "action plan"—were agreed to by 183 nations on the basis of "consensus."

A "consensus" process in international meetings is one in which everybody has to agree on everything for anything at all to get done. (One Helsinki Accords review conference was held up for weeks because Malta—Malta!—got into a snit and "refused consensus.") In Vienna, "consensus" meant that the final vote had to be 183–0 or there would be no final document. The consensus process often sets up negotiating dynamics in which countries whose governments could be criticized by their publics for "wrecking the conference"—by digging in their heels, for example, on points of moral or political principle—are at a serious disadvantage. Syria, Burma, Vietnam, and China can be as obscurantist and difficult as they want, secure in the knowledge that their people will hear only what the rulers want them to know about the conference. But open, democratic societies are placed in a different and difficult position by the consensus procedure.

Most democracies—especially those eager not to appear harsh toward the Third World—are afraid of being charged with conference-wrecking. Moreover, while many western European chanceries take exercises such as the Vienna conference—or 1992's world environmental summit—with a large grain of salt, Americans tend to think that the language of an international agreement ought to reflect at least a modicum of reality, and that commitments undertaken because of such agreements ought to be serious commitments. These points tend to put the United States at a disadvantage in these situations, and the disadvantage is magnified when the United States has a new team that is unclear about its policy goals, unfamiliar with the curve balls thrown in this particular league, and eager to get a document it can live with so that it can claim a major international success.

"Consensus" caused its usual headaches at Vienna. But the real problem, the enduring problem, of the Vienna Declaration was not the way it was produced but what it did and didn't say.

The Dogs That Didn't Bark

The most important part of the Vienna Declaration is Part II, the statement of principles. And the key to grasping the grave problems of Part II is to notice, like Sherlock Holmes, the dog that didn't bark—in this case, the affirmations that were *not* made.

The Vienna Declaration affirms the "right of self-determination," the "right to development," and the "right to enjoy the benefits of scientific progress," while hinting broadly at a Third World "right" to debt relief (meaning debt cancellation). It condemns toxic-waste dumping in Third World sites (no doubt a problem) as a human-rights violation. And it finds ample room in which to praise indigenous peoples, disabled people, migrant workers, and refugees: all of whom are, to be sure, frequently abused.

But the Vienna Declaration contains no clear articulation of the basic human rights of:

- religious freedom, or
- freedom of association, or
- freedom of assembly, or
- freedom of the press.

Which is to say, the Vienna Declaration is not serious business.

The entire experience of the twentieth century testifies to the fact that civil rights and political freedoms are the bedrock of any meaningful scheme of human rights. For there can be no effective protection of basic human rights without transparency in government, without a constitutional codification of the fundamental and inalienable rights of persons, and without a clear, unambiguous recognition that society exists prior to the state, and that the state exists to serve society, not vice versa. Yet this historical experience, in societies that are both the most free and the most prosperous in human history, was virtually ignored in the Vienna Declaration.

A "human rights declaration" that fails to reaffirm the priority of basic civil rights and political freedoms is, at best, a confession of ignorance and a self-consignment to irrelevance. But the Vienna Declaration took shape not in a political vacuum but in the political and ideological context established by the Bangkok Declaration, which was nothing less than a declaration of war against the Universal Declaration of Human Rights. For the Vienna Final Document to take so accommodating a position toward the agenda embedded in the Bangkok Declaration makes it worse than irrelevant: the Vienna Declaration must be considered dangerous, an actual threat to the protection of human rights.

The Indictment

Some examples will help establish this point.

- Paragraph 3 of the Vienna Declaration's statement of principles reads: "All human rights are universal, indivisible, and inter-dependent and inter-related. The international community must treat human rights globally in a fair and equal manner, on the same footing, and with the same emphasis."

This is simply the Bangkok Declaration tarted up for public

display. What is conceded by the statement of "universality" is immediately denied on the basis of "indivisibility, interdependence, and inter-relatedness." These three nouns may sound unobjectionable; but do not think that they are "neutral" terms. In the current U.N. context, they have very explicit meanings. To get down to specific cases: according to this formulation, the putative right to "periodic holidays with pay, as well as remuneration for public holidays" is as basic a "human right" as freedom of religious belief.

This pernicious and demeaning approach reduces human life to a (slightly) higher form of animal life. It denies a basic anthropological truth: that certain innate human aspirations reflect a quality of transcendent nobility that radically distinguishes man from his pet dog and other sentient creatures. Moreover, we have had a long, hard experience of what happens in countries whose regimes blather on about their commitment to "economic, social, and cultural rights": they tend to be poor, absolutely or relatively, and to be ruled by dictators. For the United States to agree to a human-rights declaration in which the alleged "indivisibility, interdependence, and inter-relatedness" of human rights were given equal footing, morally and legally, with the universality of basic human rights was a serious error.

■ Paragraph 6 reaffirms the "right to development" as a "universal and inalienable right and an integral part of fundamental human rights."

In the days when he was representing the United States at the U.N. Human Rights Commission in Geneva, Michael Novak used to ask whether, if there was a "right to development," there was not a corresponding "responsibility to develop." And if there *was* such a responsibility (as the notion of such a "right" would seem to imply), then what should we say about governments whose corruption, malfeasance, and economic wrong-headedness were the primary causes of their nations' underdevelopment? Would there not be, in these instances, something like a "right to get government out of the way of development"?

These would have been useful questions to pose during the Vienna debate. For, however much confusion there may have been about various schemes of economic development at the time when the Universal Declaration of Human Rights was drafted, the world has had forty-five years of experience since then, and the verdict is in. There is no general positive correlation between levels of "development assistance" and real economic development; therefore demands for "development assistance" on the basis of a rights claim take on the ever more ugly character of international extortion. Moreover, countries that want to create wealth and to distribute its benefits equitably will opt, not for state-sponsored and state-directed development assistance (which is what is implied by the "right to development"), but for market-based economic modernization (which can, to be sure, be furthered at key moments by external assistance—primarily investment).

The choice is not between "concern for the Third World" and economic realism. To be concerned—*seriously* concerned—about the gross poverty and deprivation of the Third World is to advocate those policies of market-oriented economic (and democratic political) reform that are most likely to empower the poor and to lead to real economic growth. We know, now, what those policies are, at least in general orientation. And it is long past time for the United States to do some essential economic truth-telling in international forums, and to respond, sharply and with facts and figures, to the charge that such truth-telling constitutes hegemonism or "insensitivity."

But that would require a settled American policy (one that transcends changes of administration) that we shall, publicly, in and out of season, argue that the "right to development," as it has come to be understood by the majority of states in the United Nations, is dangerous nonsense.

■ Paragraph 19–2 of the Vienna Declaration is a Castroite plea for an end to the U.S. economic embargo of Cuba. Paragraph 19–3 brings us right back to the agenda of the Bangkok Declaration.

Again, the U.N.-ese may seem, at first blush, unobjectionable: "The World Conference reaffirms the importance of ensuring the universality, objectivity, and non-selectivity of the consideration of human rights issues." But what do "objectivity" and "non-selectivity" mean in the linguistic fantasy-land that is the current U.N.? Well, "non-selectivity" means that there can be no special human-rights rapporteurs (investigators, really) appointed for specific *countries*; there can only be special rapporteurs for *issues* (like religious freedom). Thus despotic governments (Cuba, for instance) can further seal themselves off from international scrutiny. And "objectivity" means that, for example, in the case of a special rapporteur's criticism of the state of religious freedom in, say, Sudan, the Sudanese government can reject the report as being "non-objective," insensitive to cultural differences, biased, and so forth. Orwell lives, indeed.

■ Paragraph 26 of the Vienna Declaration was another victory for the Bangkok Declaration sensibility. The preceding paragraph, on non-governmental organizations (NGOs), had stated that human-rights monitors and other NGOs should "be free to carry out their human rights activities, without interference, within the framework of national law and the Universal Declaration of Human Rights." Fine. But Paragraph 26, on the media, merely states that the press should be guaranteed "freedom and protection . . . within the framework of national law"—there is no mention of the Universal Declaration and its principled affirmation of freedom of the press. This has serious implications, not only for press access to countries run by despotic regimes, but for international broadcasting services like the Voice of America, Radio Marti, and Vatican Radio. Jamming these sources of information does not, according to the Vienna Declaration, constitute a serious breach of human rights. Indeed, a clever lawyer (Ramsey Clark? William Kunstler?) could probably turn Paragraph 26 into an argument for the international illegality of Radio Marti (the U.S.-sponsored, Radio Free Europe–style "surrogate radio" for Cuba).

Thus it appears that the U.S. damage-control effort was, at best, only minimally successful. "Universality" was reaffirmed: but at the price of acquiescing to a host of silly, mendacious, or downright dangerous affirmations that may well subject the claim of universality (and the protections it has afforded dissidents) to the death of a thousand cuts.

Boondoggles

The Vienna Declaration's action plan also included a couple of dubious proposals for expanding the U.N. human-rights bureaucracy. The first is the creation of a U.N. High Commissioner for Human Rights, to coordinate U.N. human-rights activity and to serve as a kind of universal ombudsman for human rights—much as the U.N. High Commissioner for Refugees has done for the victims of war, famine, and natural disasters. The proposal, attractive in the abstract, becomes far less so in the light of current U.N. politics.

The position of High Commissioner would, like the Secretary-Generalship, almost certainly have to rotate among various regions of the world. This would virtually guarantee bad choices, or High Commissioners who could be counted on not to rock the boat. Moreover, the office of the High Commissioner for Human Rights would add yet another layer of bureaucracy to a U.N. system that is already choking to death on red tape. The money required for this initiative might be better spent on strengthening the system of special rapporteurs responsible to the U.N. Human Rights Commission. The United States supported the idea of a High Commissioner at the Vienna conference, presumably out of a concern that we be seen as "serious" about human rights; but it is not at all clear that the cause of human-rights protection will be advanced by the addition of another blizzard of paper.

The United States did oppose the establishment of a "Working Group on the Right to Development," a truly Brobdingnagian boondoggle whose creation was supported by our increasingly unserious western European allies. But the Yanks lost the argument, and another bureaucratic black hole was created into which hundreds of thousands of dollars will be sucked.

THE NECESSITY OF HARDBALL

Although the Clinton administration publicly claimed great success at the Vienna conference, its more candid members were likely to argue, privately, that given the consensus procedure, the United States made the best it could out of a bad set of circumstances. But why did we agree to a consensus-driven conference in the first place?

The U.S. delegation believed it could "solve" the problem of the Bangkok Declaration in Vienna by the discreet application of some muscle and a wide range of concessions behind the scenes:

this would avoid a public quarrel (which a vote on issues like "universality" would surely have provoked) and preserve the image of unanimity that now surrounds the Universal Declaration of Human Rights. But why is this a priority? Why should we *want* to maintain a fiction of unanimity with despots—unless the West in general, and the United States in particular, is leery of being seen as pushing its weight around? As the conference opened in mid-June, Joshua Muravchik proposed a tougher strategy, based on a more assertive understanding of the position of the United States and its democratic friends in world politics today:

> The end of the Cold War has brought down many barriers, including, it seems, the barrier that used to divide communist and anti-communist tyrants. On the other side of the coin, advocates of human rights and democracy are united across the political spectrum as never before. Why shouldn't the democracies accept the challenge thrown down by the dictators? Who needs false unanimity? Why not declare that the new dividing line in global politics is between those who honor and practice human rights and democracy and those who do not? Why not have a vote?[3]

Why not, indeed?

But such assertiveness requires leadership. That means the United States would have to accept responsibility for spearheading a reconception of human-rights work in international political and legal institutions today. The Europeans will do nothing unless the United States takes the lead, and much of the heat. And one has to wonder, sadly, whether the United States could gather itself to such a task, just now. Our people are in an isolationist mood (which in no small part reflects a failure of political leadership). The Clinton administration really seems to believe that its Republican predecessors "dismantled" America's human-rights policy, showed gross insensitivity to the Third World, and paid too little attention to the agenda that flies under the flag of "economic, social, and cultural rights." (The first two judgments are profoundly mistaken, and the third ought to be celebrated, not deplored.)

But the United States does the cause of human rights no favor when it takes the advice of former President Carter, who argued in Vienna that the democracies should be "understanding" about the "frustrations" of the countries that signed the Bangkok Declaration.[4] The United States has no shortage of problems; but it is ludicrous to suggest that we enter a discussion of human rights on an equal moral footing with the signatories of the Bangkok Declaration.

What the cause of human rights needs is an assertive United States, unashamed of its own human-rights traditions, committed to the notion that civil rights and political freedoms are the basic building blocks of decent societies, and willing to challenge the shibboleths that have fouled international human-rights discourse for two generations now. That is not, unfortunately, the United States that showed up at the World Conference on Human Rights. And the real losers were the victims of human-rights abuse throughout the world.

AFTERWORD

The Responsible Superpower

The isolationist current that one senses running strong in the America of the early 1990s is being fed by many streams. There is the nation's traditional reluctance to get involved in the hoary tribal feuds and fractiousness of Europe, Africa, and Asia. There is the widespread belief that in recent years we have paid insufficient attention to the decline of our own republican culture and society. There are concerns about the cost-effectiveness of federal spending abroad. There is a certain insouciance about world affairs in the general public. And there is most certainly a lack of leadership in the White House and the Congress.

All these factors have been exacerbated by the general Western failure, and the specific American failure, properly to mark and celebrate the end of the Cold War. We seem unable to grasp the fact that we have just played a major role in a great victory for freedom. And, having failed to take the full measure of our success in the Cold War, we worry about our capacities in the post–Cold War world.

This funk in which we find ourselves is in striking contrast to the expectations one encounters in the new democracies of central and eastern Europe. There, gratitude for American leadership in the Cold War is profound, and eagerness for American leadership in the post–Cold War world is widespread, But worry about America's seeming withdrawal into a trans-Atlantic cocoon is beginning to surface. The new democracies of the old Warsaw Pact (like the new democracies in Latin America and East Asia) do not expect the United States to shoulder the entire burden of responsibility for defining and enforcing the ground rules of world politics in the 1990s and beyond. But they fear the chaos they

231

believe will fill the vacuum if the United States, the lone super-power, abdicates the responsibilities of leadership.

And they are right to do so.

Which is not to say that the lone, and lonely, superpower can or should be the world's policeman, to trot out one of the most tired of isolationist clichés. Measuring our responsibilities accord-ing to a calculus of our interests, informed by a commitment to the gradual evolution of a measure of world order, is no easy business in the aftermath of the Cold War. In the first year of the Clinton administration, for example, we have learned—as usual, the hard way—that "multilateralism" is no substitute for coherent U.S. policy, and that the pursuit of the noblest goals can go seriously awry when our benign intentions are not mediated through a realistic appraisal of the obstacles to success. There can be mindless interventionism, just as there can be mindless isola-tionism. Moreover, there are resources and capabilities enough, in the advanced industrialized democracies, to help sustain a reason-able division of labor in world politics—if the United States understands that such things don't just happen by themselves but require American engagement and American leadership.

History should have taught us that the failure to exercise effec-tive leadership in the short term often leads to serious trouble in the long term. The paradigmatic twentieth-century case is, of course, the failure of the Western democracies, including the United States, to respond forcefully to the rise of Hitler and Nazi Germany, an abdication of responsibility that eventually led to what Winston Churchill called the "Unnecessary War," World War II. True, Serbia and all the other lightweight thug-states that have emerged in the wake of the Communist crackup in central and eastern Europe do not and cannot constitute a threat to international security on the scale of the Third Reich. But should the lands of the old Warsaw Pact implode into chaos and mayhem, we may be reasonably sure that the dangers will not remain localized: which is one reason why the new democracies of central Europe, and possibly the principal successor-states to the old USSR, should be integrated as rapidly as possible into existing Western economic and security structures. Here, as in other areas of life, an ounce of prevention (however much exertion of political will it requires) is indeed worth a pound of cure.

Moreover, it would be the height of folly to assume that the victory of freedom is secure throughout the world, and that democratic polities, free economies, and cultures that cherish and protect basic human rights are the inexorable wave of the future. There is the looming, massive fact of an undemocratic, economically boisterous, and demographically intimidating China. There is the large, unresolved question of whether a fervent Islam can accommodate itself to the structures of the free society and the moral and cultural commitments that sustain those structures.

U.S. foreign policy, by itself or in alliance with democratic allies, cannot univocally determine the path taken by the People's Republic of China or by activist Islam. But it could support the forces within China and within the sundry realms of Islam that wish to channel the tremendous energies of these peoples and cultures in ways that contribute to an enlargement of the sphere of ordered liberty in the world. To assume that such a beneficent outcome will simply emerge on its own, absent the responsible engagement of the established democracies, is to run a risk that strikes me as, at best, wildly imprudent; to assume that the established democracies will act absent the leadership of the United States is imprudence squared.

Powerful motives of economic and political self-interest ought to impel the American people and their leaders to seize the opportunities for responsible leadership in world affairs that history—and our victory in the Fifty-Five Years' War against totalitarianism—has set before us. But self-interest cannot be the only reality at work here. To go back to the beginning: we have to understand that determining the ways, means, and ends of America's action in the post–Cold War world—defining the "national interest"—is an exercise in moral reasoning as well as in political calculation. The late Charles Frankel put the matter as well as anyone when he wrote, almost twenty years ago, that "the heart of the decision-making process . . . is not the finding of the best means to serve a national interest already perfectly known and understood. It is the determining of that interest: the reassessment of the nation's resources, needs, commitments, traditions and

political and cultural horizons—in short, its calendar of values."[1]
In debating the national interest and the national purpose in the
1990s, we are, ineluctably, debating America's "calendar of values." We are debating who we are as a people, and what we want
to be, for ourselves and for the world. A greater measure of clarity
about those values might, just might, lead to greater clarity in
U.S. foreign policy.

The lassitude, sometimes bordering on surliness, that was all
too apparent in the public, congressional, and executive-branch
debates over foreign policy in the wake of the Revolution of 1989
and the New Russian Revolution of 1991 is unworthy of us. We
can do better. We must do better. Our own interests are involved.
So is the judgment of history on the moral quality of the American
democratic experiment.

Notes

CHAPTER ONE

1. See Timothy Garton Ash, *The Polish Revolution: Solidarity* (Sevenoaks, U.K.: Hodder and Stoughton, 1985); *The Uses of Adversity: Essays on the Fate of Central Europe* (New York: Vintage Books, 1990); *We the People: The Revolution of '89* (Cambridge, U.K.: Granta Books, 1990).

2. Vladimir Tismaneanu, *Reinventing Politics: Eastern Europe From Stalin to Havel* (New York: The Free Press, 1992).

3. Ibid., 3.

4. Ibid., 21.

5. Cited ibid., 33.

6. Ibid., 114.

7. Ibid., 139.

8. Václav Havel, "The Power of the Powerless," in Václav Havel et al., *The Power of the Powerless* (Armonk, N.Y.: M.E. Sharpe, 1990), 40.

9. Tismaneanu, *Reinventing Politics*, 205.

10. Ibid., 210.

11. Ibid., 285.

12. See my study *The Final Revolution: The Resistance Church and the Collapse of Communism* (New York: Oxford University Press, 1992).

CHAPTER TWO

1. See S. Frederick Starr, "Soviet Union: A Civil Society," *Foreign Policy* 70 (Spring 1988), 26–41.

2. James H. Billington, *Russia Transformed: Breakthrough to Hope* (New York: The Free Press, 1992).

3. Ibid., 6–7.

4. Ibid., 35.

5. Ibid., 37.

6. Ibid., 39.

7. Ibid., 42.

8. Ibid., 105.

9. Ibid., 112.

10. Ibid., 133.
11. *New York Times*, 7 May 1992.
12. Ibid.
13. Leszek Kołakowski, *Main Currents of Marxism 3: The Breakdown* (New York: Oxford University Press, 1978).
14. Václav Havel, "The Post-Communist Nightmare," *New York Review of Books*, 27 May 1993, 8.
15. Ibid.
16. Ibid.
17. Ibid.
18. Ibid.
19. Ibid., 10.
20. Ibid.
21. Ibid.
22. Ibid.
23. Billington, *Russia Transformed*, 128, 127.

Chapter Three

1. George F. Kennan, "The G.O.P. Won the Cold War? Ridiculous," *New York Times*, 28 October 1992.
2. Lest it be thought I exaggerate, here are Kennan's words:

. . . Isn't it grotesque to spend so much of our energy on opposing . . . Russia in order to save a West which is honeycombed with bewilderment and a profound sense of moral decay?
Show me first an America which has successfully coped with the problems of crime, drugs, deteriorating educational standards, urban decay, pornography, and decadence of one sort or another; show me an America that has pulled itself together and is what it ought to be, then I will tell you how we are going to defend ourselves from the Russians. But as things are, I can see very little merit in organizing to defend from the Russians the porno shops in central Washington. In fact, the Russians are much better at holding pornography at bay than we are [George F. Kennan, "Selections from Interviews," in *The Nuclear Delusion: Soviet-American Relations in the Atomic Age* (New York: Pantheon Books, 1982), 74].

3. Patrick Glynn, *Closing Pandora's Box: Arms Races, Arms Control, and the History of the Cold War* (New York: Basic Books, 1992).
4. Ibid., 1.
5. As Glynn points out, Lord Grey's post-war analysis was a reprise of the liberal pacifist approach to international relations (and its deprecation of the usefulness of military capability) that the foreign secretary had espoused prior to the war—the approach that had proven so disastrously inept in meeting the challenge of Wilhelmine Germany. This pattern of liberal pacifist failure-and-revival would repeat itself throughout the century. Indeed, it continues to this day, and is one source of the "no winners" interpretation of the end of the Cold War.
6. Glynn, *Closing Pandora's Box*, 42–43.
7. Cited ibid., 163.

8. This point has been conceded by Georgi Arbatov, the erstwhile head of Moscow's Institute for the Study of the USA and Canada, and a favorite of nuclear-freeze advocates during the 1980s. It may be recalled that Arbatov bitterly denied charges from American "hawks" and "warmongers" that the Soviet Union was engaged in a massive, relentless buildup of nuclear weapons in the late 1970s. Now, in a book in which he seeks (with terminal implausibility) to portray himself as a closet dissident and reformer, Arbatov writes that the Soviet Union tried to achieve, and by his reckoning did achieve, nuclear superiority over the West at precisely the time when Arbatov was blaming the "arms race" on Western hawks in the Committee on the Present Danger. "As far as nuclear arms are concerned," Arbatov writes, "we surpassed the Americans in the number of delivery systems, megatonnage, and throw-in weight in strategic arms, and also in medium-range weapons" (cited in Richard Pipes, "The Toady," *The New Republic*, 19 October 1992, 41.) Thus "the toady" vindicated (inadvertently?) the analysis of the Americans whom he once worked overtime on ABC-TV and National Public Radio to vilify.

9. Or at least that part of the administration represented by Warnke and Secretary of State Cyrus Vance; National Security Adviser Zbigniew Brzezinski took a rather different view and, according to Glynn, invested considerable time in bureaucratic struggles to temper the doves' concessionary enthusiasms. Glynn aptly notes (again harkening back to the Sarajevo Fallacy and one of its by-products) that "détente and arms control under Carter could be said to have combined the worst aspects of Roosevelt's approach to Stalin with the British radicals' approach to the kaiser" (*Closing Pandora's Box*, 286).

10. Ibid., 306.

11. Walter Isaacson, *Kissinger* (New York: Simon and Schuster, 1992).

12. Ibid., 767.

13. Ibid., 612.

14. Ibid., 613, 612.

15. Ibid., 621

16. Ibid., 436.

Chapter Four

1. Zbigniew Brzezinski, Letter to the Editor, *Commentary*, December 1990, 2.

2. Quoted in Foreign Broadcasting Information Service, FBIS-EEU-91–199, 15 October 1991, 13.

3. Quoted in FBIS-EEU-92–001, 2 January 1992, 11.

4. Stephen Engelberg, "The Velvet Revolution Gets Tough," *New York Times Magazine*, 31 May 1992, 32.

5. Jeri Laber, "Witch Hunt in Prague," *New York Review of Books*, 23 April 1992, 5–8, and Letters, *New York Review of Books*, 28 May 1992, 56.

6. Václav Havel, quoted in FBIS-EEU-91–199, 15 October 1991, 13.

7. Christine Stone and Mark Almond, Letters, *New York Review of Books*, 28 May 1992, 56.

8. Joseph Held, ed., *The Columbia History of Eastern Europe in the Twentieth Century* (New York: Columbia University Press, 1992).

9. Sharon L. Wolchik, "Czechoslovakia," ibid., 129–41.

10. John Chancellor, "NBC Nightly News," NBC–TV, 22 August 1991.

11. Editorial, *Seattle Post-Intelligencer*, 2 June 1988.

CHAPTER FIVE

1. Charles Krauthammer, "America's Case of the Sulks," *Washington Post*, 19 January 1992.

2. Jeane J. Kirkpatrick, quoted in *National Review*, 30 March 1992, 6.

3. Norman Davies, "Parallel Tyrants," *New York Times Book Review*, 22 March 1992, 3, 31.

4. *Henry V*, act 4, scene 7, lines 82–89.

5. Robert W. Tucker and David C. Hendrickson, *The Imperial Temptation* (New York: Council on Foreign Relations Press, 1992).

6. Christopher Dawson, *Religion and the Rise of Western Culture* (New York: Doubleday Image Books, 1991), 27.

7. John Maynard Keynes, *The General Theory of Employment* (London: Macmillan & Co., 1936), 383.

8. Francis Fukuyama, "Rest Easy, It's Not 1914 Anymore," *New York Times*, 9 February 1992.

9. Stanley Hoffmann, "Delusions of World Order," *New York Review of Books*, 9 April 1992.

CHAPTER SIX

1. Owen Harries, ed., *America's Purpose: New Visions of U.S. Foreign Policy* (San Francisco: ICS Press, 1991).

2. Robert W. Tucker and David C. Hendrickson, *The Imperial Temptation* (New York: Council on Foreign Relations Press, 1992).

3. Raul Alfonsin, "No Alibis for Fujimori," *Washington Post*, 19 April 1992.

4. Philip Dimitrov, "Freeing the Soul From Communism," *Wall Street Journal*, 23 March 1992.

CHAPTER SEVEN

1. Personalities aside, that disdain for "vision" was one part managerial hubris, one part domestic political calculation ("The American people are tired of world leadership"), and one part historical judgment ("Crisis management is sufficient to maintain order and stability in a post–Cold War world"). The domestic political calculation was cynical: contemptuous of the intelligence of our people, and thus contemptible. The historical judgment was just plain wrong, as the crisis catalog in the preceding paragraphs amply illustrates.

2. Paul Johnson, "Wanted: A New Imperialism," *National Review*, 14 December 1992.

3. Ibid.

CHAPTER EIGHT

1. Patrick J. Buchanan, "America First—A Foreign Policy for the Rest of Us," *PJB From the Right* 2:1 (September 1991).
2. Ibid.
3. Ibid.
4. Ibid.
5. Ibid.
6. Ibid.
7. Paul Johnson, *Modern Times: The World From the Twenties to the Eighties* (New York: Harper and Row, 1983), 232.

CHAPTER NINE

1. Harry G. Summers, Jr., *On Strategy II: Critical Analysis of the Gulf War* (New York: Dell, 1992).
2. Robert Tucker, "Justice and the War," *The National Interest*, Fall 1991, 108.
3. *U.S. News and World Report* Staff, *Triumph Without Victory* (New York: Times Books/Random House, 1992), 409.
4. John Courtney Murray, *We Hold These Truths* (New York: Doubleday Image Books, 1964), 274.
5. James Turner Johnson, "The Just War Tradition and the American Military," in James Turner Johnson and George Weigel, *Just War and the Gulf War* (Washington: Ethics and Public Policy Center, 1991) 8–9.
6. J. Bryan Hehir, "Worldwatch," *Commonweal*, 28 February 1992.

CHAPTER TEN

1. Ivo Andric, *The Bridge on the Drina* (Chicago: University of Chicago Press, 1977), 73.
2. Ibid., 75.
3. Ibid., 173–74.
4. Michael Ignatieff, "The Balkan Tragedy," *New York Review of Books*, 13 May 1993, 5.
5. See Caleb Carr, "The Humanitarian Illusion," *New York Times*, 16 September 1993.

CHAPTER ELEVEN

1. Bernard Lewis, "Roots of Muslim Rage," *Atlantic Monthly* 226:3 (September 1990), 60.
2. Fouad Ajami, *The Arab Predicament*, rev. ed. (Cambridge, U.K.: Cambridge University Press, 1992).
3. Ibid., 21.
4. To be sure, the worlds of Islam include hundreds of millions of people who do not live in the Middle East or North Africa. Some of what is argued in

this chapter has relevance to the Islamic societies of Pakistan, Bangladesh, and central Asia, and to the great Muslim states of Malaysia and Indonesia. But there are also differences. Indeed, it just may be that in Indonesia a new pattern of interaction between Islam and the processes of marketization and democratization is unfolding. Were this new, less confrontational pattern to succeed, the implications would be very significant, given Indonesia's oil resources and its position as the world's fifth most populous country. But the focus here will remain on the Levant and the Maghreb, where the encounter between Islam and the West seems likely to be sharpest for at least the balance of this century.

5. The "unsecular" experience of the United States should, of course, have proven a cautionary tale here.

6. Ajami, *The Arab Predicament*, 70.

7. As Barbara Tuchman argues in *Bible and Sword*, the genteel anti-Semitism of the Foreign Office was in sharp contrast to the romance about the Holy Land that animated many other English spirits (preeminently, Balfour and Churchill) and led to the countercurrent of British Christian Zionism.

8. Ajami, *The Arab Predicament*, 112.

9. John L. Esposito, *The Islamic Threat: Myth or Reality?* (New York: Oxford University Press, 1992).

10. Ibid., 189.

11. Ibid., 107.

12. Ibid., 168.

13. Ibid., 174.

14. Ibid., 139.

15. Ibid., 14.

16. Ibid., 19.

17. Ibid.

18. Cited ibid., 51.

19. Ibid., 19.

20. Ibid., 14.

21. Ibid., 185.

22. Ibid., 187.

23. Ibid., 189.

24. John L. Esposito, *Islam: The Straight Path*, exp. ed. (New York: Oxford University Press, 1991), 19.

25. Esposito, *The Islamic Threat*, 48–49.

26. See ibid., 56ff.

27. Ibid., 165.

Chapter Twelve

1. Michael Walzer, *Just and Unjust Wars*, (New York: Basic Books, 1977), 197.

2. Walter Laqueur, *The Age of Terrorism*, rev. ed. (Boston: Little, Brown, and Co., 1987, 5–6).

3. Ibid., 28–29.

4. Ibid., 56.

5. Ibid., 6.

6. Ibid.

7. Ibid., 6–7.
8. Ibid., 7.
9. Ibid.
10. Ibid.
11. Ibid., 8.
12. Ibid.
13. Ibid., 8–9.
14. Ibid., 306.
15. Ibid., 260–61.
16. William Safire, "Islam Under Siege," *New York Times*, 18 March 1993.

CHAPTER THIRTEEN

1. Peter L. Berger, "Are Human Rights Universal?" *Commentary*, September 1977, 60.
2. Arthur M. Schlesinger, Jr., cited in Joshua Muravchik, "Why Accept the Hubris of Tyrants?" *Los Angeles Times*, 15 June 1993.
3. Ibid.
4. This was, in fact, one of the least objectionable of Carter's sundry Vienna pronouncements. After being shouted down by Latin American radicals at an NGO forum in Vienna, Carter said that he only wanted these "frustrated" people to know that "I was not [at the forum] representing my country because I have strongly disagreed [with] and condemned the human rights policy of my country for the past twelve years." The Georgia sage also condemned the "selfish attitudes of the nations of the North who control the economic, political, and cultural power in the world," trotted out the old tyrants' saw that a family starving to death wouldn't be interested in freedom of speech, and claimed that, while the United States has invested "billions of dollars" in the Salvadoran military, none of this has benefited "ordinary people."
Plus ça change . . .

AFTERWORD

1. Charles Frankel, *Morality and U.S. Foreign Policy* (New York: Foreign Policy Association, 1975), p. 52.

Index of Names

Abkhazians, 98
Abraham, 182, 189–90
Abrams, Elliott, 216, 220
Abrams, Herbert, 69
Acheson, Dean, 71, 126
ACLU (American Civil Liberties Union), 203
Afghanistan, 52–53, 131
Africa, 4, 86, 103, 109, 117–18, 131, 182, 231
Age of Terrorism, The (Laqueur), 198
AID (Agency for International Development), 130, 133
AIDS (Acquired Immune Deficiency Syndrome), 117
Ajami, Fouad, 178–79, 181, 183, 185
Albania, 172
Alexander II, 198
Alexei II, 33, 41
Alfonsin, Raul, 104
Algeria, 155, 205
Al-Hayat, 196
Al-Salaam Mosque (N.J.), 196
American Bar Association (ABA), 69
American Revolution, 214
Amnesty International, 205
Andric, Ivo, 161–62, 171
Andropov, Yuri, 34
Animal Farm (Orwell), 68

Arab Predicament, The (Ajami), 178
Arbatov, Georgi, 237 n.8 (chap. 3)
Aristide, Jean-Bertrand, 110
Aristotle, 22, 93
Armenia, 100, 110, 163, 199
Arms Control and Disarmament Agency, 49, 53
Asia, 78, 84, 86, 98, 115–17, 129–31, 133, 169, 177, 218, 231
Asquith, H. H., 46
Assad, Hafez al-, 178, 204
Association of Soviet Lawyers, 69
Athens, 2, 213
Augustine, Saint, 192–93
Austria, 15, 21
Austro-Hungarian Empire, 47, 110, 162
Azerbaijan, 110

Baader-Meinhof Gang, 203
Ba'athism, 145–46, 178
Baghdad, 133, 144–45, 155, 177
Baker, James A., III, 89, 131, 164
Balkans, 12, 102, 111, 161–71
Bandow, Doug, 83
Bangkok Declaration, 218–20, 223, 225, 227–28

243

GEORGE WEIGEL became president of the Ethics and Public Policy Center in Washington, D.C., in 1989. A graduate of St. Mary's Seminary and University in Baltimore and the University of St. Michael's College in Toronto, he was a 1984–85 Fellow of the Woodrow Wilson International Center for Scholars. He is the author or editor of fourteen books and hundreds of essays, reviews, and op-ed articles on religion and public life. Weigel serves on the boards of several national and international organizations devoted to religious freedom and other fundamental human rights.